GRUB STREET

GRUB STREET

THE ORIGINS OF THE BRITISH PRESS

DR RUTH HERMAN

AMBERLEY

First published 2020

Amberley Publishing
The Hill, Stroud
Gloucestershire, GL5 4EP

www.amberley-books.com

Copyright © Dr Ruth Herman, 2020

The right of Dr Ruth Herman to be identified
as the Author of this work has been asserted
in accordance with the Copyrights, Designs
and Patents Act 1988.

ISBN 978 1 4456 8884 8 (hardback)
ISBN 978 1 4456 8885 5 (ebook)

British Library Cataloguing in Publication Data.
A catalogue record for this book is available
from the British Library.

Typesetting by Aura Technology and Software
Services, India. Printed in the UK.

CONTENTS

INTRODUCTION

Before we embark on this journey, we must address the title of this work. Some may wonder what Grub Street was, and whether it was a real place. To explain this, we have to start not at the beginning but at what looked like the end. We therefore enter the story at a critical point when it was gloomily predicted that Grub Street and its industry was finished. This pessimism was the result of the government's constant efforts to curb the press. None of these measures had been popular, but the 1712 Stamp Act was felt to be particularly damaging. It was a tax on the paper used for newspapers and journals, and its introduction prompted prophecies of doom from contemporary writers. Jonathan Swift's immediate reaction was negative. 'Do you know that Grub Street is dead and gone last week? No more ghosts or murders now for love or money.' Joseph Addison, one of the originators of *The Spectator*, was no more optimistic: 'This is the day on which many eminent authors will probably publish their last words.'

How wrong could they be? Well, clearly the Stamp Act did not stop the presses and the newspaper industry did not die, whatever difficulties it may have caused. In fact, just eighteen years later a feisty magazine full of 'satire and irony' entitled *The Grub Street Journal* appeared and was read widely, if grudgingly. 'Universally condemn'd and universally read,' it referred to the place nicknamed Grub Street. Dr Johnson in his dictionary shed some light on the origins of the title: 'Originally the name of a street, near Moorfields in London, much inhabited by writers of small histories, dictionaries, temporary poems whence any mean publication is Grub Street.' The Grub Street residents were hacks and were viewed with some disdain by the great writers of the day. Their pens were for hire, and the quality of the writing was less important than the fee.

I don't think I can give a better description of a Grub Street writer than one which appeared in 1720, in the supposed memoir of a young man who has abandoned his apprenticeship to a tailor and wishes to make a name for himself.

I was just come of Age, so that I had the Disposal of about Fifty Pounds, which was left me by my Uncle, to set me up; and so indeed it did, but in a different Trade from what he intended; for having, as I said before, a little smattering of Learning and a pretty good Opinion of my own Parts, I thought my self fit for an Author; with this Money therefore, I furnish'd myself with a Sword, a Tye-wig, a Cane, a Snuff box, five Reams of Paper, a Standish and a Common-place Book. I then took an handsome Lodging (not very Spacious in deed) up three Pair of Stairs at a little Ale house in the celebrated Regions of Grub Street, a Place long since renown'd for polite Wit and Learning, where I have spent my time ever since ... in writing abundance of elaborate Treatises upon all manner of Subjects, for the good of my Country and my own Belly – Two Considerations which are seldom missing in most of our modern Writers.

Over the Door of the House I fixt up a Board, like a little Sign, with these Words upon it, Here liveth Humphry Scribblewit (for that is the Name I took upon me, – when I left my Master) Who writeth all sorts of Pamphlets, Letters of Controversies, Answers and Replies, Poems, Satires, Libels, Lampoons, Songs, Ballads, Essays, Travels, Voyages, Novels and Romances, at reasonable Rates: Enquire within. — By this means I soon got into Business and have in something more than three Years publish'd above an hundred several Pieces.

So there we have what was thought of as a typical Grub Street hack, possibly not overburdened with talent but ready to turn his pen to anything. Many of them were the unsung heroes and heroines of the burgeoning press, providing the words for the printers and keeping them in business. For the insatiable readers, these hacks kept up the supply of eagerly awaited news.

Despite the variable quality of writing, Grub Street was above all an interesting place, opening windows into the lives and concerns of times and people now long gone. Some of the stories and attitudes they recorded are sad, while others are funny. Some, by modern standards, are simply weird – but they are all authentic. Although the physical reality of writers scratching away in small rooms in Central London has gone, I don't think the concept of Grub Street has disappeared. It has simply changed its name to 'media', under which guise it continues to intrigue, delight and infuriate us. Let's now go to the beginnings of the institution that is the British press.

BEFORE THE WORD

Welcome to the world of the newspaper before it has been invented. The first two chapters in this book are intertwined as they concern the febrile era of the English Civil Wars. It is easy to think of this as a time when everybody took a side and each side had a mountain of print to bolster their convictions. Punishments were brutal, and the inflexible ideologies were typical of people who have no doubt that they are in the right. They have God on their side, and the devil and his army are house guests of the opposition. Against this backdrop, we must first plot a path through the embryonic stages of the British newspaper industry to see how it was praised and reviled (in equal measure) at its birth.

Let us begin our story with the Tudors, who weren't keen on transparency. The publication of news to the general population was considered dangerous and was therefore banned in England by the Star Chamber, the powerful arm of the establishment (in truth it *was* the Establishment) which essentially ruled the country. This inner council was made up of a select few of the king's advisers and was therefore entirely subject to his or her personal rule.

The Star Chamber's fear of the widespread knowledge of current affairs in England forced the newsmen to print their work in Amsterdam.

This changed during the seventeenth century, when we see the rise of the pamphlet and a very uncivil war of words between the followers of King Charles I and the Parliamentarians. The insatiable appetite for political news, together with religious pamphleteering, fostered a mountain of texts which provide some insight into the passion behind the torrent of words, and the personalities responsible. The Parliamentarians wrote about 'arbitrary and tyrannical government', and the king responded with his own publication, *Mercurius Aulicus*, which talked about the world being abused with falsehoods and deceived with untruths. The earliest broadsheets, called 'Courantos', appeared at around this time along with over three hundred different newsbooks, all to be devoured by an eager readership.

In order to understand the task that was ahead of these early newspapers as the Civil War approached, we should set the scene. England was ruled by a king who believed implicitly he was God's gift to the nation and being divinely ordained was therefore always right. As a reaction to this there emerged a set of highly politicised people who disapproved of everything the king stood for. They saw him as tyrannical, and some went so far as to consider him and his crew as the Antichrist. This mixture was the primordial soup out of which the press emerged. Perhaps its most important element was the very outspokenness of the writers. For these pioneers, the pursuit of freedom of speech was more important than the brutality with which they were treated and the injuries they suffered. Of similar importance were the printers and publishers, who were becoming more sophisticated in terms of their marketing. These individuals and their interaction with the authorities provided an environment in which pamphlets, handwritten news-sheets and one-off scraps describing current affairs could evolve into the British press. It was loved and loathed in equal measure, and this has remained the case ever since.

Perhaps the popular image of the two sides in the English Civil War gives a false impression. We should not be distracted by the long, curly hair of the Cavaliers or the sober dress of the Roundheads – both sides were engaged in a deadly war, and the words on the page don't show the humiliation to which these writers were subjected. All we see are the pages and pages of angry sentences written by frustrated but extraordinary people. At the safe distance of 350 years, we don't feel the anger that might have been engendered by these texts, the content of which led to physical and mental suffering for their radical originators. However outrageous a headline might look today, the average British reader is unlikely to need to hide a newspaper that has been branded as seditious and treasonous. The texts that were once considered seditious are now safe to read so it is easy to forget that these pioneer journalists could be in genuine danger.

If this all sounds a bit dramatic, that's because it was. In Britain today it is generally safe for a reporter to claim the government is incompetent and even accuse ministers and members of Parliament of being corrupt and dishonest. The journalists don't expect to suffer physical retribution. And yet, 350 years ago the authors of the first pieces of what might be called journalism risked painful and brutal treatment. Van Dyke's splendid image of Charles I on his rearing white stallion is spectacular, and Lely's grim but honest-looking representation of Cromwell, warts and all, makes the Lord Protector look reliable. While admiring such artistry, we do need to bear in mind that these lofty figures might well have come to sit for their portraits having just condemned some poor author to the most inhumane of mutilations. It's tempting to keep a romanticised view of the Civil War in England in the middle of the seventeenth century, but to do so would be to deny the brutality of the era.

Putting the violence to one side, most of this chapter is set in the overheated period of Parliament's growing unease with the king. On the secular front Parliament objected to King Charles's demands for money to fight an unpopular war in Scotland, while on the spiritual side they were deeply disturbed by his brand of Anglicanism, which the increasingly radical Puritans thought far too close to Roman Catholicism. Because of their overall dissatisfaction with royal rule, Parliament did not play the game and exercised their right not to vote him the necessary funds. In a fit of pique, an angry Charles sent the MPs home, making his endless quest for funding even harder. At one point he even pawned the Crown Jewels.

In addition to all this, the radicals were further incensed by rumours that Catholics were being given favours as part of the negotiations for the king's marriage to the Catholic French princess Henrietta Maria. What made matters worse was the perception that the High Anglicanism practised at court was secretly Catholic. Pitted against Charles ideologically and then physically were the Protestant sects, large and small, who wanted to return to what they believed was a simpler and more authentic version of their faith. And with the king illegally raising taxes to fight a war they opposed, it was almost inevitable that tempers would run high. This argument escalated from an ideological dispute into the bloody conflict now known as the English Civil War. At the end of its first chapter, the victorious Parliamentarians found the captured king guilty of treason and chopped off his head. After a few more bitter years, this very acrimonious war was ended with the declaration of England as a republic. It is less commonly known that off the battlefield the war was also waged through the words which tumbled from writers' pens.

With the end of the English Civil War came the extraordinary experiment known variously as the Commonwealth, the Protectorate or the Interregnum. This ended after just ten years upon the death of Lord Protector Oliver Cromwell, the hitherto unremarkable country gentleman who had emerged as the leader of the Parliamentarian cause. Everything fell apart when his inept and uninterested son briefly inherited his title. Sick of the Parliamentarians, in 1660 the people asked Charles's son, technically already Charles II, to come back and take up the vacant post of king, the Restoration. Duly crowned, Charles II would set up a glittering, hedonistic and glamorous court in England. But even before he returned, the radical writers were busy. As so often happens, once the common enemy was defeated – in the case the Royalists – the Puritan movement splintered in myriad ways, all claiming that they had God's approval. With this split came words, words and more words. The printing presses, licensed or clandestine, toiled away and the newly born English quasi-journalism flexed its infant muscles. The factions turned upon each other, and the ensuing in-fighting produced crude, lengthy and surprisingly readable texts. And the English loved it.

Perhaps the most surprising thing about this was the fact that the 'lower orders' could read; even more alarming for the authorities, however, was what these people wanted to read. An interest in politics went far further down the social pecking order than some realised, considering how few people had the right to vote. The long reach of the printed word did not suit the rather nervous powerbrokers, of course. They would prefer the lower orders to mind their own business and not worry about things that were above their station. The lack of a vote made little difference to the level of interest among the poor, and politicians were wary of everyone knowing what they were up to. The concerns of the elite meant nothing to the wider public, who believed they had every right to be informed of what was going on in the corridors of power. As one member of the clergy wearily complained, the English were much happier attending to political gossip than to their spiritual health.

It would seem more likely that the working, labouring and often poverty-stricken lower orders would have been more interested in their next meal rather than the activities of politicians; what remote princes did in wars far away might be thought of as irrelevant to the English working man. Yet according to their contemporaries, the average subject of the time was surprisingly fascinated by the world outside. We would expect the people who might be directly affected by political activity to be interested; it is not surprising that Members of Parliament, lords, the gentry and those rare creatures, the enfranchised, read accounts of government at home or abroad. But it was said of the English at all levels, even the 'vulgar and ignorant multitude', that they liked to know what was going on outside their immediate concerns. It is easy to speculate about the literacy of anyone who could not leave a record of what they read, but given that their 'betters' are recorded complaining that the ordinary people are too bothered about topics above their station, the news must have been available. And you only needed one or two people in a village who knew their letters (and not necessarily how to write) in order to spread the word. It is difficult to get precise numbers, but according to one source as many as 60 per cent of men in the larger towns of the south and at least 30 per cent in the country could read by the time Charles I lost his head in 1649.

The result was that news, as they say, travelled fast. The main mode of communication was probably that most effective (and possibly unreliable) of systems, word of mouth. The importance of this should not be underestimated. We must take into account that in this period property ownership could be transferred by verbal agreement. In this context, any news passed on through conversation would be taken seriously and could engage even those with no literacy at all. Given this widespread interest, it comes as no surprise that the number of people hauled up for sedition makes interesting reading. In one account we are told that of the 154 Home Counties defendants accused of writing against the government just over twenty were gentry or clergy. The rest came from other, much lower ranks. It might even cause some surprise that eleven of the accused were women. The receptiveness to this 'newsmongering' among those whose literacy and access to the written word might have been thought limited is significant. The press as we know it was a little way off at this time, but there is nonetheless an indication that the readership was in place and eager to hear about the world outside.

For those who really could not read, and for whatever reason had no access to informal political discussions, there was another source of news. These were the proclamations that came straight from the royal inner circle. They were the 'truth' as the king wished it to be known. They could be regarded as early government press releases, with all the bias that might be expected from such a source. Politicians of any period are not noted for their even-handed announcements. As his reign progressed, Charles I, whose belief in the divine right of kings was unshakeable, had rapidly lost his temper with a Parliament that seemed to think it was in charge. As a result of this, he had put out some proclamations which were bound to cause trouble. For instance, his announcement of the dissolution of Parliament seems designed to be offensive. He did not mince his words, condemning the 'disobedient and seditious carriage of those ... ill affected persons of the House of Commons'. He complained that 'Our Regall authoritie and commandement, have been so highly contemned, as Our Kingly Office cannot beare'. Charles maintained to the very end that he was not at fault – how could he be when God had put him in England to rule? His message to his people was that the dissolution of Parliament was necessary because of a wicked, disruptive minority. If Charles and his propaganda team had been a bit more attuned to the political atmosphere, they would have realised that they were in fact only increasing the tension.

These official proclamations were ostensibly printed and sold to be read, but it seems self-evident that their real target was the illiterate. For the benefit of the unlettered, a local official stood in the town square or market place and read out the words. Sometimes, to ensure that everybody could see him, a stool was provided. Despite some misgivings about telling all and sundry what was happening at Westminster, Charles and his team realised it was important that absolutely everybody knew what was going on at the heart of government. As a propaganda exercise, the proclamations were intended to stop the unrepresented becoming a mob and challenging the king's authority. The recognition that the population did not want to live in a news vacuum was important. It contributed to the government's realisation that it was in their interest to give the public carefully filtered information as approved by those in charge.

In the light of this realisation, we can return to the question of how many people could actually read. (It is important to note that this is not full literacy, which would include writing.) Clearly there would have been no point in printing reams of material if barely anybody could read it. Equally, there are the physical limitations on squeezing bodies into a market square to hear the news proclaimed. Reading rates are difficult to determine, but according to one historian there was a dramatic improvement in reading figures between 1580 and 1690. The claim is that 16 per cent of yeomen were able to read in 1580, and 67 per cent by 1690. The same is true of tradesmen, whose literacy in Norwich went from

56 per cent to 70 per cent during this period. Another researcher claims that 60 per cent of men in the London and south-east could read by the early eighteenth century. Another expert suggests that 83 per cent of yeomen, 68 per cent of craftsmen and 36 per cent of labourers could read by the end of the seventeenth century. While the exact figures might be up for debate, taken together they indicate that there were many more readers than we might have imagined.

We should also bear in mind that the established religion, Protestantism, urged individuals to read the Bible independently. With this incentive, it is only to be expected that readership grew. Common sense also tells us that the explosion in the printed word indicates the growth of readership – there must have been enough people around to read what was published. This is not a scientific or empirical conclusion, but why else would printers go to the trouble and expense of producing so many items if so few people could appreciate them?

There was also the means to learn to read. By the early 1700s, there were women who took it upon themselves to teach the children in their parish to read. Some parishes would have had a regular schoolmaster come at prescribed intervals to teach reading. There is also evidence of reading being taught earlier still in the seventeenth century. There was licensing of teachers, and, maybe more importantly, there was enough demand that the historical record turns up evidence of unlicensed teachers being employed. There was an obvious appetite for education and a willingness for labouring parents to give up some of their hard-earned pennies to improve their children's education and prospects. Equally, there seem to have been enough people willing and able to take those few pennies to teach, officially or otherwise.

While it is encouraging to hear that literacy was increasing, we should not get carried away with some notions of equality in the reading material. There was a ranking of the suitability of the news for the various levels of society, with the least trustworthy being fed to the lower orders. Ben Jonson in *The Staple of News*, written in 1625, satirised the voracious appetite for printed matter and talked of news that was suitable for barbers, tailors and porters as 'apocryphal ... of doubtful credit'. Alongside this there is 'news of the faction ... Reformed news ... Protestant news ... pontifical news' and, in a strangely prescient turn, 'false news ... to the super-vexation of town and country'. Fake news was disrupting political discourse four centuries ago, just as it does today.

It is worth examining what these eager readers did upon reading an item of interest. The Early Modern literate Englishman was a great collector of scraps. The importance of this in the context of the newspaper industry is that there were newspaper cuttings stuffed into scrapbooks alongside disordered titbits about families and snippets of local gossip. Clearly these bits of the printed word meant enough to the journeymen who had learnt their letters. Why else would they preserve the doings of the world outside their very limited sphere? One example which survives is the jottings of a working man in Essex who lived through the Civil War. His scrapbook contains everything from the sale of a piece of land to a Londoner to the imprisonment and subsequent release of 'my cousin Sparhawk'. Alas, we are not told what Sparhawk did, but the scrapbook contains details of the local MP being returned to Parliament, demonstrating the importance of the printed political word to people at this level. These cuttings from the early 'newspaper' were eclectic, but the collector clearly thought they were interesting, relevant and worth keeping. More to the point, there is evidence that he thought about what he was reading because he made appropriate jottings in the margins. For this man of the countryside, London politics and the doings of the great and the good were worth recording as much as the more intimate news of family and friends.

So, we have a burgeoning readership and the beginnings of a newspaper industry. It is not outside the bounds of the imagination that this fast-growing literacy and the availability of news combined to produce the world of reporting in embryo. At the root of the print world is the thirst for news, be it accurate, false or just plain weird. We can thank the Early Modern consumers of gossip and news for showing us that the activities outside their limited personal circle was a matter of interest even then. It is no wonder that the ensuing decades saw an unstoppable growth of newspapers and journals – despite the best efforts of the elite to control the flow.

The authorities were not going to allow what we now call freedom of speech, so they created licensing laws that were frighteningly stringent. Purveyors of news attempted to circumvent these laws by printing abroad, in places such as Amsterdam, and then smuggling in the materials. But the licensers were not fools, and they outlawed the practice of binding such documents overseas and importing them. If the culprit was caught publishing material which was deemed offensive, the law called for something to remind them in no uncertain terms not to do it again.

Another problem which arose at this time was caused by the Stationers' Company, who held a monopoly on printing and publishing in England and controlled the licences mandatory to print. A landowning supporter of Parliament, George Wither, provides us with a neat case study. He even found it difficult to get his psalms into print because of the monopoly of the senior members of the Stationers. The battles he fought with the company and his persistent attempts to print without a licence saw him thrown into prison at least twice. At one point he claimed that he was having to do the printing himself because he could not find a licensed printer to do it for him. It did not help that he had been hauled up before the Star Chamber early in his literary career for a satirical treatment of the Earl of Northampton.

Later on, Wither made a plea for freedom of speech in *Britain's Remembrancer*:

Must I turne mad ...?
Yes, Yes, I must. For what soe're they be
In presse, or pulpit, dare of speech be free
In truth's behalfe; ...
(Though, at the common good, they onely ayme,
And be as strictly Carefull to shun blame
As wisdome can devise): they cannot scape
The malice of the age. ...
As if truth's friend, must needs be *Englands* foe.
These rimes, I hope, shall not be censur'd

Clearly his words fell on deaf ears. It is unsurprising that Wither, a committed Parliamentarian, continued writing after the Restoration and was arrested again. He was sent to the Tower for seditious libel at the grand old age of seventy-four. Three years later he was taken up again by the authorities, and he records being under house arrest. Defiant to the end, he died in 1667, still writing. He can be applauded for his stated aim of reaching out to 'illiterate persons'.

We have already commented on the power of the Star Chamber, and it was this court that was responsible for Wither's first clash with authority. The pursuit of an effective censorship method carried on throughout Charles I's reign and beyond. The Privy Council gave writers such as Wither headaches with their attempts at curbing the press, which, as he found out, generally revolved around licensing at this time. At one point they limited the number of licensed printers throughout the country to twenty-three, which clearly challenged Wither's aspirations – and woe betide anyone who was found to be in possession of an illegal press.

Another method of censorship was available to Charles' supremely unpopular favourite, Archbishop Laud, who wasn't even liked by his colleagues in the Star Chamber. Laud was given power to suppress offending publications with his official 'imprimatur', or authorisation, although he seems to have been routinely ignored. Laud's crime, according to his contemporary enemies, was his determination to steer the country back to Catholicism by the back door. The result of his unpopularity was a mountain of satire ridiculing him. Various cruel lampoons were directed against him. In one he was depicted fastened to a post in a cage, making him no better than a dancing bear. However hurtful this might have been, the nastiest satire was preferable to his final humiliation, which was imprisonment and execution. Further examination of Laud's unpopularity provides examples of the inventiveness of Early Modern journalists and cartoonists when they were minded to take someone apart.

Laud records some of these in his diary, and there are common themes. One that recurs is the accusation that he is letting out St Paul's Cathedral to the devil. He is described as the 'Antichrist', as a dragon spitting the poison of 'an Asp' and committing 'great cruelty against God's people', who are clearly the Parliamentarians. One pamphlet, *A Prophecie of the life, reigne and death of William Laud*, associates him with the Jesuits, who are in turn associated with the unpopular queen consort, the Catholic Henrietta Maria. For good measure, Laud is accused of causing 'the Church to sin against God'. In a further and possibly graver aspersion, he is said to be admired by the Pope and has been given the 'authority of the King' to act in a way contrary to the laws of the land, making him guilty of treason.

Another pamphleteer, no doubt trying to add a bit of humour to the grim scenario of an archbishop being thrown into prison, assumed the voice of the king's jester. The jester's name was Archie Armstrong, and he had upset Laud, resulting in his dismissal and banishment from court. In the pamphlet, Archie has a dream in which the fallen archbishop is being prepared to join Wolsey and Bonner (Catholic bishops who were involved in Henry VIII's attempt to divorce Catherine of Aragon). They were being 'whipped forward by a company of Hellish Haggs'. There is more than a note of triumph ending the pamphlet, glorying in the fact that 'noe long since no man durst speak a sillable against, but it should have been esteemed as pettie treason. But now the times are changed, and his pompe altered, and he now waites for a tryall which heretofore tried so many.' There is a tangible sense of glee that Laud had fallen so low that he could be insulted with impunity.

When any kind of law lapses, the resulting freedoms are likely to be taken up enthusiastically. In 1641, when the Star Chamber was abolished, printers who had been producing what had previously been termed 'seditious' literature had a field day. The king, his spiritual advisers and his government were now in the sights of pamphleteers and dissidents. Whether it was the result of a shrewd sales strategy, deeply held ideology or a pragmatic mixture of both, the English market for pamphlets experienced exponential growth. The Royalists would have their revenge, as we will explore later. This was by no means the end of censorship – it just swapped sides.

It is remarkable that dissenting opinion survived so well in a period when material critical of the authorities was suppressed so heavily. In fact, the threat of savage retribution seemed to mean nothing to a writer or a journalist who bravely upheld the cause of freedom of speech despite the potential for physical suffering (including the loss of body parts). A writer unfortunate enough to be working in the later reign of Elizabeth I might lose their writing hand for offering an unwelcome opinion. If they were foolish enough to believe that all views were worth putting forward under Charles I, the official reaction was almost as brutal. The unfortunate Alexander Leighton, for instance, was beaten, branded and sentenced to ten years' imprisonment; but even this is tame compared to his subsequent punishment, when he had an ear cut off and his nose slit. As an added extra, the authorities stood him at the pillory to be whipped again and then fined him a massive £10,000. The justification for this was his blatant use of inflammatory language. It was not wise to advocate a violent Puritan revolt and possibly even less wise to refer to Charles's Catholic queen as 'a daughter of hell, a Canaanite and an idolatress'. Leighton also suggested killing English bishops, referring to them as the 'trumpery of anti-Christ'. It was hardly surprising that the king was upset.

This was not the only brutal treatment meted out to a pamphleteer. Lodovick Bowyer, convicted in 1633 of publishing false tales and scandals about Archbishop Laud, was fined £3,000. While this was expensive, the more painful part of the sentence was to have both ears cut off and to be imprisoned for life. Sometimes the perpetrators got off comparatively lightly. In 1634, Mephistosheth Robyns was convicted of libels against the Archbishop of York and sentenced to a public whipping and a £1,000 fine. A publisher named Thomas Archer was merely 'laid by the heels' for an unlicensed publication, sentenced to a public whipping and a £1,000 fine.

A supreme example of a writer whose convictions (in both senses of the word) were remarkable is William Prynne, who somehow managed to upset almost the entire political spectrum. This extraordinarily brave and perhaps foolish lawyer produced a pamphlet which attacked plays, particularly the participation of females in them. Although famously there were as yet no professional actresses on the stage, women did appear in court masques. In his pamphlet *Histriomatrix*, having roundly condemned men for dressing as women to play female parts, Prynne then attacks females acting in their own gender:

> Female-Actors, are worse than male-Actors arrayed in woman's apparel ... Both of them are abominable both intolerable, neither of them laudable or necessary; therefore both of them to be abandoned, neither of them to be henceforth tolerated among Christians.

The lawyer's timing could not have been worse. It was most unfortunate for Prynne that this female fashion for acting included Queen Henrietta Maria, who shortly after this pamphlet was published started rehearsing for her part in a court masque. Naturally, Prynne's comments did not go down well. Hauled before the Star Chamber, his punishment was brutal. He was convicted of seditious libel and fined £5,000, and further punishment was delivered in the most appalling way. The withdrawal of his university degree and the loss of his place at the Inns of Court were the least of his problems. Even standing in the pillory at both Westminster and Cheapside wearing a sign decrying his own work was humiliating but tolerable. What was truly bad was that he had his ears 'shaved', or partially cut away, one at each pillory.

It is an extraordinary testament to the strength of Prynne's beliefs that he went on publishing and getting his word to the people. For this continued defiance he was tried again and convicted of sedition. The punishment was now more than uncivilised. His ears, having previously just been trimmed, were now taken off completely. His nose was slit again, and the initials 'S.L.', indicating that his crime was as a 'Seditious Libeller', were burnt into his cheeks. Unbelievably, he still went on smuggling his writing out to his public. The barbarous punishments meted out to these writers bear repeating because, whatever ideologies they espoused and whatever their relevance today, they displayed great bravery in their fight for freedom of speech, setting an example for all journalists.

Given the ferocity of the punishments handed out by the king's councillors, it was only to be expected that the victorious Parliamentarians made sure they took their revenge on Laud, who provided a handy scapegoat. As we have just seen, they held him responsible for what they saw as crypto-Catholic practices. They also accused him of being the chief mover behind the restrictive licensing practices, and of using the Star Chamber 'to prevent the printing of sundry orthodox works formerly printed and sold by authority, as the Geneva Bible with notes, &c'.

So, when Parliament had the chance, the long-suffering Prynne's particular brand of authorship became useful for the newly powerful Commons. He subsequently produced his lengthy attack on Laud in his 1645 tome entitled *A Necessary Introduction to the History of the Archbishop of Canterbury's Trial, Discovering to the World the severall Secret Dangerous Plots, Practices, Proceedings of the Pope and his Confederates both at Home and in Forraigne Parts to undermine the Protestant Religion usher the whole body of Popery into our Church, and reduce all our Realms to the ancient Vassalage to the Sea of Rome etc.* The book makes good on the claims of its lengthy title, attacking the king and his court. It no doubt went down very well after Laud's execution in January 1645. As the political tables turned, so too did the definitions of obscene and acceptable viewpoints. Perhaps we can spare one moment of sympathy for Archbishop Laud. We can see through the medium of print how quickly a member of the elite can be brought from great heights down to the absolute punishment of execution.

In the confused times of the mid-seventeenth century, it was not just the writers who suffered physical abuse – the books came in for punishment as well. The surprising violence against inert paper and board added another aspect to the trade. The sheer theatricality of an official book burning came in handy for those with an eye for profit. And what can be more spectacular for a book's publicity than to see it ceremoniously put to death? Indeed, the state employed all the trappings of a public execution in such events. A hangman was present with his noose, plus a contingent of trumpeters accompanied by assistants carrying the offensive texts. However, with the authorities unable to find every copy of the offensive pamphlet or book, this spectacular event ultimately failed to stop incendiary literature from reaching its audience. It is easy to find modern examples of the publicity generated by a book's censure: the obscenity trial surrounding *Lady Chatterley's Lover* certainly didn't do its sales figures any harm. For our forebears, the oxygen of publicity might also put the price up. One printer no doubt looked on in satisfaction as the price of one pamphlet went from 14d to a crown. For another printer it meant that not only could he charge the vast sum of 14s for the text but he also had to put on an extra print run. As one MP succinctly put it, the public burning of a book simply showed people that it existed.

There were other methods by which authorities sought to control the press; as the crown passed from the Tudors to the Stuarts, the aforementioned Stationers were kept busy checking for unsavoury opinions in the publications they rubber-stamped. Censorship is an old practice. We know now that it is a largely fruitless exercise to try to stop people thinking, speaking and writing in ways that doubt, question or criticise the government, but the state simply does not like it when someone points out its faults. And in a tyrannical state (which arguably describes the Tudor and early Stuart monarchies quite accurately) any kind of negative comment was looked upon with more than simple disfavour.

From very early on, government held the belief that it was possible to stem the flood of printed material – they just didn't quite know how to do it. For the early Stuarts, the answer was licensing. The monopoly on all aspects of bookbinding and publishing (including apprenticeships and arbitration in any trade disputes) of course belonged to the Stationers, who in return for this privilege were expected to act as eyes and ears for the government, preventing the publication of anything that the authorities did not want to see on the streets. In effect, they were to restrict the distribution of anything the current administration considered treasonous, seditious or heretical. When flaws appeared in the process, the government enacted new legislation to fix them. One thing they tried was to bolster the Stationers' monopoly and strengthen their control by an Act banning the sale of books bound by foreigners, whether in the country or not.

Such scrutiny was originally carried out by the Church. Chaplains would send approved manuscripts to the Stationers, who would make sure that all the necessary permissions were in place, allowing the work to be registered. This lengthy process might have been suitable when manuscripts were few and far between, but as printing presses proliferated the chaplains were soon overworked. They could not possibly cover the reading in anything like enough detail. In addition, there was a loophole that allowed authors to insert material after the work was seen by the Church officials and before it was passed to the Stationers. In fact, it was such a haphazard system that some books were registered before they had even been written.

Returning to Charles I and his battle with Parliament, it was not only criticism of the king's war with Scotland that was creating discord. Religious practice was a continual thorn in Charles' side, and he was very sensitive on the matter. He quite rightly perceived that his form of High Anglicanism, referred to as Arminianism, did not go down well with the growing Puritan community. Unfortunately for Charles, his religious opponents were extremely articulate and ready to do battle with language. One particular bone of contention for the Puritans was Charles' intended marriage with a Spanish (and therefore Catholic) princess. The original marriage proposal fell apart, but the atmosphere wasn't helped when he actually married another Catholic princess, who happened to be French.

The link between suspicion of all things Catholic and the licensing restrictions can be seen in a snappy little twenty-seven-page pamphlet by one Thomas Beard, a Huntingdon schoolmaster. Beard carefully conceals his name on the manuscript, while in the published version it is clearly stated that the author is Thos. Beard. Circumstances at court had changed during the production of the pamphlet: the Spanish marriage had fallen through. When we look at Beard's language, it is hardly surprising that he had been nervous of putting his name to the work at the time. His description of the Catholic Church in Rome as 'the great Whore, which corrupted the earth with her Fornication' would not have endeared him to the Spanish entourage. Beard's other claim to fame is that he taught a certain Oliver Cromwell, who clearly sympathised with his teacher.

As animosity built between the king and the Parliamentarians, the ideal conditions for a regular news carrier fell into place. The first such publication was the *Diurnall Occurrences of the Heads of several proceedings in both houses of Parliament*, which marks a very important point in the development of the press. Published weekly, it was presented as a record of the previous few days of debate in the two houses of Parliament. From the beginning it veered towards the confrontational, and although foundations for the regular newspaper were being laid elsewhere in the world, readers in England were not quite ready for this innovation. Parliament in the meantime made valiant efforts to combat the renewed flood of pamphlets from both sides, but without a more effective system in place it was pointless. There was of course plenty of news to fill as many publications as could be printed, including the declaration of war with Spain and the massacre of English settlers in Ireland by the native population.

Neither side was particularly satisfied with the press, and Parliament needed to fill the void with a new licensing process when the old system disappeared with the abolition of the Star Chamber. Having initially thought they had gained the freedom to produce whatever they wanted, the printers and publishers were soon watching their backs – the new regime was no less wary of the printed word. With the formation of a new Committee for Printing, more than fifty printers and publishers were summoned to answer for their work, and some were punished with imprisonment. But this was retrospective censorship, and it soon became clear that no sentiment could be recalled once it was published.

It was imperative that a way be found to properly license and control the flood of publications. Parliament duly created the 'Ordinance for the Regulation of Printing' in 1643, and it must have been with some satisfaction that the Stationers' Company accepted their old monopoly on the increasingly lucrative book business in all its manifestations. Once again they were allowed to pursue printers outside their register, giving the forces of authority leave to 'carry away such Printing Presses Letters, together with the Nut, Spindle, and other materials of every such irregular Printer ... to make diligent search ... for such scandalous and unlicensed Books, Papers, Pamphlets and all other Books ... And likewise to apprehend all Authors, Printers, and other persons whatsoever, imployed' in producing the offensive material, and 'all those who shall resist' would stand before 'the Houses or the Committee of Examinations' to receive 'punishment, as their Offences shall demerit'. If the printers wouldn't cooperate, the

'Captains, Constables and other officers' were permitted 'to break open Doors and Locks'. Parliament named their own trusted checkers, and publications would need their approval before registration and publication. Interestingly, there does not appear to be any record of how this particular piece of legislation was passed – no record of any official debate or discussion is recorded. The press therefore returned to watching their backs.

Perhaps unsurprisingly, the newly powerful Parliamentarians soon turned on each other. The first to fall foul of the Stationers under the new ordinance was a printer called Peter Cole, who collaborated with known troublemakers and refused to hand over the keys to his premises. His attitude speaks of the growing confidence of the press: 'Who can passe the many Locks and Bars of any the severall Licencers, appointed by you.' Parliament was less than satisfied with the writer's doubtful response, and he was eventually made to apologise publicly for his 'resistance of the Warden of my Company (and those that assisted him), in a search and taking downe a presse'. He duly declared his guilt: 'I the said Peter Cole according to the Command Committee of Examinacions, doe hereby acknowledge my disobedience [and] promise (for the time to Come) to behave my selfe.' While the words were in the prescribed format, the committee apparently did not like his delivery. However, no further action appears to have been taken against Peter Cole.

Despite Cole's contempt for the new restrictions, the various religious sects were now under the scrutiny of a highly vigilant Parliament. This included those not following the party line of Presbyterianism. This became confusing due to the myriad independent splinters of Protestantism, which all regarded themselves as following the true way. If one of these sects failed to acquire a licence, the strength of their faith meant they would simply publish their views anyway and face the consequences.

One pamphleteer who did this explained his motives in a passionate plea entitled *Inquires into the causes of our miseries.* Even the front page makes it clear that he needs no official permission to publish since he has a higher authority:

> Warranted by the God of Heaven, being ordered according to His Churches book on earth; and published for His Churches sake in the very close of this year 1644.

He goes on to explain:

> Touching my licence here, I have no *Imprimatur,* no licence to speak. To which I could answer, Yes, that I have, for by the grace of God, *Truth,* and *Reason* ... have licenced my words all along.... It will be said ... That I go a crosse-way to an Ordinance of Parliament.

His next comment is perhaps made with tongue in cheek:

> I look upon an Ordinance of Parliament as an Ordinance of God, not to be disputed, but obeyed. I kisse the hand of Authoritie ... I went, in obedience thereunto, craving a licence, though I think it my due, and ought to be given me: but could not obtain it. The truth is, if the Book bear *Independent* upon its *front,* and be thought to speak for that way (which God Himself will cleer and justifie before all the world) it is silenced before it speaks.

One such rebellious author was John Milton, the poet famous for *Paradise Lost.* He wrote a very powerful pamphlet called *Areopagitica,* named after a speech by the Athenian Isocrates. In it he pleads for freedom of the press and, perhaps even more controversially for divorce. An important statement by a significant writer, *Areopagitica*'s main argument was that words are powerful and that licensing or restricting them limits humanity. Although this was not a periodical or a newspaper, its underlying message aligned with the work of those who opposed censorship in the political press. It is a constant refrain throughout the following decades: the press's freedom must not be curtailed.

As tensions between Parliament and King Charles boiled over into open conflict in the early 1640s, there sprung up on both sides new-sheets (of several pages) prefixed *Mercurius*. The insults heard in such papers were very often extreme. For instance, in the 23 April 1643 edition of *Mercurius Aulicus*, a Royalist paper, there is the story of how Colonel Cromwell visited Peterborough 'and put them to the charge of his entertainment, plundering a great part thereof to discharge the reckoning, and further that in pursuance of the thorow Reformation he did most miserably deface the Cathedral Church, break downe the Organs, and destroy the glass windows committing many other outrages on the house of God which were not acted by the Gothes in the sack of Rome'. The report claims that Cromwell not only demanded his expenses be fully funded by the good people of Peterborough but also treated their most holy site with less respect than could be expected from infidels. The Royalist attack was reinforced with libellous claims against the so-called 'saints', as they dubbed the Puritan Parliamentarians, gleefully claiming of one politician that 'he should be termed Whore-master' and that another 'should be said to have laine with his wives owne daughter and to have gotten [her] with child'.

Reading through these newsletters, it is quite difficult to tell whether the attacks therein were meant to be taken seriously or were simply satire taken to the extreme. Was one of the 'saints' a pederast? Was another plagued with excessive flatulence? Perhaps the most unlikely accusation was that Mrs Cromwell was a nymphomaniac. These faintly ridiculous accusations did not go unnoticed, and at least one pamphlet from the Parliamentarians saw fit to respond that the Oxford *Mercurius Aulicus* was full of 'lies, forgeries, insolences, impieties, prophanities, blasphemies and popery'.

Possibly the most outrageous claim of all came from one issue of *Mercurius Aulicus* in which it was claimed that while the Royalists were at church like good Christians, their 'holy rebel' prisoner was spied buggering the keeper's mare. As the author of this piece of scurrilous tittle-tattle points out, the Parliamentarians were always reminding people how godly they were, and such activities were clearly not in keeping with their claim. Another publication, *Mercurius Caelicus, or a Caveat to all the People*, did not pull its punches when warning the good readers not to believe a recently produced *Royalist Almanack* because it was a 'Collection of untruths, raked out of a dunghill of Mercurius Aulicus' and was an 'Infectious disease now raging at Oxford', referring to the seat of Royalist government since they had been forced to leave Westminster.

It comes as no surprise that at the heart of this war of words the core complaints focused on religion. The king and his party were deemed crypto-Catholics and the Parliamentarians claimed themselves as the practitioners of the true Protestantism. The king's writer, they say, claims that the Parliamentarians have 'thrust out of the Church the Lord's Prayer, the Creed and the Ten Commandments.' However, claim the good Puritans, 'we have thrust out only all the vaine babblings, and repetitions of Popish Anthemes, Litany and Responses with all the other idle profane fopperies which the bishops brought into the church.' The opposing side was not averse to answering in kind: as we have seen, Cromwell's visit to Peterborough is likened to Alaric's hordes descending upon Rome in 410.

Amid all this squabbling, some people were not inclined to listen to either side. A one-page pamphlet appeared in October 1647 entitled *Mercurius Medicus or A Soveraigne Salve for these Sick Times*. One verse (of two) runs:

> We judge of things but by the second hand
> …
> And we in vaine rely on humane Lawes
> When heaven it selfe doth plead the righteous cause;
> Nor King, nor Parliament may we rely on,
> Tis God must teach us, not those sit in Sion

Despite the efforts of censors, snippets of Parliamentary news inevitably leaked out and were included in the early newspapers, and such offerings generally appear to have been written by those close to the action. Voters and non-voters were eager for information on election results. It was useful to be kept up to date with the composition of the Commons since an MP might have been expelled for anything, be it Royalist tendencies, ideas too radical even for the Puritan Parliament or plain old-fashioned financial misconduct. In any of these situations, people wanted to be able to look in a news-sheet and find out who had replaced the MP. This kind of news is hard fact, and has to come from reliable sources.

So how did these little gems of truth get to the English reader? In the early days, it appears that there was a lucrative business going on within the very Houses of Parliament. One reliable communication channel from Westminster was run by the parliamentary clerks, who were not averse to augmenting their income by selling handwritten accounts of various activities. These included committee proceedings and lists of MPs. However, this very important function disappeared when the printed news-sheets ('separates') made their revolutionary debut (of which more later).

In an age without the internet, telephones or reliable international transit, people had to find other ways to find out what was going on. While fantasy and groundless gossip clearly played a role, with word of mouth to help it, much news made its way around the country through the medium of letters. News was also disseminated by professional writers, who were particularly important in the transmission of information to those in the countryside. While some could rely on letters from well-informed friends, for these others it was necessary to pay for the privilege. The service was considered trustworthy, and the information would be copied and circulated between friends and acquaintances. It was this service that marked the beginnings of professional journalism, where the writing was done for money and not simply for a political cause.

Getting news by letter wasn't cheap: the fee could be £20 annually for a country gentleman to receive news from the capital. Such correspondents were active enough, sometimes sending clients as many as four letters a week. Such supplies of information were treated with great respect; indeed, the recipients treated these regular letters with such reverence that they were bound into volumes for future reference.

However, as we have seen, there were restrictions on writing about domestic news. Relaying it was therefore tricky, particularly as it was commonplace for mail to be intercepted. As a result, or perhaps simply because English political life was somewhat dull before the Civil War erupted, a lot of these newsletters were full of things happening elsewhere.

The extraordinary thing to remember about newsletters in this period (and they lasted right through to the eighteenth century) is that at their inception in the early 1620s they were priced at practically the same level as the mass-produced 'separates', despite their production being considerably more labour-intensive. The printed 'separates' could sell for anything between sixpence and

2*s* per issue, and to match this price the letter writers copied away at breakneck speed to meet deadlines. For the individual subscriber, the cost could be shared by pooling funds with neighbours and sharing the letters.

The number of actual readers receiving news by letter is difficult to calculate, but it must have been huge. We can only imagine how the well-thumbed papers were passed around to interested friends and how far word was spread by those passing on these snippets of news, gossip and half-truths by word of mouth.

The last rung in the ladder of receiving news was hearing it read out aloud in marketplaces and other public areas. One brave soul was reprimanded for reading out his newsletter every market day; he cannot have been the only one. An entrepreneurial publican is recorded as having sold news items at a halfpenny a time. Not surprisingly, accuracy was an issue. There is nothing new about false news, and there was really no way of knowing the reliability of what was available. There was even a pecking order regarding the veracity of what was being read. Surprisingly, newsletters were at the top while rumour languished at the bottom of the scale.

One thing newsletters were careful not to include was editorial comment. That came later, in the hysteria of civil war. Even then, it was several decades before the major surviving newsletter service, written by William Dyer, became markedly partisan. His political bias was obvious in the 1705 General Election, when he commented on the Whig victory in Abingdon that 'fortune had favoured the wrong side'. Dyer was vociferously Tory, so any pretence at impartiality had been abandoned by then.

We have talked about serious newswriting and the questions concerning its accuracy, but there was also a proliferation of ballads, poems and verses. These often scurrilous works were circulated in inns and alehouses. As always, it is useful to have a good example of how disrespectful these anonymous poets and songwriters could be. Who better to choose as a subject of scorn and disparagement than the hated Duke of Buckingham, favourite of the possibly bisexual James I, and who went on to become an advisor and trusted companion to James's son Charles I? Buckingham's story is that of someone pulling themselves to the top of the political tree, and it lends itself to satirical comment by those who would dare.

Buckingham first found himself a place at court through family connections. Young, handsome and with impeccable manners, he soon caught the eye of King James. He became a favourite and was openly fawned upon by his majesty, and by 1615 the two were sharing a bed. We don't know whether or not this indicated a homosexual relationship, but such an eventuality would not have gone down well. On the other hand the King made no secret of the fact that he 'loved the Earl of Buckingham more than any other man... Jesus Christ had done the same as he was doing ... for Christ had his John and he had his George'. The rumours surrounding the pair were not helped by the pet names that the king and his favourite had for each other: Buckingham referred to himself and James as 'slave and dog', and James talked to Buckingham as 'Dear Dad and Gossip and Steenie'. In addition to all this, James loaded Buckingham with honours, money, land and titles, giving rise to considerable disapproval. Alas, Buckingham's delight in purchasing beautiful properties overtook his considerable income. The Treasury had to bail him out, and he started selling titles for money. He ultimately became the symbol of all that was corrupt and rotten in the state of England.

As if this weren't enough to make Buckingham supremely unpopular with the Catholic-hating English public, he also played a major part in the negotiations between the French and English in the marriage of Prince Charles to Henrietta Maria.

The antipathy towards him was only increased when the duke, who came from a Catholic family, refused to condemn the arm of Protestantism known as the Arminians. These were simply the equivalent of today's High Anglicans, but they did not impress the increasingly Presbyterian House of Commons, who regarded them as crypto-Catholics.

Unsurprisingly, Buckingham's role in a tangled web of poorly conducted diplomatic activities and a disastrous war which Parliament refused to fund brought about his downfall. His presence as a scapegoat for all the things going wrong in the country saw him impeached by Parliament. He was eventually assassinated by a disgruntled soldier who believed he had been passed over for a promotion.

The harvest of all this unpopularity and blame for the ills of the world was an outpouring of poems and ballads against Buckingham. In this, he provides an interesting case study in quite how bold the anonymous writers were willing to be. A spirited example is a so-called 'Answere to the Lower House of Parliament'. It purports to be Buckingham's response to the accusations levelled at him, and gives us a good idea of what the bottom rung of the news world might write to influence the lower ranks. The poem starts:

Avaunt, you giddie-headed multitude
And doe your worst of spight: I never sued
To gaine your votes, though well I know your ends
To ruine mee, my fortunes, and my friends;
...
Or that by rapine I fill up my coffers
Nor that an office, in church, state or court
Is freelie given, but they must pay mee for't;
Nor shall you ever prove I had a hand

I' th' poisoning of the monarch of this land;
Or the like hand by poison to intox
Southampton, Oxford, Hamilton, Lennox

And so the poem goes on, talking about his 'fowle lust'. In other poems there is talk of 'a great and wealthie state, not govern'd by the master, but his mate'. And there was even more: 'O Lucifer, thou must resign thy crowne; For thou shalt meet a duke will put thee downe.' The epitaphs are equally unpleasant: 'Pride lies here, revenge and lust, Sorceries and Avarice all accurst … he sinfull liv'd and dyed with shame, His flesh now rotts.' Out of such an industry would spring the modern press.

2

THE REAL BEGINNINGS

The thirst for news was growing across the country, and it was taking many forms. Just as the Ancient Greek heroes found the Hydra difficult to kill, with one decapitated head immediately replaced by two more, the English government was struggling to suppress the published word. Writers and booksellers were simply refusing to lie down and accept repressive regulations and heavy-handed censorship. We have seen how the news was disseminated through various channels, from handwritten newsletters for wealthier patrons to scurrilous pamphlets for the masses. Now we encounter the next stage in the development of this newsmongering.

The printed word was proliferating, and alongside the pamphlets there began to appear short-lived regular titles. These were the first brave attempts to produce publications which might be recognisable as newspapers in that they had some continuity and were produced in numbered issues. They carried a consistent political message depending on their affiliation, and they displayed their title in a masthead. Meanwhile, newsletters were still circulated and the gentry maintained their faith in the accuracy and integrity of their contents. But with tempers inevitably rising in line with an increasingly confrontational political atmosphere, people took up their ideological positions. And, very much like today's readership, they wanted to have access to opinions and news that reflected their own beliefs. The Government became increasingly watchful of the printed word as the rage of party politics took over. As one writer put it, 'Carmen and Coblers over Coffee draw up Articles of Peace and War, and make Partition Treaties at their Will and Pleasure'. There was no shortage of writers eager to fuel the fascination with politics. Inevitably, accusations of dishonesty and manipulation abounded.

We can chart the progress of the press through the entertaining, vicious and plain sensational insults flung across the political divide in the form of Royalist or Parliamentarian pamphlets, 'separates' and other one-off publications. Everybody was desperate for news. They would follow the vicissitudes of foreign wars, particularly those which touched on English sensibilities, just as international sports are followed today. Even those who couldn't read for themselves would pester their more literate friends to find out what was going on in foreign parts. Those who lived in London made their way to St Paul's Cathedral or the Royal Exchange to discuss the wars between Catholics and Protestants across the water.

Religious tolerance was not a virtue generally appreciated at this time. The printed sheets read or listened to were normally translations by Protestant Huguenots and the Dutch in the Low Countries. Quite apart from the risk of draconian physical punishment and financial penalties, taking a 'balanced' view was commercial suicide. Marketing, even when it is implicit rather than a defined management function, is a key factor in building readership circulation. It would not only have been politically incorrect to sell anything that openly supported the Catholics but also virtually impossible in the world of print.

A large readership was therefore achieved by responding to the largest common denominator. In seventeenth-century England this included support of the courageous Protestant armies, even if they were foreign ones. It was seen as the surest way to sell newsprint. News reports confirming that God was on the Protestant side were what the English wanted to see – and this was duly provided by the English pre-newspaper scene.

In the run-up to the early newspapers, it is important to examine the quirkier examples among the Civil War pamphlets, ballads and stories. Their significance lies in the way they represent their readers' opinions. Some of the comments and sentiments might seem odd to our eyes, but the pamphlets, ballads and ephemera are in tune with their audience. The first example is surprising in the approach it takes to many supposedly outrageous actions, including styling one's hair. It's entitled *Women, or, a Spie for Pride: shewing the unlawfulnesse of any outward adorning of Haire, either in laying forth the Hair, or in crisping of the Haire, or broidered Haire of all women, declared fully by the Scripture. Also those Scriptures and Objections answered, which are seemingly made for it.* Printed in 1644, one 'RW' is identified as its author, and he makes no bones about his thoughts on his 'drunk, whore[ing], cozen[ing], lie[ing], steale [ng], murder[ing]' contemporaries. While the condemnation of murderers, liars and swindlers is only to be expected, it is certainly odd in that it includes a long digression on the subject of hair. Although it has to be said that the writer's knowledge of hairdressing techniques is impressive, his lack of tolerance is symptomatic of the age.

Something that also strikes an unusual note in this seventeenth-century rant is what appears to be a command to dress according to rank. He says, 'For your gold and silver is lawful for to wear, by such persons in whom the Lord is pleased to bestow this worldly wealth upon.' By implication, this is a command not to dress above the reader's station because God looks graciously upon the righteous and rewards them materially. His next target is cross-dressing: 'It is indecent in man's sight for a woman for to go in mans apparel.' Some women did indeed go out in male clothing, partly to avoid unwanted attention from men. Overall, 'RW' lays down firm rules for how to present oneself as well as condemning bad behaviour.

Such intolerance was common, and a good example can be found in a case study of a cleric, Thomas Edwards, who managed to upset the authorities. This example also serves to illustrate the way the press was developing and using the printed word as a weapon. Edwards fought his battle through pamphlets and articles, and his opponents responded in kind. Eventually, the rivers of text became streamed as other writers joined in and the press could be said to have self-organised as writers with similar ideologies joined forces. Thomas Edwards is referred to as a 'controversialist' in the *Dictionary of National Biography*. He started out as a conventional English clergyman, graduating from Cambridge, but he never quite managed to get a regular parish. In the days of the tussle between King Charles and the Westminster Parliament, the clergy were in the thick of it and Edwards appears to have been permanently in trouble. He was an interesting character with what sounds like a talent for rubbing people up the wrong way. Very early in his career he preached a sermon so problematic for the ecclesiastical hierarchy that he was furnished with a signed certificate publicly declaring that he had gone against the rules of the Established Church. His argument was that in moments of crisis one should follow one's conscience, even if this meant not following the teachings of the bishops.

Despite this black mark with his superiors, Thomas's vitriolic attacks on various disorderly Protestant sects briefly made him a useful tool in the Parliamentary establishment's war against them. He proceeded to trash the various splinters of English Protestantism in rambling attacks. To prove his unsavoury claims, he presented letters supposedly sent to him by interested parties. Their authenticity may be questionable, but the provenance of source material was not a cause for concern when religious tolerance had become a dirty word. The Established Church, the orderly Presbyterians and the radical sects were fighting an ideological war, and the difference between fact and fiction was not a consideration.

In his most infamous work, *Gangraena*, Edwards took pains to list the many Protestant splinter groups and their heinous errors and practices. These 'Independents' included Brownists, Chiliastes or Millenaries, Antiromians, Anabaptists, Manifestarians or Arminians, Libertines, Familists, Enthusiasts, Seekers and Waiters, Perfectists, Socinians, Arians, Antitrinitarians, Antiscripturists, Scepticks and Questionists. Displaying a talent that is almost enviable, Edwards managed to infuriate them all by writing about them as heretics. Unfortunately, his ability to upset people was only matched by his ability to get his timing disastrously wrong. Unable or unwilling to see the risk in what he was doing, Edwards was soon in hot water with the Parliamentarians; at the time of *Gangraena*'s publication, members of Cromwell's New Model Army and a large proportion of the House of Commons adhered to one or another of these sects.

As an indication of Edwards' methodology we can look at a selection of his claims. Some were plainly ridiculous, while others were faintly amusing. For instance, according to one of Edwards' informants one sect had dressed a cat in a child's suit of clothes to be baptised. Frustratingly, he doesn't explain the reasoning behind this and leaves the reader assuming they did it to ridicule the act of baptism. A less amusing practice concerned the baptism of 'many weakly ancient women naked in rivers in winter, whereupon some have sickened and died'.

A number of the alleged practices concern the lascivious behaviour of these wayward sectaries, and there are the inevitable stories illustrating their lustful nature. A popular accusation levelled by their enemies was that the men used their authority to conduct themselves in lewd practices, while the female members were also lustful and uninhibited. Edwards' contribution to this popular belief was a claim that one sect abused young maids, 'Citizens' daughters'. The story went that the abuse took place very early in the morning, the girls having been tempted out of their fathers' houses at midnight to be baptised while the parents were asleep. A further typical example 'for a certain truth' involves a member of the Seekers sect who 'sought to gain the good will of a Virgin to be his wife, and when she consented ... he propounded that they might lie together at night, at which motion she [was] startled, saying not till we are married, to which answer this Seeker replied, that marriage was but an idle Ceremony'; once he managed to get her to agree, they 'were now man and wife before God, having promised one another, whereupon they went to bed together and next morning after the Seeker had satisfied his lust he ran quite away, and left his bride, and instead of one Seeker there were two, the daughter thus forsaken and her mother (who was a widow) to seek after him.'

In direct opposition to these tales of debauchery, he also declared that once the Independents had gone through their strange baptism rituals their services were disappointingly dull. The beautiful singing of psalms and prayers was banned, leaving only talking and preaching. Elsewhere he states that they tried to ruin other people's church services by keeping their hats on 'in a contemptuous manner'.

Some of the stories are more macabre. There was, for instance, 'one Goodwife in Colchester' who 'brought forth two children both dead, the one a perfect child, the other was born ... with a vestigial head on his chest with only one arm, and the other arm being rather the lump of an arm, ending in two fingers, with something like a thumb coming out of one side of it; there was one perfect foot and one severely malformed'. The cause of this as explained by Edwards seems ridiculous to modern eyes. He ascribed this tragedy to the father 'of this Monster [who] is a Separatist, frequenting their congregations. An enemy to the baptising of his own children; the Mother a hearer in the separated congregations likewise, who resolved heretofore, that if ever she had any more children, they should never be baptised.' Edwards further insisted that this strange tale had to be true because 'this Relation is affirmed by those of trust and understanding that saw this Monster, and know the parties'. Authenticity and checking of sources, as we have seen, was not always a primary concern for the Early Modern hack.

And then we go from the sad and the reprehensible to the slightly threatening, in a letter claimed to be from a man to his vicar:

Pardon my boldness in imparting to you that which hath lately befallen me. I was in the company of some Aminomians that were very importunate with me to forsake your teaching, and come among them and harken to their Preachers, and they prevailed with me so far, that I gave them my promise to hear their Preachers, but the night following I had such a terrible dream which made me break my promise with them; for I dreamed that the Devil would have pulled me out of the bed, and carried me away with him, then I cried out in my deep so loud, that I waked them that were in the Chamber, Lord Jesus help me Lord Jesus help me – then me thought the power of God came on my right hand, and rescued me from Satan: This I take for a warning from God.

With printers and booksellers coming to the realisation that there was demand for a regular source of news, and with their growing awareness of what the public liked to read about, forerunners of the newspaper appeared in which there were anecdotes and stories just as bizarre as anything Edwards could come up with. The first publications that might be called 'newspapers' – in the sense that they were not loosely related one-off pamphlets – were the 'Corantos'. Originally printed in Amsterdam and shipped to England, these were single sheets bearing snippets of news. Because of their Dutch origins, they were unlicensed and out of the control of the Stationers' Company. They began to arrive in England around 1620, but enterprising printers were soon producing their own home-grown versions.

The content was quite international; for instance, there is a particularly heartfelt plea, printed in England, said to be from the unfortunate King of Bohemia, the Calvinist Frederick V. Frederick started off as the Elector Palatine of the Rhine, and a staunch Protestant with a particular place in English affection as he was married to the daughter of James I. Meanwhile, Bohemia had decided that as Protestants they were no longer comfortable under the Catholic rule of the Holy Roman Emperor. So, expecting the Protestant powers of Europe to rally round and support their somewhat rash move, they offered the crown to Frederick. In predictable response, the Catholic forces drove him out of Bohemia so that he ended up as a rather distinguished refugee in The Hague. In a Proclamation printed in English, he complained:

We doubt not but that it is known and more than notorious unto all as well within as without the Empire, into that most miserable

Estate this Crowne of Bohemia with the incorporate Countyes thereunto adjoining, hath been plunged and reduced by their Advisers and their Assistants, Aiders and abetters, not only without lawful precedent causes but also of mere envy, and an unsatiable desire of revenge; whereby most cruelly and barbarously, yes more than the Turkes, Tartarians and Infidels there tyrannized upon.

There are six pages to this document, and whoever wrote it relied on a readership that was either very interested or very patient. Having said this, the writer is well aware of the trigger words and phrases which would have attracted interest. There is mention of the 'shedding of innocent Christian Blood', more 'cruell and unspeakable tyranny' and 'the molestation of godly Christians'. This is all very moving, and no doubt appealed to its fiercely anti-Catholic readers. The shame was that it made no impact whatsoever on the political stage, and the unfortunate Frederick spent the rest of his days languishing in his Dutch exile. However, the fact that it was printed and published in English clearly indicates that the publisher felt confident that there was a market for foreign news as early as 1620.

Not every publication was so clear in its purpose. One pamphlet, dated October 1621, appears haphazardly composed, an almost random mixture of snippets of news. It would have been interesting to have seen the reaction of the avid news-reading public when they opened it up. Among its contents, it tells of the flooding in Ferrara, where 'we are certified that not long since, the River of Adie, over flowed the bankes, and not only there, but in the land of Verona, drowned 18'. Not quite so stimulating for anyone not trading with the Continent are the reports of imported goods. On the other hand, there was an entertaining report on how the excitable foreign aristocracy conducted themselves. They might have wondered if English lords would react as violently as the 'Marquise Centrerione, a Genovesian, was also come thither with 2 Gallies, ...: where being in the Castle of Ovo, hee had a quarrell with 2 Spanish souldiers, to whom he gave two blowes on the eare, for the which he was committed to Prison, and ... presently condemned to dye, but by the Vice-Roy and the Marques De S. Croce his life was begged, but yet condemned to be eight years Prisoner, to pay 10,000 Crownes for a fine, and his 2 Gallies to serve'. Whatever the justice of being sentenced to death for clipping two soldiers round the ear, it confirmed to the English reader that foreigners were volatile and unreliable. As the reduced sentence on appeal was still an eight-year stint and a fine, they may nevertheless have sympathised with the quarrelsome marquise.

Even today we can see the appeal of some of the stories. For instance, there was a piece about English soldiers who were fighting abroad in the Palatinate. In common with many English holidaymakers today, these seventeenth-century troops missed their favourite tipple. Unlike the English of today, however, they were forced to go further than simply finding an English bar, and with commendable entrepreneurial spirit the soldiers were in fact teaching the Germans to make 'Good English Beer'. This no doubt warmed the hearts of the readership. However, not every item was so flattering to the English. One item, while not explicit, left readers in little doubt about recent English diplomatic activities in Regensburgh, where 'many women and Gentlewomen, who never before had any children, have been brought to bed since the late Dyet and Assembly'.

As any political journalist in a repressive regime will know all too well, reporting on government activities is hazardous when your aim is to supply truthful information to voters and others. There is also the need to balance this with keeping the politicians on your side so that any information which is passed on and published is accurate. If the only likely outcome of stepping over the line is a reprimand from an MP or a party official, it is probably worth the risk. It's a lot more problematic when the charge is sedition, and we have seen that this might mean something considerably more painful than a ticking off. In the seventeenth century, writers had to be careful and often remained anonymous.

A major hurdle was the total ban on the reporting of speeches in Parliament. According to contemporary opinion, reporting Parliamentary debates was dangerous. The Members were nervous of releasing too much information to the king or his subjects. If a printer, bookseller or writer ventured to publish the proceedings, the consequences, as we have seen, could be both physically and financially painful. But somehow the secrets of the chamber escaped. The system was not watertight; Members wrote to each other and kept journals, and we have seen that parliamentary clerks could make a pretty penny leaking the proceedings they recorded. If somebody wanted to know what was in a speech, they could pay a clerk the prescribed fee. This fee increased if the customer requested the details of committee meetings. For the party faithful, these fees were worth paying. Parliamentary proceedings with appropriate commentary were invaluable as propaganda. There was a natural appetite for knowledge of what the Members were saying, and there were always people who were prepared to take some risks to fulfil the market's appetite for news. One stationer was given a 'sharp reprimand' for printing a speech in 1640, although if this is all that happened to him then he came off lightly.

It was against this backdrop that the *Diurnalls* appeared, purporting to give almost verbatim accounts of what was going on in the chamber. The 18 July–25 July 1642 instalment of *A Perfect Diurnall of the Passages in Parliament*, for instance, records a number of things that we can examine here. On Monday 18 July, 'the House of Commons being met, Letters were read, which came from Sir John Hotham, intimating that the Cavaliers had many approaches near the walls of Hull & had burnt two Mills near the Town, but he made such opposition against them by Canon that from the Town that they were quickly forced to fly'. So this was a victory for the brave Parliamentarian soldiers, and a demonstration of the way the king's army would happily destroy anything in their way. Next we have misguided priests: 'Then one master Barton a Minister of Buckinghamshire was brought to the House as a Delinquent for reading in his Church at Salisbury His Majesties last Declaration, notwithstanding the Parliament had made an order to the contrary and after examination he was admitted to the Gatehouse for his contempt.' There is also evidence of Cavalier brutality: 'Information was given that the Cavaliers did violently force the common Soldiers (many of them being desirous to desert their present employment) to dig and make Trenches, holding their naked swords over them and threatening to kill them if they will not cheerfully obey their commands.'

These single-sheet publications increased in size and became 'newsbooks' of between eight and twenty-four pages or more. While these early 'newsbooks' did not really feel like a coherent publication, they developed and eventually became more of a series. Between 1622 and 1641, the British Library records an increase in the number of titles to fourteen. These newsbooks, which form such a significant part of the history of the British press, lacked sophistication but they were widely available to the public. By way of advertising his intention, one publisher made the following declaration:

If any gentleman, or other accustomed to buy the weekly relations of news, be desirous to continue the same, let them know that the writer, or transcriber author, of this news, hath published two former Newes, the one dated the second, the other the thirteenth of

August, all which do carry a like title, with the arms of the King of Bohemia on the other side of the Title-page, and have dependence one upon another; which manner of writing and printing he doth purpose to continue weekly, by God's assistance, from the best and most certain intelligence. Farewell, this twenty-three of August, 1622.

These brave words indicate a quiet defiance, and this determination to keep the reader informed ran through the early days of the newsbook. Until the ruling powers found a way to control the flow of information, they could never be sure of keeping the lid on rebellion. Repressive regimes always pay attention to the media, and in Stuart England the battle for the printed word was fought long and hard.

The reporting was clearly biased on both sides. A good example of this is the *Perfect Diurnall of all the proceedings of the English and Scotch Armies in Ireland*, produced in 1642, which is based on a report to Parliament. The first page sets the tone with the comment that the troops were passing through land with 'rich soil, by many pleasant seates' which was 'too good for so barbarous and wretched a people as inhabited it'. The general drift of the piece is to lay out in no uncertain terms who is in the right and who is in the wrong concerning military action in Ireland. Indeed, the rather anodyne front page of this work belies the bloodcurdling content of this account of the violence that was taking place across the Irish Sea.

In a nutshell, the Irish Catholic gentry rebelled against the new Protestant regime in England. Reporting as it is back to the Parliamentarians in England, this particular work leaves the reader in no doubt that the Protestants are blessed by God and the Papists are prepared to burn and forsake their villages to deprive the Parliamentarians' New Model Army of any provisions.

The Irish are called cowards; they are accused of trying and failing to ambush the English army. They are spreading false news about the defeat of the brave Protestant soldiers. The writer appeals to the reader to 'pray with us, that God will please to continue in gracious blessings, and prosper. *Amen.*'

There is one last thing to observe about the publication of parliamentary proceedings. There was a scrivener who kept a stall in Westminster Hall, where he quietly turned out regular reports of parliamentary proceedings. This man, Samuel Pecke, somehow appears to have been considered relatively innocuous, only being arrested twice during his publishing career. No doubt he kept his head below the parapet as much as was possible. It may be that he made every effort to keep his reports as accurate as he could, and was therefore shown greater toleration.

To reflect on what we have discovered, by the time Civil War was underway the two sides had drawn up their battle lines in prose. Pamphlets accusing the enemy of indulging in ghastly, godless and monstrous behaviour abounded. While most content was written anonymously for obvious reasons, people knew the men and women responsible for these sheets. Historians have identified that one of them was a certain Nathaniel Butter.

Sadly, he presents us with a case study in the mismanagement of a bookseller's business in England in the mid-seventeenth century. The unfortunate Nathaniel was sufficiently well known – perhaps we should say notorious – to be the inspiration for a character in at least three plays on the contemporary stage: The first was Ben Jonson's *The Staple of News* (1626), and he also featured in John Fletcher's *The Fair Maid of the Inn* and James Shirley's *Love Tricks*. These playwrights were not complimentary about the burgeoning newspaper industry. It is described as 'monstrous! Scurvy! And stale! And too exotic! Ill cook'd! And ill dish'd!' While this is not a very flattering description of the 'newsmongering' trade, it was the inevitable result of sensationalism and misreporting that often went with the job.

While many of the pioneers of the nascent press have disappeared from the record, some are known to us. Particularly important was the trio responsible for a *Coranto* made up of writer Captain Thomas Gainsford, moneyman Nicholas Bourne and star of the show Nathaniel Butter, who had become the model for so many stage characters. Mr Butter's presence in three plays is not the only mark he left on the dramatic world, either; we can thank him for printing the first edition of *King Lear*. This aptly demonstrates that such men were not simply newspaper proprietors but had a wide portfolio of print works.

Unfortunately for Butter, he was seen as the public face of his business, which seems to have resulted in him being the one who was punished for any transgressions. He may have been singled out for official scrutiny so often because he insisted in taking a strict Protestant Calvinist standpoint and was a little too uncomplimentary about the government. Whatever the case, when the Royalist authorities cracked down on news publishing Butter bore the full brunt of their displeasure. His crime was to be found to be publishing 'dangerous' material, which basically meant anti-Catholic. The fact that he was publishing this material was not surprising given the antagonism the country felt towards the Catholics, and while we may think of this prejudice as undesirable and illiberal it was in fact problematic from a diplomatic perspective as well. This was a period when international relations were strained. Butter was arrested several times because ambassadors from Catholic countries objected to his tone. He did not buckle under pressure, however, and carried on producing *Corantos* for the benefit of his readers.

Butter's story begins to become quite complicated here. Despite their chequered history, Butter and his colleague Bourne were elected to the governing body of the Stationers' Company, and this august institution very generously bailed Butter out in some of his worst moments. Bourne definitely had an eye for the market, later producing a newsbook specifically for the many French Huguenots who fled to England. Butter, on the other hand, was not so canny. While the Stationers' Company were willing to help him – surely indicating some tension between the Stationers and the government – Butter's story is a litany of prosecutions. When the *Corantos* were banned, he was warned to stop reporting the news. However, his life went from bad to worse when he was sent to debtors' prison in 1643. His fellow Stationers again came to the rescue and helped him out. Sadly, this pioneer of the newspaper business died 'very poore'.

The greatest objection to the *Corantos* was always the fear that someone would print something which brought down the wrath of the country's allies. There was disquiet among Charles I's court and the people at large because the king had tried to make an alliance with the French. Disappointingly for him, the French didn't seem to agree with Charles's sentiment that the Hapsburgs' Holy Roman Empire was the enemy. The French instead favoured harassing the Protestants, which they did, persecuting the Protestant Huguenots. This in itself was bad news for the Anglican English, but what really riled the nation was that the French employed an English fleet as part of this aggression. After this rather cheeky move, Charles changed tack and decided to treat the French as an enemy rather than an ally. However, he was not favoured by fortune and after several disastrous attempts at beating the French at sea he signed a peace treaty in 1629. The relationship with France was becoming increasingly troubled – a state of affairs not helped by the presence of Charles's French consort, Henrietta Maria, who had become deeply unpopular. While there were a number of reasons for this ill feeling, religion was the main driver. Henrietta

Maria was an openly practising Catholic, and she did not hide her antipathy to the Parliamentarians.

Before Charles gave up on his war with France in 1629, a great deal of attention was paid to the reports that were coming into the country. They needed to be checked for their accuracy, and to eliminate any comments that might prove incendiary. We have seen that this was achieved through the clergy taking initial responsibility for approving texts and then handing over the material to the Stationers' Company. This would have remained a perfectly acceptable system except that the Stationers themselves were becoming unreliable, and 'false and scandalous' things were slipping through. So what was the solution? It was clear that somebody would have to go in to check the checkers. In fact, the ultra-sensitive Charles wasn't keen on any news getting through at all. His secretary, Viscount Conway, had made the point in 1627 of 'his Majesties dislike of the libertie taken in printing of weekly Courantoes and Pamphletts of newes without anie rule or warrant'. The Stationers, not surprisingly, took heed and warned Nathaniel Butter to mend his ways. They had proved helpful to him, but he was the most prolific publisher of foreign *Corantos* and when he clearly neglected their advice and was imprisoned six months later it was predicted that *Corantos* might well be in short supply thereafter.

With the drama of Henrietta Maria's Catholicism, Charles's war with France and dismissal of Parliament, and then the great tumult of Civil War, the public thirst for news was insatiable. And amid all this there emerged a new space that gave people the opportunity to discuss the news: the coffee shop. Like their modern counterparts, the first coffee shops were places to meet and talk. One poem mocking the topics routinely discussed in the coffee houses confirmed that 'the one talks of news [and] ...stores of [papers] are to be found'. In London the coffee shops flourished, providing the latest newspapers and pamphlets for their patrons to read. Soon such locations were opening up around the country in cities and larger towns. They were a centre for eclectic conversations, and topics included politics. Likeminded men could meet and chew over all the latest news and gossip. Women, of course, didn't frequent these places except to serve the coffee. It was very much a man's world.

So, we have an avid and growing readership; we have an expanding mass media; we have public spaces for the discussion of current events. We also have tremendous political divisions pushing the public into political consciousness. It is little surprise that coffee shops flourished, attracting as they did likeminded people and therefore ensuring a reader could find congenial reading material and companionship in a specific venue. If one has a particular axe to grind, it's good to join fellow axe-grinders to reinforce the belief that one is right.

Much like today, the early newspapers blatantly carried their politics on their sleeves. This is particularly true of the two rival newspapers funded by the two main protagonists of the Civil War, the Cavaliers (or Royalists; also known as 'Oxford', because that was where the king set up his Parliament when he decamped from London) and the Parliamentarians (who had taken over Westminster). Any notions of editorial independence and accurate reporting concerning these two parties can be discounted. Instead, the escalating mudslinging of these early news carriers is simultaneously shocking and entertaining. False news and sensationalism were part of the mix, and while seventeenth-century newspapers lacked celebrity gossip they were remorseless in their attacks on the opposition. Indeed, there were some incredible pieces in the years we are focusing on; often it is hard to believe that they were intended to be taken seriously.

Let us look at an example from the output of the two camps. In the Royalist corner we have the aforementioned *Mercurius Aulicus*, the news organ of the government situated in Oxford. In the Parliamentarian corner we have the *Mercurius Britannicus* of Westminster.

The *Aulicus* issue scrutinised here bears the subtitle 'Communicating the Intelligence and affaires of the Court, to the rest of the Kingdome' and gives the date as Saturday 30 April (1643). The pages are divided into sections, generally with a date line on the progress of the war and the disgraceful actions of the Parliamentarians. The focus of these items is the noble attitude of the king, as in a 'Proclamation from His Majesties ... for the relief of all such Soldiers as are or shall be maimed in His majesties Service' who will be 'rewarded with some liberal Pension'. In comparison to this, the wicked and disrespectful House of Commons via the Common Council of London have 'pulled down to the very ground the Crosse in Cheapside, an ancient and glorious Monument of Christianity ... in so triumphant a manner, with sound of Trumpet, and the noise of several instruments, as if they had obtained some remarkable victory of the Christian Faith'. Furthermore, they have 'defaced all the glasse-windowes in the Cathedral Church off Westminster' and were about to deface the tombs of the kings and queens of England. One can only imagine the outrage this kind of news would have engendered in the loyal gentlemen in the shires.

The opposition pamphleteers countered with their own version of events in *Mercurius Britannicus*, subtitled 'Communicating the affaires of Great Britaine for the better information of the People'. A typical statement of this equally unbalanced publication from December 1643 reads, 'I thought it beneath my pen to dip into the lies and follies and calumnies of such an Oxford Pamphlet ... I tooke my pen ... have discovered the lies, forgeries, insolences, impieties, prophanities blasphemies, popery ... printed at Oxford, formerly a University, now a garrison of popery.'

In the *Mercurius Aulicus* we at last have a publication that comes out regularly, retains the same format, has a consistency of content (albeit clearly biased) and claims to detail current affairs in an orderly fashion. Immediately we have something that is recognisable in a bookseller's window, something that the Royalist or Parliamentarian can pick up to revere or deride according to their own views. This is a breakthrough. Just as today, when a reader picked up an identifiable newspaper, in the seventeenth century they knew the political view that the content was likely to represent. When a seventeenth-century Royalist picked up a *Mercurius Auculus*, then, they knew from page one of the issue for Sunday 31 December 1643 that satisfaction and outrage would be the order of the day. How could they disagree with the statement that 'God hath blessed His Majesty since this day twelvemonth'? And of course there is the horror of the rebel Parliamentarians spreading the word that 'for as much as thou and we know that the King and Queen have brought all this mischief upon us, therefore we beseech thee to separate and divorce those two asunder as farre as the East is from the West'. This new fount of information, having started its life in Oxford, was soon being published in a slightly different format in London as well.

Just as today, the issue of false news was raised in this issue of *Mercurius Auculus*: 'The world hath long enough beene abused with falsehoods: And there's a weekly cheat put out to nourish the abuse amongst the people and make them pay for their seducement.' To vary the menu, the editors threw in a little bit of controversy by describing a visit from two aldermen with a petition from the City of London. They came to ask the king if he would consider returning to Parliament in London without an army, promising to do their best to protect him. Perhaps with some justification, the king pointed out that they were unlikely to be able to protect him given that they couldn't protect themselves from 'wrong and violence'. The detail in this dense, five-page issue is impressive, with day-to-day reporting of letters to and from the royal court in Oxford. Reading the text gives a good idea of the trouble between the king and the capital. Some passages read like pure fantasy, but nonetheless the *Mercurius Auculus* filled a need. One story is typical of the myths of loyalty and love that each party would put out: as the aforementioned aldermen left Oxford, they saw a soldier and offered him a piece of gold. The 'poore man (poore only in outward fortunes) returned the Gold againe, and withal this answer, That the King did not suffer His soldiers to want anything and therefore that he had no need of the Roundheads money.'

The stories the *Aulicus* delights in are clearly those that put the Roundheads in a bad light, particularly showing them acting violently towards decent ordinary citizens. A few days after the above issue came the news 'that it is reported strongly that the Gentlemen of Hartfordshire, deputed by and for that County to tender their desires unto his Majesty; as they returned homeward with his Majesties Gracious Answer thereunto ... were met with and assaulted on the way by certain troops of horse on the Parliament side, beaten dispersed and very barbarously used.' The publication continued for a time, eventually closing down in 1645.

The Roundheads' view of this onslaught on their integrity and worthiness can be summed up in a few words from a pamphlet of 1653. While the author of this defence of the Lord Protector begins by stating that 'the invention of printing was doubtlesse at the first one of the most laudible and profitable discoveries that could have been made by man,' his opinion of its abuse is plain. 'Since the mystery of it grew common, and the permission in a manner general, it hath been a pestilent Midwife to ... Error in the Church and Sedition in the State.' If there was one thing the Roundheads could do well it was to throw insults, and another anonymous writer had earlier attacked Sir John Birkenhead, the author of the *Mercurius Aulicus*. The eight-page rant is a stream of abuse, including the assertion that Birkenhead is a 'learned liar', that his work 'is like an unconscionable physician who for lucre sake feedeth up the malignant humours which liye in the body of his patient', and that 'he is of those that would have the King to be a Tyrant rather and men that live in his Kingdom to be used like slaves rather than like loving subjects.'

On the Parliamentarian side, the 5 September 1643 issue of the *Mercurius Britannicus* quickly makes itself clear: '*Mercurius Aulicus* is rewarded with a place at court, he is one of the new patentees and hast a Commission to lie for his life, for the better advancement of his Majesties service.' *Britannicus* goes on to have a dig at Henrietta Maria: 'Alas good Queen how hath she been troubled in counselling his Majesty in providing Armes and Ammunition and priests and Jesuits and crucifixes.' *Britannicus* gives us a list of the lies that his rival has to perpetuate:

That [they] should not fight suddenly with the Parliament Armies, but that they labour by all meanes to corrupt their Commanders first and to be sure to work treachery before

That if they see either Papists, priests or other in or about Court or his Majesties Army he never publish it to the disservice of his Majesties cause

That all robbings, plunderings, ravishings, or what other act may be committed be called faire usage and generous behaviour

Once it became clear that there was a market for regular titles like *Mercurius Aulicus* and *Mercurius Britannicus*, innovation was in the air. Amazingly, and perhaps with an element of bravery if the quality of the artwork is considered, there were even some illustrations. The depictions of King Charles I and Henrietta Maria on the front page of *Mercurius Civicus* (18 July 1643) are bad enough that a charge of treason would have been justifiable even if the publication had not been Parliamentarian!

But there was a little light relief, and before we head off to the post-revolutionary court of Charles II it is worthwhile to take a look at what the 'ordinary' folk were reading or having read to them. In the previous chapter it was revealed that there were a lot more readers than we might have thought. But we should also remember that many of these 'new' readers were not necessarily as sophisticated as the audience of the court or parliamentary journalists. We have already noted that there was a general belief in magical portents, such as the following story of the strange sight of a foal being born in Wales: 'a brave new Colt come into the world, with new shooes on its feet, and the Nailes so closely and handsomely clinched, that her verily beleeve, that the best Farrier in the world could not have set them better on. ..., yet her must nor dissemble the feares which by reason of this Portentous birth, her Nation is in, viz that the sad imployment for horse and the Iron age of warre will continue.'

Meanwhile, in Northamptonshire there are strange doings which are considerably more sinister. A heavily pregnant woman who had, according to the pamphleteer, spent too much time with the 'conventicling sectaries' and 'vaine babbling and erroneous sycophants' was worried about her child being baptised with the sign of the cross, since they had convinced her that it was a 'pernicious, popish and idolatrous ceremony'. Despite the advice of two reverend divines, she decided that she would rather her child was born without a head 'than to have a head to be signed with the sign of the cross'. Wringing his hands at the fact of said poor child being born without a head, the pamphleteer laments that the

Kingdom of Albion is made 'a laughing stock' and pleas for 'one Lord, one faith, one baptism ... and that we may jointly agree in love'. Alas, such noble sentiments were not the order of the day in those troubled times.

If we are to believe the pamphleteers, monstrous births brought on by misguided religious affiliations were not uncommon. Take for instance the unfortunate Mary Adams, who, having claimed that she was impregnated by the Holy Ghost, declared the original Virgin Mary an imposter and announced herself the true Virgin Mary. She also claimed that the child within her was the True Messiah. This was a very serious claim, and she was thrown into prison to await the delivery of the baby, which took eight days and was apparently extremely painful. The net result of this labour was a dead child so deformed that the midwives had it buried immediately. Mary herself, rotted and covered from head to foot in 'botches, blains, boils and stinking scabs', did not feel able to ask for forgiveness and is said to have torn out her own bowels in a moment of privacy.

The cause of all this misery and deformity was deemed to be Mary's abandonment of Anglicanism for Anabaptism. From there it is suggested that, like an addict who feels the need for ever greater stimulation, she moved onto the notorious Familists of Love, and that when this was not enough she became a Ranter. According to the writer, this led her to believe that there was no God, Heaven or Hell but that Creation came by providence. More sensationally, it was supposedly a tenet of her faith that 'woman was made to be a helper for man and that it was no sin to lie with any man, whether Batchelor, Widdower or married but a thing lawful and adjured thereunto by nature'. In the context of the times, Mary's greatest transgression was to have joined the contemporary equivalent of a cult rather than remaining in her Anglican faith.

Since the readership both in London and the countryside ranged from the upper to lower echelons, there were budget options; for as little as a penny, a book of ballads could be bought which appealed to every level of society. While some of these ballads were based on legends, others were similar to today's stand-up comedy, offering a wry take on the foibles of the great and the good. Sold by itinerant 'chapmen', collections of these works came to be known as chapbooks.

The choice of reading material was therefore very wide, offering something at every price point and covering a huge of range of topics from scandal to politics (subjects which often merged). As we have seen, a fair amount of superstition and bias was an essential part of the mix. It is fairly safe to say that there was something for everyone. Having looked at *Corantos*, pamphlets, ballads and other printed and handwritten material, we can close this chapter with something a little different. This is a ballad written on the death of Charles I:

A DEEPE GROANE, FETCHD At the FUNERALL of that incomparable and Glorious Monarch, CHARLES THE FIRST,
King of Great Britaine, France and Ireland, &c. On whose Sacred Person was acted that execrable, horrid and prodigious murder:
The Judgement hall's remov'd to Westminster.
Hayle to the Reeden Scepture the Head, and knee
Act o're againe that Cursed Pageantrie.
The Caitiffe crew in solemne pompe guard on
Mock'd Majestie as not to th' Block, but Throne,
The Belch agrees of those envenom'd Lyes;
There a Blasphemer, here a Murd'rer dyes.
If that go first in horror, this comes next,
A pregnant Comment on that gastly Text.
The Heav'ns ne're saw, but in that Tragick howre,

Slaughter'd so great an Innocence, and Power.
Bloud-thirsty Tygers! could no streame suffise
T'allay that Hell within your Breasts but this?

The pamphlet containing this poem purports to have been written in 1649 by the 'Ordinarie Poet to Charles II named as John Quarles'. Quarles wasn't an official poet, but the extract above gives some indication of the feelings engendered by the death of the unfortunate Stuart. This leads us to the reign of his son, the Merry Monarch, Charles II, and the beginning of newspapers in earnest.

3

THE RESTORATION, THE MONARCH AND THE PRESS

When Charles II came to the throne, he and his government were appalled at the freedom the nascent press had enjoyed during the Commonwealth. The Act they introduced in 1662 was therefore an attempt to exert control over the printing trade, once again through the medium of licensing and a very tight control over the printers. But as we shall see in this chapter, illegal printing presses proliferated despite the government's best efforts. Their inspectors battled against the printers, but by the end of the Stuart period the press had established itself as a powerful force.

We will begin when the handsome young King Charles II rode into London on 29 May 1660. It was his thirtieth birthday. Parliament had given up their groundbreaking experiment, and it was time to restore the monarchy. At this point, the gentlemen and ladies of the press may have felt apprehensive about the likelihood of losing the hard-won 'freedom' enjoyed by the press during the Commonwealth. To be fair, that freedom was more the result of a lack of control than a move towards liberalism, but it was still a state of affairs they cherished. In their favour was the fact that

Parliament had tasted independence, which meant that the country would never again tolerate an absolute monarch. They only needed to look across the Channel to the increasingly autocratic Louis XIV to remember the dangers of an overmighty monarch.

But the new king, Charles II, was not like the old one. He was pragmatic, and his years in exile had made him shrewd and realistic. His Declaration of Breda, in which he laid out in general terms what conditions would bring him back to London, included a certain amount of tolerance to the dissenting sects – provided they did no harm. The Citizens of London may have harboured hopes of much greater spiritual freedom as they cheered him on.

On the other hand, Charles II no doubt remembered the trouble such free thinking had given his father. He had plenty of advisors who profoundly disagreed with any policy which did not require considerable toeing of the Royalist party line. With a deeply held belief in the Divine Right of Kings, Charles was not going to simply let the print industry have its own way. Almost from the moment the crown was placed on his head, plans to control the press were activated and treacherous writers who dared to air their independent views were slapped down hard. So strongly did Charles feel about this matter that one of the first things the new government did was to pass legislation governing the press in the form of the carefully constructed 1661 Act 'for Safety and Preservation of His Majesties Person and Government against Treasonable and Seditious practices and attempts'.

This new Act was explicit that one of its targets was the dissenting Roundhead writing community, 'because the growth and increase of the late troubles & disorders did in a very great measure proceed from a multitude of seditious Sermons Pamphlets and Speeches'. The ideology of the Commonwealth was dead and gone, and so was 'defaming the Person and Government of your Majestie and your Royall Father'. The new king was not happy that 'assertions have been seditiously maintained in some Pamphlets lately printed' that the upper and lower houses of Parliament had a legislative power without the king. So, 'if any person or persons at any time after [24 June 1661] shall maliciously and advisedly by Writing [or] Printing [argue such, they] shall be deemed declared and adjudged to be Traitors and shall suffer paines of death'. Furthermore, if someone was foolish enough to accuse the king of being a 'Heretick or a Papist or that he endeavours to introduce Popery' they would be punished. Finally, if anyone were to 'declare any Words … to incite … hatred or dislike of the Person of His Majestie or the established Government' they would be debarred from 'having holding enjoying or exercising any place Office or promotion Ecclesiasticall Civill or Military or any other Imployment in Church or State'. In simple terms, toleration did not extend to criticism of the new regime. Depending upon the severity of the criticism, the guilty party could lose their head or their job.

It appears that sometimes the judges were just too heavy-handed, and at least one Lord Chief Justice found himself, probably to his great surprise, on the receiving end of a judgement from a parliamentary committee. He may well have asked himself what he had done. It appears that the man in question, William Scroggs, had actually gone too far in his zeal for controlling the press. The committee heard about one defendant, a bookseller who 'was brought before the said Chief-Justice, by his Warrant, and charg'd by the Messenger …, that he had seen some Parcels of a Pamphlet … in his Shop'. The fury unleashed upon the unfortunate bookseller was out of proportion to the crime:

> The Chief-Justice told him, he would make him an Example, use him like a Boor in France, and pile him and all the Booksellers and Printers up in Prison, like Faggots; and so committed him to the King's-Bench, swearing and cursing at him in great Fury.

And when he tendered three sufficient Citizens of London for his Bail, alleging, Imprisonment in his Circumstances would be his utter Ruin, the Chief-Justice replied, the Citizens looked like sufficient Persons, but he would take no Bail: ... And a while [the accused] was committed by the said Chief Justice, and Bail refused, for selling a[nother] Pamphlet ... he declared to them he would take no Bail, for he would ruin them all.

Scroggs then apparently went on to commit another unlucky bookseller 'for selling a Book called, *A Satyr against Injustice*; which his Lordship called a Libel against him'. The unfortunate bookseller, Jane Curtis, had a husband and children whom she appears to have been supporting. Whatever her circumstances, 'her Friends tendering sufficient Bail, and desiring him to have mercy upon her Poverty and Condition, he swore by the Name of God she should go to Prison; and he would shew no more mercy than they could expect from a Wolf that came to devour them; ... and prosecuted to her utter Ruin'. The judge then did it yet again, this time to stationer Edward Berry, who was committed and 'accused of selling, *The Observations on Sir George Wakeman's Trial*; and though he tendered [£1,000] Bail, yet the Chief-Justice said, he would take no Bail, he should go to Prison, and come out according to Law'.

These were all blatant miscarriages of justice as there was no law on the books upon which to pin a prosecution. Despite this, it took about eighteen months before the last defendant could be freed, even though there was nothing the judge could legally charge him with. The esteemed judge also got a little cross at another trial when his fellow judges decided they couldn't uphold a law that didn't exist. He explained that 'they would insinuate, as if the mere selling of such a book was no offense: it is not long since, that all the judges met, by the King's command; as they did some time before too: and they both times declared unanimously, that all persons that do write, or print, or sell any pamphlet that is either scandalous to public or private persons; such books may be seized, and the person punished by law. And further, that all writers of news, though not scandalous, seditious, nor reflective upon the government or the state; yet if they are writers (as there are few others) of false news, they are indictable and punishable upon that account'. Once again the term 'false news' appears. Scroggs was eventually stopped, but in the meantime he had a field day with his prosecutions. The parliamentary committee which addressed the complaints against him ruled that he had overstepped the mark on these and 'others of the like Nature' and that 'the refusing sufficient Bail in these Cases, wherein the Persons committed were bailable by Law, was illegal, and a high Breach of the Liberty of the Subject'.

But there were further surprises. Lord Chief Justice Scroggs had also sent out warrants requiring the Messenger of the Press to seize 'such Books and Pamphlets ... in any Bookseller's-Shop, or Printer's Shop or Warehouse, or elsewhere whatsoever, to the end they may be disposed of, as to Law shall appertain. Likewise if you shall be informed of the Authors, Printers or Publishers of such Books and Pamphlets, you are to apprehend them, and have them before me, or one of his Majesty's Justices of the Peace, to be proceeded against as to Law shall appertain.' The committee ruled that 'the said Warrants are arbitrary and illegal'. It was a small triumph for fair play and freedom of the press. Justice was almost seen to be done as impeachment proceedings against Scroggs were begun, but they were dropped and the king subsequently awarded him a pension of £1,500 per year. Such examples serve to remind us that, despite the popular myth of an easy-going Charles II, the king was prepared to ignore the law to back his own supporters.

The judges' ruling on the maverick Scoggs sounds encouraging, but it was the exception rather than the rule. In general, the legislature erred on the side of intolerance rather than liberalism. Meanwhile, there remained the challenge of selecting somebody to spearhead a rigorous search for traitorous publications. The king's sidekick, the Duke of Newcastle, had some big ideas. He advocated limiting the teaching of literacy, and would have put in place some extremely severe press restrictions. His opinion was that people who could read chose things which made them think, and newspapers gave them something to think about. He felt that 'when most was unlettered it was a much better world'. The Duke of Newcastle was a particularly aristocratic peer, however, and he certainly wasn't going to dirty his hands ferreting out ink-stained journalists and printers. His ideas therefore remained on the drawing board.

But the noble duke was probably pleased to see that after the chaos of the Commonwealth the new monarchy reverted to one of its favoured methods for controlling the press – the licensing system. The system that emerged, however, would have been very confusing for printers. There were specialist licensers for different types of publications, with the Church responsible for anything that wasn't historical, political, heraldic or legal. Universities had to license books intended for them.

The whole system was thrown into disarray in 1679 when the licensing laws needed renewing and a row blew up over Charles's brother James. James, Duke of York, was heir to the throne. He was openly Catholic, and was never going to prove a popular choice as monarch for the largely Protestant English public. He was anathema to the radical Members of Parliament, who wanted to exclude him from the succession. With the government lacking effective control over the press, James's critics in Parliament were free to contribute to an increasing tide of anti-Catholic literature. There was no legal machinery that James's supporters could use to prosecute them. Tired of the unruly Members, and annoyed at his lack of power, Charles simply prorogued Parliament.

He tackled the unfettered press using the Privy Council, with his bulldog Surveyor of the Press, Sir Roger L'Estrange. We will return to Sir Roger later.

Even with Parliament prorogued, and the Privy Council hunting down the dissenting press, there was still an irritating problem. As we have just seen in the Scroggs case, judges had ruled that publishers of unlicensed books could not be prosecuted because there was no law to enforce such an action. As is often the case with autocratic kings, when somebody told Charles 'no' he simply sacked them and found somebody who would say 'yes'. Eventually, a new set of judges would rule that they 'may by Law prohibit the printing & publishing all News Bookes & Pamphletts of News whatsoever not licenced by your Authority as Manifestly tending to the Breach of the Peace & Disturbance of the Kingdome', essentially putting a block on the news. This state of affairs would hold until 1695, long after Charles's reign had ended.

In the meantime, the licensing system was still in play. However, as the demand for reading material steadily increased, more printers entered the industry. Inevitably, the burden on the licensing authorities increased. Even getting perfectly innocuous material licensed became more and more cumbersome. Something had to be done, and the select group of politicians who held sway over the government decided that offending pieces of print could be deemed treasonous. The problem of course was that it was like using a sledgehammer to crack a nut. Essentially, to secure a charge of treason required developing much more complex legal procedures than those necessary to lodge a mere infringement of the licensing laws. A treason charge involved time-consuming judicial decisions that must be applied individually to each publication. Gathering the necessary evidence for prosecutions necessitated the employment of spies, and the whole business became very messy. Treason was a very serious crime, requiring the accused to have actually advocated regicide. Most publications that came up for consideration for charges of treason were simply anti-government, or critical of some political stance. They weren't at all treasonous in any sense of the word.

The law was failing to keep up with the burgeoning press, and it was urgent that the authorities find another way to deal with it. The next thing they tried was the introduction of something called *scandalum magnatum* – seditious libel – which, broadly speaking, implied publishing material to arouse disaffection against the government. And it was undeniable that this type of press was on the increase. The licensing laws were proving unfit for purpose.

So far, we have seen that the authorities made various unsuccessful attempts to control the press through the courts. It has also become clear that monarchy favoured keeping their own bulldogs to attack the enemy press, with the irascible Scroggs being a prime example. Another was the ardent Royalist Sir Roger L'Estrange, who proved to be perfect for the job. There was no doubt that he operated at the extreme end of the Royalist spectrum, and that toleration and liberalism were not words that featured anywhere in his vocabulary. During the Commonwealth he had been violently anti-Parliamentarian, to the extent that he was sentenced to death for spying. He managed to escape, fleeing to Holland and returning when Charles II took the throne.

His ideas on the control of the press were stated, hysterically rather than clearly, in a pamphlet whose snappy title left nothing to the imagination: *Considerations and Proposals in Order to the Regulation of the Press, Together with Diverse Instances of Treasonous, and Seditious Pamphlets Proving the Necessity Thereof*. This work was published in 1663, the year in which he was awarded the job of surveyor/licenser of the press. First of all, the little book declared it was L'Estrange's sacred duty to find seditious publishers. His employers gave him carte blanche to publish anything he liked from his own pen while suppressing anything objectionable from other authors. Sir Roger established responsibility for the work at every level of production and distribution. He indicated that everyone involved would shoulder guilt, from the authors and compilers down to the stitchers, the binders and the coachmen who transported the bound copies. He proposed that anyone in the print trade caught with a book he considered seditious was as bad as the author, and would be punished accordingly. The approach was retrospective: 'The same Reason that prohibits *New Pamphlets*, requires also the Suppressing of *Old ones* (of the same Quality) for 'tis not the *Date*, that does the *Mischief*, but the *Matter*, and the *Number*.'

In tandem with the uprooting of sedition, L'Estrange also felt there were too many printers. The solution was simple: those he deemed surplus to requirements should simply be closed down. As we saw above, the peripheral trades also had to bear some responsibility for the material that was produced, so they too would require official approval. L'Estrange's system called for the interrogation every single person who had ever been associated with printing or publishing, including foreigners. Just how the government would carry this out was not addressed. His proposals became increasingly surreal and impractical as he went on. One of the almost impossible stipulations was the requirement for guilty printers to identify all the recipients of their texts. L'Estrange justified his views by claiming that the proliferation of seditious texts rendered the English nation 'cheap in the eyes of the world'.

Alas, for L'Estrange authority caved in when the licensing laws expired and he lost his role and position. For the many printers and writers he had pursued, revenge was sweet as they took the opportunity to attack their former licenser. L'Estrange hit back in a pamphlet called *A Short Answer to a Whole Litter of Libels*. He railed against being 'pelted with Libells, in the rate of ... two or three per week'. However, to his credit L'Estrange wasn't only a destroyer of printed works; he is also credited with the creative and innovative input of a newspaper called *The Observator*, which showcased groundbreaking editorials. *The Observator* was a real publication which answered to the name of newspaper, with consecutively numbered issues. His contribution to the development of the medium is therefore significant, and the editorial is something that would be developed in various ways as the next century progressed. It was certainly an important weapon in the vicious war of words between the two newly formed parties in Parliament: the Whigs, who were defined by their implacable opposition to the succession of the Catholic James, and the Tories, who supported his succession.

Another important element of the newspaper in these early days was the changing attitudes of the more enlightened politicians. One of the outcomes of the growth of the press was that the people in charge of the country came to realise that while requiring careful handling, the press could be put to good use rather than always being a nuisance. We have already noted that the proceedings of Parliament were kept secret. We have also seen that in reality this was a pointless exercise since even without the clerks' illegal reporting service there was a gallery where outsiders could hear the debates. It was even more difficult to keep these proceedings secret when it was possible for interested outsiders to tuck themselves away in corners and cubby holes to hear what was going on. The government tried prosecuting, fining and incarcerating printers who leaked news from Parliament, but the interest in the proceedings at Westminster proved more attractive than the threat of retribution.

Parliamentary activities are always of interest, but the fascination with politics ramped up to an unprecedented degree when the Catholic James II acceded to the throne. For Protestant England, this development was simply not to be tolerated. And once the parliamentary debates leaked to the public, the coffee houses buzzed with discussion of the juicy bits. We know these public spaces acted as debating chambers for information gleaned from Parliament, where one could find details of votes held in the upper and lower houses. Sometimes the details were even printed and left in a pile for anyone to see.

Even the most insular of Members realised that some decisions on the publication of parliamentary proceedings had to be made. On 24 March 1680, the commons debated the hot topic of printing the votes. The following exchange sums it neatly:

> **Mr Secretary Jenkins**: I beg pardon, if I consent not to the Motion of 'printing the Votes, &c.' Consider the Gravity of this Assembly; there is no great Assembly in Christendom that does it – It is against the Gravity of this Assembly, and it is a sort of Appeal to the People. It is against your Gravity, and I am against it.
>
> **Mr Boscowen**: If you had been a Privy-Council, then it were fit what you do should be kept secret; but your Journal-Books are open, and copies of your Votes in every Coffee-house, and if you print them not, half Votes will be dispersed, to your prejudice. This printing is like plain Englishmen, who are not ashamed of what they do, and the People you represent will have a true account of what you do.

The MPs came to realise that their voting patterns were being published whether they agreed to it or not. And while they might want to filter what was released, they also needed to guard against the potential falsification of their votes. The MPs, in short, wanted their constituents and the general public to see that they were doing a good job for their voters (of which there were a limited number), but equally wished to appease those who constituted the 'mob', who could quite easily make lots of trouble if provoked.

During the so-called Exclusion Crisis, when many members of Parliament made clear their desire to prevent the Catholic James from taking the throne, they came up with an idea that had a profound and positive effect on the British press. For the first time, votes were published officially under the watchful eye of the Speaker, and newspapers were not allowed to carry the votes. Debates were still secret. Having said that, it was impossible to keep these things out of the public eye entirely, and there were plenty of unlicensed reports of parliamentary debates floating about. Nevertheless, the first brick in the wall had been knocked out.

The regular publication of parliamentary votes was not the only development at this time. There was also the government's mouthpiece, *The Gazette*. This started when the Royalist government was driven to decamp to Oxford once more, not by the Roundheads this time but by a more dangerous enemy: the Plague. The idea was to create a newspaper which gave only serious information. The British Library, which holds a huge digital collection of early newspapers, has it beginning on 7 November 1665 as the *Oxford Gazette*. It appeared twice weekly, and its content included 'foreign despatches, government notices and also news relating to trade and business'. Samuel Pepys described it in his diary entry for 22 November 1665 as 'very pretty, full of news, and no folly in it'. On the court's return to London, the *Oxford Gazette* became the *London Gazette* with issue number 24 for 1 February 1666. The paper is often said to be the first English newspaper, and is still in production. It was made up of a single sheet printed on both sides. The journalist responsible for the paper was Henry Muddiman, the man who put together a newsbook named *Mercurius Publicus Comprising the Sum* and *Kingdomes Intelligencer*.

Muddiman remained an editor of the *London Gazette* right up until 1688, and until 1703 there was even a French translation for circulation abroad. The *London Gazette* still publishes government notices each weekday, and is the oldest surviving English newspaper and the oldest continuously published newspaper in the United Kingdom. The character of the paper was not intended to be sensational, and it carried some exciting news in a very dull way. We have seen the sensational and bizarre reports coming out of the Commonwealth, so the more sober tone adopted by this official newspaper makes a change. Even the most exciting foreign news was reported in the most mundane manner. In the first London issue, Algerians are reported as setting fire to German ships and drowning sailors on vessels identified as Dutch and French. A bizarre Jewish immigrant to Smyrna was calling himself the Messiah and promising to raise someone from the dead. Overall, it reads like a melange of stories touching on foreign affairs and a manifest of ships coming and going.

One paragraph nestling among the foreign wars which was definitely meant for English eyes was a veiled threat to wine merchants who had not paid for their licences. The Exchequer indicated that it was ready and willing to prosecute such transgressors. The threat is so subtle, however, that the offending businessmen might not notice it. Perhaps these traders received more personal and effective instructions and the *Gazette* was merely fulfilling its purpose as the official organ of government.

One other titbit is worth mentioning: when the Great Fire of London raged, the various printers found they had to print the *Gazette* outdoors in a freshly dug graveyard.

As the politics of the capital changed and a new set of politicians gained control during the reign of Charles II, they made it clear that they had no compunction about upsetting the Dissenters and Nonconformists. This new grouping of politicians became what is popularly known as the CABAL – a mnemonic made up of the first letters of their names. This new set of politicians could have been manufactured expressly to annoy the Members of Parliament. There was Thomas Clifford, a Catholic; the Earl of Arlington, who was eventually charged with popery, corruption and betrayal of trust; the Duke of Buckingham, famously hated by Parliament and eventually pursued for 'popery' and pro-French sympathies; Anthony Ashley, the purported founder of the Whig Party, who was loathed by the Tories and eventually arrested for high treason; and the Duke of Lauderdale, responsible for the suppression of Scottish Dissenters.

The importance of these characters in the development of the press is that, with their power and their Catholic leanings, CABAL did not endear themselves to the Protestant population, particularly the Dissenting and Nonconformist groups – and these two groups turned to print to make their position absolutely clear. It was a form of protest they had mastered in the years of the Commonwealth and before, with the printed word becoming their weapon of choice against those who did not share their convictions. Now, with a Catholic prince as heir to the throne, they really did have something to get their teeth into. With such an imminent threat to the nation's established religion in the form of the succession, the atmosphere became increasing tense, including as it did the fabrications of Titus Oates, a perjurer who sent anti-Catholic paranoia into overdrive with his spurious claims of a papist plot to kill Charles II.

This unpleasantness, however, provided a breakthrough for the press. It also marks the beginning of a link with the modern political press, as it is now that the infant Whig and Tory parties formed and lined up against each other in Parliament. Towards the end of the century, the lapse in the licensing laws gave the journalists a welcome freedom as they sharpened their poison pens. But it should be clear by now that the government's control over what was published was already incredibly weak in the face of such an overwhelming mountain of print. There was so much to write about, and newspapers were sprouting up all the time – and they were becoming more and more like our modern conception of newspapers. For instance, in the 28 July 1679 issue of the *Domestick Intelligence* a 'crime report' appeared with a story concerning a convoy of coaches travelling between Bath and Bristol. The travellers were set upon by some 'well-armed' highwaymen who appeared to be 'souldiers', who robbed them all 'to a considerable degree'. One passenger's servant 'fell very briskly upon one of the robbers, and knocked him down, but being overpowered by the Thieves, they beat and abused him very much'.

This being the seventeenth century, we also have to allow for some supernatural activity. So in another story it was a 'credible relation' that a milkmaid sitting by a cow was rained upon by drops of blood coming from the heavens. This is placed next to some serious comment concerning the threat King Louis XIV of France posed to world peace. Following straight after this international news item, there is a report of a drunken farmer's grisly murder at the hands of his equally inebriated neighbour as they walked home from market. These news items are rounded off by information from Virginia in the New World that 'the Indians have of late killed and destroyed many of the English inhabitants of that Countrey, as they were Travelling from one plantation to another, and that it has been usual of late years for them to commit the like, which if not timely supprest, it is to be feared it may have an ill influence upon the Affairs of that country.' All of this is packed into two pages of print.

The printer/publisher of this muddled but entertaining paper was Benjamin Harris, a Baptist and therefore a Dissenter. Not to be outdone, a Tory produced something with a curiously similar name: *True Domestick Intelligence*. With a bare-faced cheek, the second publisher accused the first of being a 'Pamphlet Napper and Press-Pyrat'.

The stories in the second publication are just as varied and interesting. For example, a 1679 edition records an incident over the recent election at Westminster when 'Mr Taylor did vilifie and bespatter one of the candidates there, which Mr Price vindicating, drove Mr Taylor into such a passion as to fling a glass of wine into Mr Price's face, which he retaliated with a Blow on the Face, at which Mr Taylor stepping back, drew his Sword and Run Mr Price into the left pap to the heart'. If ever a story were needed to prove how important politics was to the English at the time, there is the proof.

If we are looking for celebrity news, there is a report in the *Faithfull Mercury* of 25 July 1679 that the Duchess of Cleveland is back in town. Why is that interesting? Because the very notorious duchess was the king's main mistress, and wasn't afraid of people knowing it.

The year 1679 was a bumper one for the early newspapers. In July the Licensing Act expired and within six weeks the 'newspapers' began to sprout like grass after a heavy rain. They showed a harder edge as they began a tradition of mudslinging which gradually developed into an art form. The remarkable and significant feature of these papers was their fierce political allegiances. They were by and large completely loyal to their own avowed faction, either Whig or Tory. The Tory newspapers were generally not aligned with Catholicism, but they were behind James's succession and an increase in tolerance towards 'popery'.

So what form did this thrust and parry of sharp words take? The best way to demonstrate the antagonism between the two sets of writers is to quote them. We have already met the staunchest supporter of the king and his brother in Sir Roger L'Estrange, who, having lost his job as licenser, went from gamekeeper to poacher. And of course the other journalists, still smarting from his acerbic attitude towards them, thought they would take their revenge.

His view in the 1680s that only the most government-friendly or anodyne publications should be licensed no longer seemed to apply, and the press was becoming more confident and controversial. A very short-lived publication named *The Observator Observed* appeared and provided an example of the attacks on the former licenser of the press. It was vicious, particularly if we bear in mind that the country was still deeply conscious of religious differences so any references to such matters were serious. The paper referred to L'Estrange as having 'the mark of the beast' and rejoiced that he 'cannot hang his padlock' on the press. Significantly, he is accused of stifling all 'Pamphlets against the papists' and then putting the 'guineas and groats' in his pockets. According to this journalist, L'Estrange was overwhelmingly motivated by money. This particular paper was entirely devoted to attacking L'Estrange, but there were others which managed to combine these attacks with at least a modicum of news.

One of these papers, the *English Intelligencer*, is interesting for the way it reflected the direction of English politics. This seems to have presented a more ordered approach to the structure of the page. There is at least a nod to layout, with domestic news positioned at the beginning of the two pages. There follows a fairly comprehensive view of the affairs of Europe, mostly concerned with the threat of the French king. However, the issue of 21 July 1679 began with a trial of Catholics and 'Romish' priests. This was not a sensational report, but curiously it did list the names of all the members of the jury. The next story is a good one, containing a tale which would have resonated with any driver, from cabbie to coachman. It appears that a gentleman, 'a disbanded officer', had a disagreement with a coachman who asked for more money than the fee originally agreed. The outcome was rather extreme, with the 'Gentleman' drawing his sword and running through the unfortunate coachman.

Another paper from a couple of years later demonstrates how the press was reflecting public concern about the threat posed by the increasingly troublesome Louis XIV across the Channel. The journalists did not fail to comment on Louis' constant requirement for more money to fund his aggressive attitude to Europe. The *Protestant Courant* of 27 April 1682 tells of the French king's demands from religious institutions in his own country, which it claimed would inevitably lead to 'Domestick troubles'. This could be considered a sign of a certain maturity creeping into journalism. The reporting is measured, and it is evident that an effort has been made to practise straightforward, factual journalism. However, old habits die hard and the paper also features a rant against 'Popish' rivals.

At this time, another British press tradition was developing in the form of hard-hitting satire. The British press has undoubtedly developed what might be called a merciless or even vicious side. This arguably stems from the constant battles staged between the authorities and the journalists in these early days. Inefficient censorship meant that early satirists found loopholes. In the near future, British literature would enter a phase referred to as the Augustan. This was a time when giants of satire such as Jonathan Swift and Alexander Pope honed their craft, and it was also a time when journalism became professionalised. Moreover, the era would be blessed with a handful of enlightened statesmen who understood that newsprint could be useful. However, before satire could walk it had to crawl.

To demonstrate the early days of satire, we will have a look at an irreverent little pamphlet which follows a theme that the reading public might well recognise. It was one used by Ben Jonson in his comedy *The Devil Is an Ass*, and is based on the premise that the English are so bad that even the Devil can't cope with them. The satire in fact centres on two rival newspapers, one of which was written by L'Estrange. The pamphlet, *A Pleasant Conference upon the Observator and Heraclitus*, describes the antagonism between the Whigs and the Tories. The devil's servant warns his master about Plotters' Island, obviously England, where the inhabitants are so unruly that any attempt to conquer them will fail. The Whigs will 'out-pray' the Devil and the Tories will 'out-swear' him. Taken as a whole, the population of the island is 'quarrelsome, Mutinous, Seditious, Turbulent, restless', and, significantly, it is all because of 'a certain devilish engine' invented by the devil – the printing press.

All through this text, the theme remains that the 'Goosequillers' are everywhere, 'into the field, skirmishing continually'. Half demon and half man, these creatures wage war against each other through the medium of the pamphlet. The Devil's servant advises him that the first port of call should be a coffee house, where one could do the reading essential to keep up with each party's latest argument. There the Devil would find 'a table of an acre long [covered with] nothing but Tobacco pipes and pamphlets', and seats which immediately 'fill with mortals, leaning upon their elbows ... and studying for argument to revile one another'.

The pamphlet also hit the spot when it touched on the great threat of the day – Louis XIV, whose ambition to control Europe seemed to know no bounds:

[The] French King ... is resolved to make himself the universal monarch of it to which purpose he daily goes on, vexing, tormenting and incroaching upon his neighbours that no-body can live in quiet for him. No league will hold him, no faith will bind him up ... if you mind him of his treatie-attestations, he presently shrugs up his shoulders and laughs at ye.

Louis was not in favour of a free press, but by the end of the seventeenth century the arguably more enlightened English authorities were increasingly interested in what the print industry could do for them. These savvy politicians eventually realised that, rather than abuse printers and shut down presses, it would be a wise strategy to use talented writers to put the party's point of view to the population, which would prove more attractive and accessible than a parliamentary speech.

With the government now considering a more conciliatory approach to the press, more professional journalists began to appear. These new writers were not simply hacks. They did not throw papers together from scraps of intelligence collected from various sources, reliable or otherwise; nor were they utterly committed ideologues from one side or another, writing with the hand of God guiding them. Some were politically aware, and despite their journalistic balance would have been committed Whigs or Tories. Arguably some of the finest prose ever written appeared in this Augustan age, and the print trade expanded. Writers were becoming ever more innovative at this time, and many of the writers in this period were ground-breaking novelists, essayists and stylists.

While the press was growing and developing, if there was one thing that acted as a catalyst for its explosion it was the lapse of the Licensing Act in 1695. There is some mystery as to why Parliament failed to renew such an important piece of legislation. One theory is that a canny politician realised that the printed word could win him elections, and we will look at how the politicians eventually came to realise the print world could be useful as well as a nuisance.

Journalism now became a paying occupation, and some of the greatest names in the literary canon put their hands to producing propaganda. However, despite this newfound alliance between the authorities and the authors, successive governments were still plagued by illegal and troublesome printing. There was thus another concerted effort to hold back the tide of words. These attempts culminated in the stamp tax of 1712, fifty years after the restored monarchy began its battle to restrain the press.

We have now moved on in time to the end of the seventeenth century and the first decades of the eighteenth. After James II was deposed – or, as some say, abdicated – he was replaced by William III and Mary II, who were crowned as constitutional monarchs. Their coronation oath stated quite explicitly that they would 'solemnly promise and swear to govern the people of this Kingdom of England ... according to the Statutes in Parliament agreed on and the laws and customs of the same'. This is a very different scenario to Charles II's horror at Parliament's belief that they held the legislative reins. This major advance in the political infrastructure also heralded a turning point in the growth of the press in Britain. There was a tangible confidence in the air.

In the last years of the seventeenth century, the people and the law were the catalysts for the next stage in the growth of the British press. Key among the people responsible was Robert Harley, Secretary of State for the Northern Department and a major figure in the Tory Party throughout the reign of Queen Anne, who succeeded William and Mary. Harley, who was later raised to the peerage and became the Earl of Oxford, had many faults. The queen complained that he would never arrive 'at the time she appointed' and 'often came drunk'. To crown it all, he behaved towards her 'with bad manners, indecency, and disrespect'. There is probably some truth in these complaints. However, we cannot deny his genius when it came to employing writers. He had the foresight to recognise the potential power of the pen. He was certainly more enthusiastic than his sometime colleague the Whig Lord Godolphin, who 'ever despis'd the Press, and never cou'd think a Nation capable of being influenc'd, by the Mercenary Productions of a few Libellers'. This opinion was voiced until

Godolphin 'felt the Effects' of the satirists' pens. He and many of his fellow politicians did not have the vision of Harley. To some extent they were frightened of the media, which prompted them to fight the journalists rather than work with them.

It has to be said that Harley was fortunate to have the likes of Jonathan Swift (famous for *Gulliver's Travels*) and Daniel Defoe (equally famous for *Robinson Crusoe*) to write for him rather than a limited selection of old hacks (although he had some of those, too). For balance, we will also look at one or two who worked for the Whigs. Whatever side they were on, these writers mostly moved in the same circles. Some were close friends – two in particular were almost certainly lovers. They were variously motivated by money, advancement or influence. They were level headed for the most part, and understood the job they had to do.

Harley's team included Swift, a high-minded cleric who rejected payment. A Tory to his core, Swift felt his mission was the defence of the Church of England against the encroachment of Nonconformists and, horror of horrors, the Catholics. Swift hoped to be rewarded with an English bishopric, but in the end had to settle for the post of Dean of St Patrick's Cathedral in Dublin. Swift was a brilliant satirist, and certainly a forerunner of the most cutting exponents of the art today. Daniel Defoe was a different case. A serial failure in business matters, Defoe wrote for money. Naturally rather Whiggish through his Dissenter background, he wrote and worked on the principle that more words meant more money.

Also included in this list is a woman who, while not a household name, is significant in the field of women's journalism. Her name was Delarivier Manley. This feisty, talented lady was possibly the first professional female political journalist in the English language. She was not the first woman to write for a living, but her engagement with Cabinet-level politicians was remarkable. With a colourful private life, she had a genius for making a little bit of scandalous gossip go a long way. She was paid on an irregular basis by Harley, usually after a great deal of cajoling if her surviving letters are anything to go by.

Manley and Swift were Hanoverian Tories, staunchly committed to the royal line remaining Protestant. They knew each other well, working together and agreeing on many issues; they were particularly united in their dislike of Defoe, whom they had never met. One notable opponent of theirs was Sir Richard Steele, a Whig MP, playwright and literary stylist. Queen Anne's reign has been called a Golden Age, and considering the number of distinguished writers active at the time it was certainly a period which stands out as innovative and creative. This is particularly true of the rapidly developing genre of satire. The writers of this period set the bar very high for future generations.

While Harley's awareness of the positive power of the press should not be underestimated, the government could still be ruthless with unauthorised print. Anybody publishing anything deemed beyond the pale would still find themselves hauled before the authorities. Indeed, entire production teams found themselves in troubled waters. So while the lapse of the Licensing Act *could* have been the gateway to a completely free press, the government in fact stayed on the lookout for seditious material. Indeed, within a year of taking the throne Queen Anne was already nervous that the press was too independent. She spoke in the Houses of Parliament and declared, 'I think it might have been for the Public Service, to have had some further Laws for restraining the great License, which is assumed, of publishing and spreading scandalous Pamphlets and Libels; but, as far as the present Laws will extend, I hope you will all do your Duty, in your respective Stations, to prevent and punish such pernicious Practices.'

Of course, politicians have to take notice when something starts upsetting the queen, and the government duly tried to bring back the treason laws – once again with a notable lack of success. They had to haul the offenders before a judge and jury, who would then decide whether the offending text was treasonous. In fact, in one singularly unsuccessful raid the government arrested fourteen printers and then had to let them all go again. Unfortunately for the exasperated government, treason laws were labyrinthine and the defendants were entitled to all sorts of rights, such as production of witnesses and proof for a prosecution. Simply accusing a printer of treason was not satisfactory, so the problem of anti-governmental propaganda wasn't going to go away. The authorities had to look back to older techniques for prosecuting printers, writers and publishers. At their wits' end, they went back to using the seditious libel laws.

Each of our star writers (except Swift, an ordained minister whose identity was closely guarded) was hauled up before the law to answer for something they had produced. So while the concept of licensing may have gone, there was by no means a propaganda free-for-all. The new proposal was that libel be defined not only as something said to the detriment of an individual, but also to a whole government.

What is it that changed to allow this flourishing professionalism among the press in the half century since the Restoration? We can't look to technology; it's not as though social media had taken over and turned everyone into a citizen journalist. True, the Licensing Act had lapsed, but the state continued to go after members of the press for seditious libel. One suggestion is that in the late 1600s writers found a way round the laws of libel by being 'ironic'. There are obviously problems with this; one major drawback is that the reader needs to have a sense of humour, and the writer needs considerable skill. Nonetheless, it possible that the British talent for satire and irony had its origins in the need to avoid prosecution while making a critical statement.

In preparation for the next chapter, it would be useful to look at some of the individuals who were key to the next stage in the development of the British press. Their talent helped shape the industry, and as publications became increasingly sophisticated these characters stamped their different styles on the printed page. The first is the aforementioned Daniel Defoe, who seemed to be able to turn his hand to anything. He was an undercover agent, travelling the country in disguise and reporting back to Harley on the mood of the people. He also produced a number of newspapers, one of which, the *Review*, became the official organ of the ruling moderate Tories. He is most famous today for his novels, of which *Robinson Crusoe*, *Moll Flanders* and *Roxana* are probably the best-known. But beyond all this, Defoe created two remarkable works that were somewhat before their time – one of which put him in the stocks.

First came *The True-Born Englishman*, a satirical poem which attacked xenophobia and racism, particularly in relation to attitudes to the Dutch William III. In a truly modern-sounding comment, Defoe explains that 'I only infer that an Englishman, of all men, ought not to despise foreigners as such, and I think the inference is just, since what they are to-day, we were yesterday, and to-morrow they will be like us.' One wouldn't want to argue with that.

However, his other significant satirical pamphlet was so subtle that it landed him in the stocks. It was meant to be taken as ironic, but the joke was completely lost on the oversensitive Whigs. *The Shortest Way with Dissenters* purported to be written by a High Tory, and recommended sweeping and brutal punishments for anyone who didn't conform to the Church of England. One suggestion, made with tongue firmly in cheek, was that 'one severe Law [should be] made, and punctually executed, that whoever was found at a Conventicle, should be banished the

Nation, and the Preacher be hang'd'. He goes on to explain that the established Church of England is like Christ on the cross, with popery on one side and the Dissenters on the other. In a major sense-of-humour failure, the Whigs took this to mean that followers of these branches of Christianity should be treated as thieves and literally crucified, 'the doors of Mercy being always open' to them if they returned to the Anglican fold. When the outraged Whigs – who were advocates of toleration for the wider Christian Church – discovered that Defoe had written the piece, they promptly fined him and put him in the stocks.

Defoe was genuinely puzzled at the government's failure to understand his sarcasm: 'If any Man take the Pains seriously to reflect upon the Contents, the Nature of the Thing, and the Manner of the Style, it seems impossible to imagine it should pass for any Thing but a Banter upon the high-flying Church Men.' Defoe was eventually pardoned, and as part of the deal agreed to work for Harley, who was part of what we might call a coalition government. He began his journalism career with *The Review*, the mildly Tory periodical that he wrote single-handedly for ten years. A ground-breaking work, *The Review* was described as 'his great achievement'. It showed that thoughtful journalism could be used to influence readers, and it also showcased the political essay. Using persuasion rather than invective, it discussed the importance of trade and what was to become economics. *The Review* is a fine example of journalism's growing maturity at the time.

While Defoe's first periodical merits considerably more space than can be spared here, it contains one observation which is probably as relevant today as it was when it was written in 1712: 'What an age of Contradiction and Inconsistency do we live in? And what is it that must bring us to the use of our reason?' One of the abiding qualities of some of these early journalists is that they have a grasp on reality that resonates today.

Jonathan Swift, the man who wrote *Gulliver's Travels*, was another writer hand-picked by Harley. A Tory defender of the Church of England, Swift was principled when it came to money and deeply affected by the sufferings of his fellow man. Always one to write from the heart, he was angry much of the time and sometimes sailed a little too close to the political wind. His impeccable and perfectly targeted satires were biting attacks on corruption, cruelty and the exploitation of the powerless. His skill can be demonstrated in a brief description of what is perhaps the most perfect piece of satire: *A Modest Proposal for Preventing the Children of Poor People in Ireland, from Being a Burden on Their Parent or Country, and for Making Them Beneficial to the Publick*. The premise here is that the Irish are so poor that their only economic resource is the children they produce. He proposes that the children should, like piglets, be allowed to grow up to the age of twelve months; beyond this, they become too tough. The suggestion is that Irish babies are edible and can be sold to the gentry as a delicacy. To maximise the profit, their skins will make excellent gloves. This horrifying notion is meant as a metaphor for the way that English landlords in Ireland took all the profit and left their tenants starving.

One begins to understand how Swift is softening the reader up for the final horror when he makes a ridiculous statement: 'I have reckoned upon a medium, that a child just born will weigh 12 pounds, and in a solar year, if tolerably nursed, increases to 28 pounds.' In closing, Swift offers that 'this food will be somewhat dear, and therefore very proper for landlords, who, as they have already devoured most of the parents, seem to have the best title to the children'. Suddenly the satirical thrust of what is being suggested is clear. The brilliance of Swift's wit shines through.

Aside from the satire, Swift also wrote very serious pamphlets and was responsible for several issues of the first of the heavyweight Tory periodicals before he was removed from the editor's chair. As brilliant as he was, Swift was also very independent and this made him too much of a loose cannon. One of his pamphlets caused so much uproar that he only avoided prosecution thanks to Harley's protection, and he was never really trusted again. He was replaced by the racy Delarivier Manley, whom Winston Churchill described as a 'woman of disreputable character paid by the Tories' to be consigned to 'the cesspool from which she should never have crawled'. This reaction stems from Manley's leading role in the vicious treatment of his ancestors, the Duke and Duchess of Marlborough, at the hands of the press. Manley is largely unknown today, except in academic circles, but she was feisty, fearless and went for the jugular. She had an interesting private life, marrying her bigamous cousin and taking as a lover the Governor of Fleet Prison, who managed to get them both hauled up for fraud. She also lived with her printer (more on him later), and possibly had some kind of affair with the co-founder of *The Spectator*. As well as all this, Manley was the gambling companion of Barbara Castlemaine, Charles's notorious mistress. When she wrote about scandal, she knew what she was talking about.

One of the most successful areas of the British press even today is the exposure of celebrities behaving badly, and we need look no further than Manley for an early expert in the field. Manley's nose for scandal was legendary in her own lifetime. She was a pioneer in the dubious arts of the gossip column. The unfortunate result of this talent for sniffing out the seamier activities of public figures was that she made enemies. Early on in her writing career, this High Tory seems to have engaged in an unlikely love affair with the committed Whig Sir Richard Steele (he of *The Spectator*). It came to grief, resulting in a very public spat which apparently began when Steele wouldn't lend Manley a coach fare. Such an affair might still make the gossip columns today, but it also sums up the small, overheated world in which the two writers lived and worked.

Sir Richard Steele came from a very similar social grouping to Manley, although he had been born in Ireland. He had been a soldier, and he started his first newspaper while he was editing *The Gazette*, the government organ. His political loyalties lay with the Whigs. He began *The Tatler* in 1709, with the avowed intention of raising the moral standards of the nation. He declared, 'I shall take upon me only indecorums, improprieties, and negligences, in such as should give us better examples. After this declaration, if a fine lady thinks fit to giggle at church, or a great beau come in drunk to a play, either shall be sure to hear of it in my ensuing paper.'

The stage had been set, and very soon *The Tatler*, which was decidedly not a newspaper, mostly carrying only social commentary, became one of the first lifestyle magazines. Its declared mission was to educate the public in polite behaviour. The very first words of the new publication read, 'It is both a charitable and necessary work to offer something whereby such worthy and well-affected members of the commonwealth may be instructed, after their reading, what to think; which shall be the end and purpose of this my paper.' There was even an introductory offer: 'I therefore earnestly desire all persons, without distinction, to take it in for the present, gratis, and hereafter, at the price of one penny.' It is arguable that we might find such sentiments patronising, and just a little bit annoying, but there was definitely a move to improve society.

While *The Tatler* started out with very little hard news, it did offer something new from the very first issue on 12 April 1709, theatre reviews:

On Thursday last was acted ... the celebrated comedy called *Love for Love* ... There has not been known so great a concourse of persons of distinction as at that time; the stage itself was covered with gentlemen and ladies, and when the curtain was drawn, it discovered even there, a very splendid audience …. All the parts were acted to perfection: the actors were careful of their carriage, and no one was guilty of the affectation to insert witticisms.

Despite his soldiering background, Steele represented the gentility of the coming age. There was even a Society for the Reformation of Manners at this time – and Steele, of course, was a fully paid-up member.

In marked contrast, his sworn enemy Manley seemed to embody the licentiousness of the Restoration and the easy morals of some of her contemporaries. Manley made her name highlighting bad behaviour rather than encouraging gentility and politeness. She did spend a few days cooling her heels in the Tower as a result of her outrageous reports, but the fact that she changed people's names to protect their privacy helped her get away with it – as did the simple fact that the stories were true.

Manley was Robert Harley's preferred choice of editor for a run of *The Examiner* when he was leader of the Tories. It's a little difficult to pin down how she got the job, which she took over from Swift; all that can be said is that the Tories were in disarray, with rebellious backbenchers openly challenging the moderate Harley to take a tougher line. He believed they needed the official Tory publication to act as a rallying point, and Manley's description of the unruly MPs as 'the best House of Commons that ever sat' was expressly intended to flatter those difficult backbenchers.

Alongside these publications were a whole raft of newspapers that, while unknown today, were just as partisan and notorious. The names of these were confusingly similar: *The Post Boy* (Tory), *The Protestant Post Boy*, *The Flying Post* (Whig), the *Flying Post and Medley* (Whig). The words poured out as they lined up in their factions to attack each other with an arsenal of abuse of breathtaking range. They flung insults, innuendos, half-truths, false news and propaganda at each other. Once more the press was becoming increasingly anarchic, despite the government hunting down and arresting the printers, writers and booksellers.

Finally, the government made yet another attempt to control the press. In August 1712, the Tory government decided to tax newspapers by the sheet. This was not particularly successful; it was difficult to administer, and did not seem to raise much in the way of revenue. However, a penny on full sheets and a halfpenny on half sheets was something, and a shilling on advertisements provided further funds. It suited the government that their enforcers could be increasingly heavy-handed, with property seized and offending printers thrown into gaol. Better still, the law said such offenders could be left in gaol to ponder on their misdemeanours until the Secretary of State felt they had learnt their lesson. Once again, life as a printer was becoming difficult.

4

THE WAR OF THE WORDS

All through Queen Anne's reign and beyond, the Whigs and Tories slugged each other in accordance with what one writer called 'the Art of Political Lying'. The period is rich in examples of seditious and probably libellous stories in periodicals, newspapers, pamphlets and even song sheets. Reporting was dubious, and publishers found ways around libel laws. But the new century also saw a step forward for authors: for the first time, some proudly put their names to their work. The biographies of some of the main players make good reading, and their punishments (which for some included spells in the Tower and the stocks) did little to curb their enthusiasm. Innovation was in the air, and periodicals began to appear in growing numbers. This era saw the birth of *The Examiner, The Guardian,* and *The Spectator.* The use of *noms de plume* and invented characters also proliferated alongside the self-identifications, and vicious personal attacks were common.

On 11 May 1710, a large woman swept into the Stationers' Company and registered her authorship of another book in her series of scandalous fictions. With her tales of excess among the glitterati of Queen Anne's England, she enjoyed a large Tory following and held a fascination for the Whigs, who were her main target. A particular statute had just been passed in Parliament, and she was determined to take advantage of it. The lady in question was Delarivier Manley, and she was indeed among the very first to make use of the *Act for the Encouragement of Learning, by Vesting the Copies of Printed Books in the Authors or Purchasers of such Copies, during the Times therein mentioned*, commonly known as the Statute of Anne. This was a huge step forward for authors as it acknowledged their rights. The text of the Act ran:

> Whereas Printers, Booksellers, and other Persons, have of late frequently taken the Liberty of Printing, Reprinting, and Publishing, or causing to be Printed, Reprinted, and Published Books, and other Writings, without the Consent of the Authors or Proprietors of such Books and Writings, to their very great Detriment, and too often to the Ruin of them and their Families: For Preventing therefore such Practices for the future, and for the Encouragement of Learned Men to Compose and Write useful Books; May it please Your Majesty, that it may be Enacted ... That from and after the 10th April 1710, the Author of any Book or Books already Printed ... shall have the sole Right and Liberty of Printing such Book and Books for the Term of One and twenty Years.

Much as it is today, the practice of reproducing work without an author's permission was all too common, and nobody – particularly an impecunious writer – wanted someone else to profit from their labours. There were, of course, times when the last thing an author wanted was to be identified with a supposedly seditious work. For instance, Manley's *New Secret Memoirs and Manners of Several Persons of Both Sexes from the New Atalantis*, published in the previous year, had got her thrown into the Tower of London for a couple of weeks, although she was released without charge.

The new volume which she had arrived to register was *Memoirs of Europe Towards the Close of the Eighth Century, Written by Eginardus, Secretary to and Favourite to Charlemagne and Done into English by the Translator of the New Atalantis*. This was a bit of a mouthful, and the book was commonly known as *Memoirs of Europe*. This was a bold move given her past imprisonment, but Manley was known as a committed Tory and her party was in line for a landslide victory – which duly arrived that year – so no doubt she felt safer than when her first volume had appeared in 1709.

While Manley's writing might have represented the more scurrilous end of the spectrum, there were others who were pushing at the boundaries of libel. The range of insulting language used by writers of all political persuasions shows their increasing confidence. This chapter will look at the interesting and innovative techniques employed as the two political parties clashed in this war of the words.

The most familiar method at this point is probably the scrutinising of public figures' private lives to find something that would discredit them. This was a particularly fruitful exercise, since very few of the major figures of the day appear to have behaved themselves. For instance, Manley included her former patron Barbara Castlemaine, Duchess of Cleveland, in her 'secret histories' although there was little that she could write about the amoral mistress of Charles II which would surprise anyone. Today she would be described today as a predatory cougar, with conquests including the ambitious twenty-one-year-old John Churchill, later Duke of Marlborough.

To return to the development of the press, a variety of formats were popular by this time. Some have since disappeared, and some we might find odd. One of the most common was a dialogue specifically set up to provide information on certain issues from a particular political standpoint. In some ways it was an early version of a very partisan FAQ on current affairs. These dialogues featured an informed individual who would correct the views of his mistaken friend. The conversations sometimes continued over several issues of the publication. They usually placed a particularly naïve gentleman, often a countryman, visiting the big city in the company of a knowledgeable, world-weary friend. The naïve countryman asks about current news and is told the true state of affairs by his friend.

For instance, in L'Estrange's *Observator* the conversations between the Whig and the Tory end with the Whig agreeing with the Tory, and declaring himself full of admiration. This rather unnatural dialogue is meant to illustrate policies, principles and decisions to those people who didn't quite understand them, hopefully winning over the undecided in the process. There is no doubt that these 'conversations' are contrived. L'Estrange's *Observator* specialised in this method, as did his extreme Tory *Observator in Dialogue*. L'Estrange's original made no bones about its allegiance; in an early issue of 2 July 1681, the two protagonists questioned each other on the true nature of the Whig and the Tory. The Tory is 'as Honest and as Loyall with One Arm or One Leg as ... with two' and the Whig 'never remember[s] benefits, nor Forget[s] Injuryes' or 'Repent[s] of any Wickedness'. The Tory support is absolutely unquestionable. We will see that this format continued into the eighteenth century.

Alongside these quite serious texts there are lampoons and poems, some of which are outrageous while others are panegyrics. At the height of the hostilities with France they were often about the Marlboroughs, treating them as either greedy or patriotic depending upon the authorship. There are dream sequences, including one written by Robert Harley, and an abundance of amusing satires. And of course there is the out and out rant, straight and to the point and often offensive. One of the distinguishing features of this period and its satire is that much of it is absolutely personal, *ad hominem*. The writers cover their backs by either using codenames, redacting letters or employing allegory where it is blatantly obvious who they mean. For instance, any poems or pamphlets attacking someone called 'Robin' are directed against Robert Harley, and the term 'great lady' usually refers to Sarah Churchill, Duchess of Marlborough, and her purported arrogance and pride.

Mocking or supporting individual Whigs or Tories seems to have been a very good trade for the scribblers of Grub Street. For instance, here is a typical offering from the Whigs:

S[ara]h: tho' thy Tory Foes, now prate
Once at home they shaking sat
Whilst thou abroad did Toils endure
To keep 'em from the Foe secure

The ballad writer here is clearly very much on the side of team Marlborough. The piece is a reminder from the Whigs of how much they owe the great general. Alternatively, a Tory sympathiser might want to read a pamphlet where the duchess is deemed 'chief sufferer' among The Petticoat Plotters, a club made up of the wives of the politicians following the fall of the Whig party. These 'impoverished' ladies bemoan the loss of their status and, most importantly, their income. They are forced to give up servants, with one unfortunate woman reduced to a solitary footman for her coach (down from three) and, horror of horrors, she is now dressed by her chambermaid.

Others pieces are much more focussed on attacking the Marlboroughs, who are described as War Wolf and She Wolf.

They 'both together shall combine infected with th' ambitious itch of being very great and rich'. Another one is subtitled 'Turned out of Court at Last'. We might conjecture that these are cheap pamphlets and ballads and that they are aimed at the barely literate. If so, it can be suggested that an impressive portion of the population had the level of background knowledge required to understand them. One ballad points out that while going to war was the right thing to do, now is the time for peace. Although undated, it would have appeared at the time of the end of the war with France, when the Tories were advocating an end to hostilities.

One of the weirder pamphlets is entitled the *Duchess of Marlborough's Creed* and essentially equates her with a bunch of radicals who were 'conceived by *phanaticism*, born of *sedition* and *rebellion*'. Such highly political pieces of ephemera indicate that politics was as much of a feature at the roughest end of the market as it was in the rarefied works written for the elites.

To really understand the depth of feeling at this time, we need a case study where both sides of the political divide felt compelled to put out a mountain of pamphlets. An excellent place to start is with a celebrity who caught the public eye and found himself in the midst of a media storm. The extraordinary cleric Dr Henry Sacheverell achieved notoriety through a sermon. He was regarded with disgust and adulation in equal measures by the two factions. It may seem a little odd that a clergyman of the Church of England could achieve something approaching rockstar status, but it is even stranger to consider that he reached these giddy heights of celebrity because of a controversial sermon. The homily in question was called *The Perils of False Brethren*, and was delivered on 5 November 1709 at St Paul's Cathedral. This was not just a ninety-minute rant but a scathing attack on the Whig policy of toleration of the Dissenting community or those Protestants who did not belong to the Church of England.

It was feared that such openness might herald a more accepting age, with rights of religious freedom potentially being granted to Quakers or Presbyterians, whom Sacheverell referred to as 'monsters and vipers'. The sermon, as was usual, was subsequently published (possibly without the permission of the Lord Mayor) and immediately sold like hotcakes, soon reaching the phenomenal figure of 100,000 copies.

The Whigs felt that they could not allow this right-wing defiance of their policy to go unpunished. The sermon was strong stuff, but it might have been a mistake for the preacher to refer to Godolphin, the Lord Treasurer, as 'Volpone' (the Fox). It was admittedly his popular nickname, indicating that he had a reputation for being sly, but it was not one to use in print and was bound to upset the Whig ministry. The Whigs therefore brought Sacheverell before the House of Lords, accusing him of 'high crimes and misdemeanours'.

It is sometimes the case that governments don't read the mood of the people very accurately, and such was the case in the Sacheverell furore. In truth, their lack of understanding of the public zeitgeist was monumental. There was rioting the night before the trial, with Dissenting chapels torched and destroyed, which should have been sufficient cause for alarm. Additionally, the reporting in the flood of pamphlets concerning the trial should have been a big red flag. It simply didn't occur to the government that it would have been better to let the sermon sink without a trace under its own weight. By giving Sacheverell the oxygen of publicity, they made the problem much worse.

Joseph Addison in *The Tatler* illustrates how the country was gripped by the trial of this flamboyant clergyman. He complained on 1 March 1710 that 'the eyes of the nation' are turned upon Sacheverell, and found that he could write about nothing else. In the British Library there are listed 273 pamphlets and other publications associated with Sacheverell during his trial and for the two years following – this, of course, only includes those that have survived the test of time. The Tory press in particular went into overdrive. The trial seemed to bring back the feelings which had run so high some sixty years previously, with the divisions of the Civil War seemingly kept alive. For instance, one ballad could have been written during the previous century, as it attacked the Presbyterians who 'seem devout' but whose words 'at Conventicle virtuous be but nauseous at home to Modesty'. Because this was the age of sexual slur, the Presbyterian at home 'hates all common whores' but clearly enjoyed them when they 'ply in private'. The ballad finishes with anger at the treatment of Sacheverell. Ironically, the pamphlet carries the title *Now's the Time to Tell the Truth*. In fact, the truth probably had very little to do with it.

Of course, there were also passionate Whigs who advocated the most severe punishment for Sacheverell. The *Whiggish Observator* of 5 November claimed that the cleric and his party were seeking to 'raise the Church against the State' and had previously suggested in September of the same year his 'madness is supported by a Faction[al] hatred'. The preacher even cropped up in an announcement about a seditious sermon preached in 1628, when the offending preacher was described as 'the Sacheverell of those days'. *The Review of the State of the British Nation* argued that it was dangerous to question the 'High Gentlemen' who were putting Queen Anne's right to the throne in danger. They stopped just short of calling Sacheverell 'Jesuistical'.

In this case we can see the early beginnings of promotional material, with enterprising marketeers of the day producing handkerchiefs with Sacheverell's head printed on them. No doubt the overwhelmed ladies who queued up to hear the trial could weep into their linen or wave it triumphantly, depending on the outcome of the proceedings. There was also a matching fan to hide behind if it all became too much. Respectable artists had their names ascribed to works such as a 'Metzotinto-Print' which claimed to be by T. Gibbons. It was 'false and counterfeit' according to an angry disclaimer in the *Supplement*.

Physical violence erupted when the London mob adopted Sacheverell and conducted him to the trial. The hordes of volatile supporters made it their business to encourage due respect from less demonstrative onlookers, who were forced to cheer and raise their hats to his coach as it rolled past on its way to the Westminster trial.

There were even printed reports of the reactions of the rest of Europe, although their veracity is uncertain. The *Daily Courant* in June 1710 told readers that their foreign correspondents felt the whole affair reflected badly on the English. The Allies (fighting with Britain against the French) supposedly considered that 'never were the Liberties of the English Nation more violated than since the Revolution' and questioned the accession of a 'foreign family' (the Hanoverians) over the rightful heir who was 'banished out of the Kingdom ... when he was but six months old'. (This refers to the Old Pretender, James, who had left England with his parents during the Glorious Revolution of 1688.) A comment ascribed to a French reporter is equally damning but attacked the Tory reverend: 'He is often obscure, but 'tis because he has a mind to be so; he contradicts himself, but because he has a mind to contradict himself.' *The Courant* was written by Samuel Buckley, and appears to have had no political bias. It was started as a channel for foreign news, and these two 'letters' balance each other out. However, since Buckley's friends in the print trade were all Whigs, it might be fair to assume his personal feeling on the matter.

So here we have Sacheverell, whose trial was so popular that one estimate gives an audience of 2,000 people, with seating in Westminster Hall specially designed by Sir Christopher Wren. Female fans were particularly enthusiastic and devoted to their idol. Decades later, the whole affair was still current enough for Hogarth to include a print of the cleric on a wall in *A Harlot's Progress*. However, not all the pamphlets took the topic seriously. *The Officer's Address to the Ladies* puts it well: 'When we accost our kind shees in the park we are whispered Are you for the Doctor? ... God bless the Doctor says the Stroller in the Strand.' The writer observed that in order to remain present throughout the trial one star-struck fan was willing to subsist on a paltry chicken leg. Cooling her heated emotions with her Sacheverell fan and dabbing her eyes with the doctor's face on her handkerchief, the Tory lady may have been horrified to know that even the whores of Drury Lane were the doctor's creatures.

To return for a moment to the copyright laws, this trial also led to the first lawsuit under the Statute of Anne. Given the sensitivity of this case, and the general rioting and mayhem it produced, it was not surprising that the order went out from the House of Commons that 'nothing, that shall be said by any Member of this House, or by any Person, that shall be produced as a Witness in behalf of the Commons of *Great Britain*, in the Trial of Doctor *Henry Sacheverell*, be printed, or published, without the Leave of this House'. In direct contravention of this order, however, the trial of the good reverend was published alongside 'an Impartial Account' of what passed 'in the last session of Parliament relating to the case of Dr Henry Sacheverell'. Unfortunately, according to the official sources 'No such Book is printed or to be printed', said the *London Gazette* on 10 June. One week later, a further advertisement appeared telling the public that the account of the trial was now being published by the Tory bookseller John Morphew, and that the Whig bookseller Jacob Tonson had 'misrepresented' and 'falsely and maliciously' printed a version. Not surprisingly, it was Jacob Tonson who was appointed the official printer for the trial, although the appointment of an authenticated outlet did little to stop the flood of alternative coverage. One pirated version even appeared in Dublin, although there is a suspicion that this was actually authorised by Tonson. However, as the official printer, Tonson sued all comers – to little avail.

The writers did not just use prose to make their point. The popular ballad form was going strong, and in one such work, *The Blacksmith*, the bottom line is clear:

> Here's a Politick Parson of late does pretend
> To show the Queen's right from God does descend
> A mischievous Doctrine and very ill penned ...

While reading this we need to bear in mind that the spectre of Louis XIV hovered just across the Channel and that the memory of James II, ousted from the throne twenty years earlier, was still fresh. Both were believers in the divine right of kings, and, as we have seen, the upsets caused by Charles I and his 'divinity' were remembered for their disastrous consequences. Another ballad rings as true today as it did then:

> These Nations had always some Tokens
> Of Madness in Turns and by Fits
> Their Senses were shattered and broken
> But now they're quite out of their wits ...

In the interests of balance, here is a self-explanatory Tory ballad which seems to refer to their landslide victory in the 1710 elections. It is somewhat more sympathetic to the doctor:

> He spoke and instantly was join'd
> By birds of every sort and Kind ...

And to the Eagle's Throne apply'd
For her compassion on his side ...

The Royal Eagle in her Breast ...

Then wisely gave Command that those
Who had been his inveterate foes
No longer should be seen at Court
Or to her Palaces resort.

If nothing else, the Sacheverell case is interesting for the mountain of press it generated. This latter-day media frenzy can only be compared nowadays to the most violent of Twitter storms.

By 8 December 1703, the publication called the *Observator* had changed its allegiances and also its author. It was now helmed by John Tutchin, and supported the Whigs. One suggestion is that the continued use of *Observator* was an ironic reference to L'Estrange's earlier High Tory publication which used the same format. The irony is highlighted by the use of one Sir Roger (clearly a reference to L'Estrange) as the naïve Tory mouthpiece who is corrected by the wise author. Tutchin was a Whig through and through, having fought in the Monmouth Rebellion, which aimed to put the Protestant but illegitimate son of Charles II on the throne in place of the legal but Catholic heir, James, Duke of York. As an author, Tutchin began the eighteenth century by getting himself prosecuted for libelling the Dutch favourites of William III, only escaping punishment because he changed their names slightly.

He began his *Observator* in 1702, and by early 1704 he was in trouble again. He wrote an impassioned piece against the barring of Dissenters from voting with an almost revolutionary idea of expanded suffrage: 'And I'll leave this consideration with You, Whether the people of England can be said to be duely Represented in Parliament, when such vast Numbers of Free-holders and Freemen are Deny'd the Priviledge of Chusing Persons to Represent them.' Tutchin was charged but absconded. When he was finally brought to justice, he was acquitted on a technicality.

Before we leave Tutchin and his dialogue, there is another representative issue of the *Observator* that shows some development in the scope of the newspaper. In November 1709, the Sacheverell issue was on everyone's lips. The topic occupies the first two pages of the relevant *Observator* issue, but then, interestingly, there is reporting on various things including some very detailed analysis of the silk weavers' trade, which has been badly affected by the war and the death of the queen's consort, Prince George. Nobody is buying ribbons and silks; the situation is dire. Workmen have to be laid off, and families starve. The *Observator* follows this coverage with a series of economic details on consumer confidence, particularly concerning the habits of the 'middling' class, who follow the fashions set by the court. The reporting includes politics, economics and some social comment – a clear step forward from the haphazard content of earlier publications. Tutchin's onslaught against the Tories was relentless, and he even managed to get into trouble while Parliament had a distinctly Whiggish flavour. Times change, however, and the newspaper industry followed.

In 1710, the political atmosphere changed dramatically when the Tories won a landslide victory in a general election. A number of publications now went head to head. One of the major confrontations was between *The Examiner*, the Tory party's sponsored publication, and the Whig *Medley*. *The Examiner* was born on 3 August 1710. Jonathan Swift soon took it over, writing thirty-one issues between September 1710 and June 1711. He was followed in the editor's chair by Delarivier Manley. But whoever was responsible for the writing – and this appears to have been a very well-kept secret at the time – its sworn enemy was the Whig

Medley, written by Arthur Mainwaring, the loyal secretary to the Duchess of Marlborough. The very first issue of the *Medley* shows the contempt with which it held the Tory organ:

> The Examiner himself, tho young and almost an infant, is already dropping into his grave, where he will be bury'd in everlasting Oblivion with Roger L'Estrange ... and the rest of his short-liv'd predecessors.

Swift showed even more contempt, coolly commenting that it was 'every Medley against every Examiner' and 'whose indefatigable, incessant Railings against me, I never thought convenient to take Notice of, because it would have diverted my design, which I intended to be of Publick Use. Besides, I never yet observed that Writer, or those Writers, ... to argue against any one material Point or Fact that I had advanced, or make one fair Quotation.' The Whigs were certainly gunning for the *Examiner*. They may even have been enjoying the fight; they certainly thought it a sufficiently serious threat to devote so much time, energy and paper to it.

When another of the Marlboroughs' employees took up the cudgel with a pamphlet called *Bouchain in a dialogue between the late Examiner and the Medley*, they again used the conversational technique. The better-informed *Medley* led the conversation and proved its superiority over its naïve friend the *Examiner*. The topic was the siege of Bouchain in the interminable War of the Spanish Succession, but it could have been anything that gave the Whigs an excuse to launch an attack on the Tories. This time, however, the Whig author was a clergyman named Francis Hare, another of the duchess's retainers (he had been the tutor of the Marlboroughs' only son, who died aged sixteen). The pamphlet follows a well-trodden path in which the *Examiner* has just arrived from the country and is therefore ignorant of Marlborough's great triumph.

This criticism would be more applicable to Manley than to Swift, the former having set off on a summer holiday around this time. However, Hare probably didn't know that she was behind the issues in the summer of 1711. If he had found out, he would have been incandescent. The antagonism between Manley and Sarah Churchill, Duchess of Marlborough, was personal, with Manley's output containing a great many pointed and even cruel attacks on the duchess. However, the *Medley* representative is relatively gentle and sticks to politics while the *Examiner* seeks to undermine the victory at Bouchain by downplaying its significance. Of course, the *Examiner* is proved wrong. The *Medley* chides the *Examiner*, accusing it of labouring to promote 'publick Hatred' despite the fact that gratitude would be more appropriate. Triumphant, the *Medley* finishes its speech: 'For shame my friend; leave off these Practices.' The *Examiner*'s reply is so unlikely as to be laughable. Suddenly struck by the heroic profile as given by the *Medley*, the *Examiner* admits to a newfound great esteem for the duke, and to having previously been 'employ'd for a particular end'. This was actually true of Manley, who was paid to write pro-Tory propaganda, but not of Swift, who felt it was beneath him to write for financial gain.

However vicious we think the newspapers are today, it is unlikely they would get away with the kind of accusations, slights and unsupported rumours that were prevalent at this time. The duchess, bold as she was, found it difficult to stomach the unrelenting attacks that Manley launched at her. The duchess's secretary, Mainwaring, having read the first attacks, called them 'nauseous' and opined that 'there is not a word in it relating to [the duchess], but very old, false, and incredible scandal'. The duchess's mother was represented as a depraved witch. While this sounds laughable to us, the burning of witches was not so far from living memory at this time, and in a superstitious age it was a sinister accusation.

In the *Examiner* – a serious political periodical, not a scandal sheet – there are elaborate allegories through which to view Queen Anne's former favourite. Under the cloak of anonymity, the duchess is set in a vast palace. Not surprisingly, it is described as a 'dazzling, unwieldy structure ... built amidst the Tears and Groans of a People harassed with a lingering War, to gratifie the Ambition of a subject, whilst the Sovereign's Palace lay in Ashes'. This of course refers to Blenheim Palace, the huge gift of the queen to the duke on his great victory at the 1704 battle of the same name. The allegory's central character, the Goddess, sat upon a gold throne, her 'beauty mixed with Disdain'. She 'had Contempt for inferior Objects' and the only image 'in which she took delight' was her own. This rather terrifying creature was accompanied by Envy and Wrath. Add to all this a full house of snakes, whips and bloody robes, and it is little wonder that the faithful Mainwaring in the *Medley* complains that the *Examiner* 'abuses her Majesty and all the Parliaments that had a hand in the building of Blenheim'.

It was just as well that the identity of the duchess had been disguised under various names. The abuse was spiteful and well targeted. Her talent for making money means she was depicted as grasping and greedy. Granted, she happened to be one of the richest women in England but she was also an astute businesswoman. The pamphlets do not fail to comment on her arrogance, particularly with the queen. Her acknowledged beauty made her vain in her enemies' eyes, a common refrain in ballads. If we look at the following examples, her unpopularity becomes explicit.

A WAR WOLF shall at first appear
To whom a Female soon shall joyn
Infected with the ambitious itch
Of being very great and rich ...
Yet this I'll venture to unfold

That the too ardent Thirst of Gold
Will prove the cause of their undoing ...
And palefaced Death within his clutches
Will soon catch both the Duke and Duchess

In another ballad she is called 'a bitch with a broom'. Meanwhile, the Whig writers tried to defend their leading lady and when she was replaced in the queen's trust and affection by an upstart, her distant cousin Abigail Masham, a Tory, the Whigs got busy. Their accusations were outrageous. They suggested that Masham had seduced the queen, hinting at lesbianism and 'dark deeds at Night'. They accused her of piercing the royal heart and claimed that she had been given a ministry to run. She is also said to have been illiterate and treasonous. All of this was a complete fiction. One final thrust at Abigail was a fictional conversation between Masham and Louis XIV's scheming mistress Madame de Maintenon, in which Masham is asking advice on how to get ahead in the court.

This nastiness was standard fare for the press the time. As long as writers were careful to be a little circumspect with the names, they would be pretty safe. When arrested by the Whigs on the publication of her first book of scandal, Manley pleaded that the stories were already out there so she was only regurgitating what everybody knew anyway. How could that be seditious?

A bit of good advice never goes amiss, and we will now look at a spoof Tory document purporting to explain how to get ahead in politics. Named *The Art of Political Lying*, this little pamphlet from 1712 gives a wry breakdown of how to use rhetoric. It was first thought to have been written by Swift, but it is more likely to be the work of the multi-talented Dr John Arbuthnot, a brilliant satirist and a royal physician. Whoever wrote it, they did so amid the turmoil of party politics, when the truth, as always, was the first victim. The pamphlet looks at the value of truth where politics is concerned and poses the unanswerable question of whether it is advisable for ordinary folk to know what's really happening. The question is put very succinctly by the writer, who claims to have found the material in an unpublished manuscript that should be required reading for any would-be politician. The premise is that 'there is more art necessary to convince people of a salutary truth than a salutary falsehood'. The conclusion, which still resonates today, is that while a citizen has the right to the truth from his neighbour, his family, his wife and his servants, he has no right to political truth:

> The government of England has a mixture of democratical in it, so the right of inventing and spreading political lies is partly in the people; and their obstinate adherence to this just privilege has been most conspicuous, and shined with great lustre, of late years: that it happens very often, that there are no other means left to the good people of England to pull down a ministry and government they are weary of, but by exercising this their undoubted right: that abundance of political lying is a sure sign of true English liberty: that as ministers do sometimes use tools to support their power, it is but reasonable that the people should employ the same weapon to defend themselves, and pull them down.

Essentially, the people have as much right to believe lies as the politicians have to invent them.

Some of the ideas relate directly to people and incidents that contemporaries would have recognised. One comment, for instance, was clearly meant to refer to the Duke of Marlborough. The hero of Blenheim was notoriously careful with his own money but was happy spending taxpayers' money on the War of the Spanish Succession. He was also accused of peculation, of creaming off the money intended for supplying the troops into his own pocket. The work's advice for dealing with such a man is that 'you will be unsuccessful, if you give out of a great man, who is remarkable for his frugality for the publick, that he squanders away the nation's money; but you may safely relate that he hoards it: you must not affirm he took a bribe, but you may freely censure him for being tardy in his payments: because, though neither may be true, yet the last is credible, the first not.'

There is plenty of advice for the aspiring politician when trying to discredit a rival:

> Of an open-hearted, generous minister, you are not to say, that he was in an intrigue to betray his country: but you may affirm, with some probability, that he was in an intrigue with a lady. He warns all practitioners to take good heed to these precepts; for want of which, many of their lies of late have proved abortive or short-lived.

Other suggestions that are uncomfortably resonant include admonitions not to frighten the people too often with the same terror, and not to lie in ways that 'exceed common degrees of probability'. It all seems distressingly familiar as he compares the two-party system. There is plenty of guidance for would-be politicians, but perhaps the best advice is that the heads of parties should not believe their own lies.

Among the other journalistic techniques employed, there is the rant. One example in particular serves two purposes, not only ably representing a very angry Tory but also being written by a Whig as a very clever satire. It also concerns the freedom of the press, therefore touching on many of our key topics. Called *The Thoughts of a Tory Author concerning the Press*, it begins in comedy and ends in deadly earnest. This piece of satire was written by Joseph Addison, cofounder of *The Spectator* with Richard Steele. The premise is that the Tories, who are still in power after their landslide victory in 1710, don't want to limit free speech. It isn't long before Addison, masquerading as a Tory, lets his mask slip. Now comes the rant, which is a complaint about the way the Tories have treated the Duke of Marlborough,

> ... the most illustrious character in this Kingdom ... yet his merit has rendered him invulnerable ... If he deserved the usage he has met with from us would he not exclaim against the infamous license of the press, and for suppressing it for ever? ... I cannot help saying so; tis between you and me ... a man thus abused ... [is] willing to enlarge the liberty of the press than to lessen it, let our Reflections look the other way, and I fancy you will grant with me that tho whatever is infamous in the license of printing should be restrained yet Whatever is true and decent whatever the law may allow may and ought to be permitted.

Although rants come in all shapes and sizes, they all have in common this hectoring tone and a way of telling the reader exactly what the rest of the world is doing wrong, what they should be doing, or a combination of both of these and a further promise that anyone who doesn't agree is going to hell. Tolerance is not something that features in this type of work. The general theme is that disaster is around the corner for those who disagree with the author's sentiments.

One of the most serious rants during Anne's reign involved three of the greatest writers of the time: Sir Richard Steele, Daniel Defoe and Jonathan Swift. The whole argument began with the much-anticipated end of the War of the Spanish Succession, when a weary Louis XIV gave in and agreed to the Peace of Utrecht in 1713. This series of treaties demanded among other things that France demolish the defences of Dunkirk. The French were simply not doing this, which upset the Whigs. In 1713, Steele was a fully-fledged Whig MP. He clearly had a momentary lapse of his normally acute sense of what constitutes useful propaganda, because he published a pamphlet called *The Importance of Dunkirk Considered*. This was fine, and sold very well (three editions in the first week), but it also had the Tories gunning for him.

The Tories chose to interpret the piece as an attack on the queen. Steele had used an unfortunate choice of words: In the *Guardian*'s 7 August edition he says quite mildly: 'The British nation expects the immediate demolition of it.' The Tories took their time, but by October had moved their biggest gun into position. Swift produced *The Importance of the Guardian Considered*, and went straight to the point: 'Mr. S[tee]le in his Letter [has] given us leave to treat him as we think fit, as he is our Brother-Scribler but not to attack him as an honest Man. That is to say he allows us to be his Criticks, but not his Answerers, and he is altogether in the right for there is in his Letter much to be Criticised, and little to be Answered.' The piece is vindictive and directly insulting, describing Steele as the 'Author of two tolerable Plays'; furthermore 'the Company he kept ... hath given him the Character of a Wit. To take the height of his Learning, you are to suppose a Lad just fit for the University, and sent early from thence into the wide World, where he followed every way of Life that might least improve or preserve the Rudiments he had got. He hath no Invention, nor is Master of a tolerable Style.' There is clearly no love lost here. It gets worse: 'After the first Bottle he is no disagreeable Companion.' And then: 'Being the most imprudent Man alive, he never follows the Advice of his Friends, but is wholly at the mercy of Fools or Knaves, or hurried away by his own Caprice.'

Once Swift had finished tearing Steele apart he got down to the point of the piece, which was to make Steele appear to be disrespectful to the queen. The form of words used certainly do give that impression so it is no wonder the Tories seized upon them as a means to shut down a very effective Whig propagandist. With little thought for the consequences, Steele wrote, 'I, though a mean Fellow, give Your Majesty to understand in the best method I can take, and from the Sincerity of my GRATEFUL Heart, that the British Nation EXPECTS the IMMEDIATE Demolition of Dunkirk; – as you hope to preserve Tour Person, Crown, and Dignity and the Safety and Welfare of the People committed to your charge.'

It was bad enough for a Member of Parliament to be giving the queen orders, but Steele followed it up with another pamphlet which called the succession into question, suggesting that the Catholic James III could be lined up for the post, and Swift went into action again in *The Public Spirit of the Whigs*. While this was written as part of a battle between the two satirists, it has some more general resonance with political writing on both sides (although Swift would never be likely to see this and certainly not admit it), as he reflects upon 'The generosity and tenderness wherewith the Heads ... of a struggling faction treat those who will undertake to hold a pen in their defence. And the behaviour of these persons is yet more laudable because the benefits they receive are almost gratis. If any of their labourers can scratch out a pamphlet they desire no more; there is no question offered about the wit, the style, the argument.' The party is just grateful that there is propaganda going out on its behalf.

Swift tears Steele's pamphlet to pieces, with its 'long, dry' preface and interminable dedication. But he reserves his really mordant comments for another attack on Steele's education. He does not mince words – unlike Steele, who has a 'confused remembrance of words since he left the university but has lost half their meaning' and puts them in according to how they sound rather than what they mean. It was a shame that Steele managed to upset the Tories so badly. If he had considered the thumping Tory majority before committing his thoughts to paper, he might have been more circumspect in his suggestions.

The upshot of all these attacks was that Sir Richard Steele, Member of Parliament, was accused of sedition and expelled from his seat. As the *History of Parliament* puts it, 'his appearance on the Parliamentary scene ... was brief but dramatic. After only a month's attendance in the 1714 session he was expelled for printing a resounding denunciation of the Tory administration, thereby achieving renown as a martyr to the Whig cause.' This was the power of words in the early years of the press. However, we can see that times have changed; a few decades earlier, he could have lost his ears.

We have now come to an extremely important development in the British press – the journal. Conveniently enough, it was Steele who was responsible for this innovation in the form of titles such as *The Tatler* and *The Spectator*, alongside his friend Joseph Addison. While the content may have changed, the titles have survived to this day. *The Tatler*, established in 1709, also marked a watershed moment in the history of manners in the United Kingdom, which is increasingly reflected in the tone of publications during the rest of the eighteenth century. After a Restoration filled with scandal, hedonism and bad behaviour there was a move to improve the ways in which the population conducted itself. We have already mentioned the Society for the Reformation of Manners, founded in 1691. In contrast to the overt political slanging matches, the saucy stage plays and the barely disguised sex scandals, the intention of *The Tatler* was to raise the general level of behaviour among its readers. For instance, in the Lincolnshire countryside the founding members of the Spalding Gentlemen's Society approved of the periodical as 'instructive and entertaining', assisting them in the knowledge and appreciation of 'polite literature'. These periodicals used an essay format, like a weekend supplement, and did not overtly concern themselves with politics.

But it is interesting or even alarming that Steele held a very low opinion of his readers. There is a warning that 'readers such as were not born to have thoughts of their own' run the risk of having their 'noddles' overrun, believing everything they see in print. He adds, 'What I am now warning the people of, is, that the newspapers of this island are as pernicious to weak heads in England, as ever books of chivalry to Spain; and therefore shall do all that in me lies, with the utmost care and vigilance imaginable, to prevent these growing evils.' If chivalry turns the head of Don Quixote and sends him chasing after windmills, what will reading newspapers do to the 'weak-headed' average Englishman? The contents of the periodical comprised a mixture of comment, gossip and, despite the stated avoidance of politics, attacks on the Tories. *The Tatler* lasted two years until 1711, when Steele joined up with his friend Joseph Addison to start *The Spectator*.

Perhaps the most important point of these papers was that they were instantly successful without the assistance of any political sponsorship. Addison reckoned optimistically on 60,000–70,000 readers. Subscribers ranged from coffee houses to private individuals, with as many as twenty readers for each copy on average. With several issues per week, *The Spectator* was a seriously successful magazine. Copies were taken as far north as Scotland, and reading groups sprang up round the country. People sent the paper out to their friends in the provinces so that country gentlemen and ladies could experience the atmosphere of the capital as Steele invented a variety of informants (a bit like a pressroom full of staff journalists and correspondents but without the necessity of paying them). They were ostensibly scattered around London, with Steele's character Bickerstaffe, a man with his ear to the ground, recording what he 'heard' in the various coffee houses. How exciting that might feel to the homebound rural reader, who could enjoy the tittle-tattle from Will's Coffee-house, St James's Coffee-house, or White's Chocolate house. Each had their speciality: White's was good for stories of romantic liaisons, Will's was a source for opinions on plays and St James's was good if you needed to know the latest from the battlefield.

To show how far the reading public had come in appreciating a more sophisticated report of what they might hear in a coffee shop around this time, if their sensitivities would bear it, an example can be found in the *Weekly Comedy* – essentially an early *Private Eye*. In the popular dialogue format, a cast of very unlikely characters discuss modern life. A selection of their names gives an idea of the flavour of the piece. We have Snarl, an unhappy ex-captain. Alongside him are the merchant Truck and the news writer Scribble. The delightfully named Squabble, a lawyer, is also present along with Whim, an entrepreneur, and Scanall, a poet. Also appearing in this satiric weekly are Plush the quack doctor and Prim the beau. The scene is set, and after the niceties of introduction there is an indication of a particularly revolting stage act at Sadler's Wells. We are spared the grisly details, but it is performed by a 'Hibernian cannibal' and once witnessed will cause the expulsion of bodily fluids at 'both ends'.

While Steele sought to reform society through his own methods, other writers were using another tactic. Right at the beginning of this chapter there was a mention of the popularity of scandal, and so to round off this chapter we will move from polite misdemeanours to more scurrilous goings-on. Once again, to turn to a real expert in the field we shall quote from Manley, who had refined *ad hominem* and *ad feminam* sexual innuendo down to a fine art. We've already seen how she treated the Duchess of Marlborough, but she had some much racier stuff on other high-profile figures. The duchess was merely depicted as greedy, arrogant and vain, with a hold over her equally greedy husband and the queen. Manley had an armoury of insults and accusations to level at other Whigs, which might be true in their essence if not in their final form. Written in the popular allegorical style, the names are changed to protect the author. There was no attempt to protect the innocent, because there is very little innocence to be found.

Some of these stories are particularly insulting. In the *New Atalantis* Manley writes of Lord Somers, a Whig elder statesman whose lover

> ... acted more in the Quality of a Nurse than a Mistress. And to show to what a Height ... she cared for him, that so she could but reign, no matter by what Methods. She used to lead her old Patrician into the costly Bath, where she caused him to be attended by bright, half-naked, dazzling Beauties; new and till then unseen, their shining Hair with a graceful Flow showing their Prime of Years, and unassisted Charms. .... There Virgins were instructed by their Corrupter.

Clearly, Somers 'had ... an imaginary, [rather] than a real Occasion for a Mistress'.

She also tells of Earl Cowper's mistress and two illegitimate children, and his brother's involvement with a Quaker heiress who died in mysterious circumstances. The earl was a former Lord Chancellor, and his brother was a very senior high court judge.

The public couldn't get enough of these naughty stories about Whig politicians. In the unlikely event that they didn't recognise the names behind the pseudonyms, keys were printed which were supposed to be separate from the book but were occasionally bound with it. The books sold very well – particularly, one suspects, to the people who knew the targets intimately. It is difficult to resist relishing gossip about someone you have actually met. Lady Mary Montague, who knew a great many important people and married the ambassador to Turkey, wrote to her sister:

> I am very glad you have the second part of the *New Atalantis*; if you have read it will you be so good as to send it me? And in return I promise to get you the key to it. ... But do you know what has happened to the unfortunate authoress? People are offended at the liberty she uses in her memoirs and she is taken into custody ... I was in hopes her faint essay would have provoked some better pen to give more elegant and secret memoirs ... but now we shall be teased with nothing but heroic poems with names at length ... so daubed with flattery that they are the severest kind of lampoons, for they both scandalise the writer and the subject alike that vile paper *The Tatler*.

Lady Mary declares she is in 'a violent passion about it'. She was a feisty lady herself, championing inoculation against smallpox and following a young Italian lover around Europe.

The British press at this point in the early eighteenth century was finding its feet, becoming organised and relatively sophisticated. While publicly correcting the waywardness of politicians was still a focus, it was also becoming more subtle. The fashion for Manley's scandal passed, and Steele's elegant reprimands took its place. This period also saw the beginnings of a recognition that women might want something different, as we shall see in the next chapter.

5

SOMETHING FOR THE LADIES

Very early in the development of the press came the realisation
that there was money in writing expressly for women. The
early publications targeted at women contained recipes, poetry,
mathematical instruction and advice. We have seen that journals
such as *The Tatler*, while not expressly for the female reader,
made a concerted effort to attract women by including tales
of love and marital bliss. The agony aunt, that stalwart of the
woman's magazine, made her debut with the *Athenian Mercury*
in the 1690s, answering questions from either gender. Moreover, a
publication named *The Female Tatler* was considered a nuisance by
a Grand Jury and told to clean up its act, which largely consisted of
scandalous tales about 'persons of honour and quality'.

In 1709, Richard Steele resolved to produce a periodical 'which
may be of entertainment to the fair Sex, in honour of whom I have
invented this Paper'. While Steele made this claim, his periodical,
The Tatler, fell far short of really being a woman's magazine. But
to give it its due, Steele's elegant work at least invited the ladies
to read and enjoy his efforts. Why, then, didn't someone write

something specifically for them? There was a gap in the market, and one would be forgiven for thinking that nobody came forward to fill it at this time. If we dig deep enough, however, it becomes evident that this wasn't quite the case. In fact, the women's press, or at least writing targeted at women, had its beginnings in the seventeenth century. We are not discussing novels here but the material which we might find in women's magazines these days. While few, there were publications purporting to be for the fairer sex.

Generally, as we saw in previous chapters, early newspapers filled their columns with political invective, snippets of foreign news and some rather random items. If we are to understand exactly what is available for the lady reader, then, we will have to look at some publications which do not fall easily within the defined notion of newspaper or periodical. There is a certain amount of latitude in what follows, but it is easiest to understand what was written for women by looking in some detail outside the shelf labelled 'weekly' or 'daily'.

We will need to cut a path through a chaotic and unruly set of publications once more, but it will be worth the effort because the texts available illustrate contemporary attitudes towards women and give an idea of what women were expected to know in this period. We will look at works which were specifically aimed at women, considered suitable for their delicate minds; some are alien to our sensibilities while others are surprisingly modern. On the other hand, some publications mentioned women in their title but were entirely unsuitable for 'ladylike' ladies. With this in mind, if we are to travel in a consistent direction I propose we go from the virtuous to the scurrilous.

To begin, we need to understand how a virtuous lady behaved in the late Stuart period. It is hardly surprising that there were publications which were written specifically to give guidance on this matter. *The Accomplished Ladies Rich Closet of Rarities or the Ingenious Gentlewoman and Servant Maids Delightful Companion* is intended to be the complete instructional handbook. While it includes 'servant maids' in its title, it is really a reference manual for the gentlewoman to show her how to instruct her staff. The duties of the lady of the house were many and varied when it was published in 1687, and the instructions covered everything from distilling spirits and creating perfumes to cleaning spots from clothes and making sauces. It also advises on delivering babies, potentially vital given the relative remoteness of many great houses.

The little volume is truly comprehensive. As well as being practical, it also advises on how to conduct oneself from infancy to extreme old age. In short, following its instructions will not only make you a better woman but will help you in your 'advancement' and render you 'acceptable in the eyes of great ones'. There are some gems, which read today are frankly bewildering. For instance, when engaged in carving, the reader is told to 'throw not anything over your shoulder'. While this is no doubt very sensible, one wonders why the carver needs to be reminded of it. Moving on to social behaviour, there are some useful tips on speaking in company: 'Let [your conversation] not taste of Confidence, Affectation or Conceitedness, nor border on the obscene.' Again, anyone can agree that it is better not to sound affected, conceited or obscene, but one might ask what is wrong with sounding confident.

This all sounds quite useful, if restrictive. The whole book takes on a slightly surreal air when one inspects some of the more bizarre instructions for medicines. Perhaps one of the least appealing cures is for thinning hair. Firstly, pigeon droppings had to be collected and burnt. A brew was then concocted, combining the burned dung with various plants and sugar, and the hair was washed in this unappealing brew. Rather more attractive is a cure for dropsy (a term covering all forms of water retention) that involves drinking two gallons of ale with the addition of a few herbs. Clearly this is unlikely to cure the condition, but after so much beer the patient is unlikely to notice or care. Perhaps the most depressing part of the book is the colour-coding of newborn children: if they are red when delivered, this means that the mother need not worry too much about them; if, however, they are white, they are likely to die. Even at a time when so many mothers and babies died in or soon after childbirth, this seems a particularly insouciant piece of information.

This book will take the reader from maidenhood to old age, and the advice varies in its usefulness. Some of it holds as true today as it did 300 years ago because it is perfectly sensible. It is still advisable not to wear anything that would 'appear ridiculous and cause laughter'; nor should 'a woman of fourscore [eighty] 'be clothed in 'the garb of a Gentlewoman of sixteen'.

The work moves through sections which advise on management of staff including an 'Experienced Cook-Maid and Cook, or Directions for the newest and most Excellent way of dressing Flesh, Fish and Fowl of all sorts, and in divers manners; as also making Pyes, Tarts, Custards'. With her domestic duties out of the way, the lady of the house will clearly have some leisure hours to fill and naturally there is guidance on what she can respectably do to amuse herself. The conventions of the day inevitably put some restrictions on activities, but there are some acceptable pastimes which can be seen one hundred years later in the writings of Jane Austen.

The lady is permitted to dance, but there is a reminder that first she must make sure she has learnt the steps. She can also play music, draw and write poetry. These are all perfectly acceptable. She could even take up engraving. Curiously, the author says it is in order for young ladies to see stage plays. Since we are now looking at a book published in 1687, at the height of the Restoration comedy, this does seem like a controversial suggestion. The stage was awash with bawdiness, marital difficulties, greed and general sauciness. Many Restoration comedies are hilarious to this day, but they are full of immorality and the triumph of vice over virtue. The respectable females of the household would surely be permitted to see some Shakespeare, the tragedies from the likes of John Dryden or even his genteel comedies, but it was difficult to avoid smut on the public stage at that time.

If the female members of the family manage to survive to a marriageable age, there is plenty of advice for them on love and marriage. What is offered is given in the context of the day, so it is understood that when an eligible young woman has made a marriage she might not find her new partner entirely satisfactory. In such cases the book recommends passivity in a wife: 'Be peaceable and pleasant towards your husband, not being Angry when he is at any time so but pacifie him with winning and obliging words.' If the husband is very young and given to 'Excursions', he can be brought to better behaviour by his young wife's 'good example'. It would be foolish not to point out at this stage that in a country riven by venereal disease and allegedly teeming with runaway wives who have clearly given up trying to reform their husbands this is a fatuous piece of advice. But we should remember that this is the ideal, and perhaps the young wife should not be disillusioned too soon. Other domestic relationships could be more successful, and there are wise words on how to treat your servants: 'You must be courteous and affable, but not over familiar, least it beget contempt.' One must also make sure that servants do not dress above their station in 'gaudy' attire.

For the established wife there follows the essential section on rearing your children. It's actually written directly to the young lady, but it would perhaps be easier to assume that the mother or the governess is interpreting this advice for them. On that subject, while Victorian novels often star governesses who are poor, unloved daughters from impoverished households, such as the eponymous Jane Eyre, this little seventeenth-century book says that it is not 'morally possible for any person to be a good governess unless she has herself been the Mother of Children and had the bringing them up'.

Another publication that serves as a foundation stone for ladies' periodicals is *The Lady's New Year's Gift or, advice to a daughter*. Purported to have been written by Lord Halifax, it contains what would nowadays be considered quite incendiary opinions, for instance: 'There is inequality in the Sexes and that for the Economy of the world the Men who are to be the Law-givers (had the larger share of reason bestowed upon them) by which means your sex is the better prepared for the compliance that is necessary for the better performance of those duties which seemed to be most properly assigned to it.' The writer therefore appears to be another advocate of the 'women wield their power through their looks and their tears' school of thought, suggesting women handle drunkards and abusers with their feminine wiles. This little book was apparently written for Halifax's daughter in the first place. Lord Halifax didn't need the money, so he didn't have it published; instead it was pirated, wowing the reading public in no less than fifteen editions. It also appears that its condescending attitude to women had international appeal, for it was translated into French and Italian. In a sexist, male-dominated society, it remained popular for decades.

If this was the general attitude to women during the last years of the seventeenth century, we might seek to find something that was considered suitable for them. Of course, in the prescribed reading there should not be anything which would lead them into any kind of moral downfall. Novels were considered rather dangerous since they dealt largely with romance and, as Lord Halifax succinctly puts it, 'it is one of the Disadvantages belonging to your Sex, that young Women are seldom permitted to make their own Choice [in a husband]; their Friends Care and Experience are thought safer Guides to them, than their own Fancies.'

Having examined these early publications – essentially books on conduct – our next task must be to consider what else was purported to be written expressly for women. And so we get to the publications that were accounted safe for ladies to read, and unlikely to corrupt or excite them too much. We actually find a truly mixed bag, much of which sits at odds with what they might have been read in the general run of newspapers. If we are truly honest, the content is dull by today's standards; indeed, it is actually very easy to see the women getting bored with them and turning back to the politics of the day. In *The Spectator*, Steele himself reports on a visit to the theatre:

> I could not but take notice of two parties of very fine women, that had placed themselves in the opposite side-boxes, and seemed drawn up in a kind of battle-array one against another. After a short survey of them, I found they were patched differently; the faces on one hand being spotted on the right side of the forehead, and those upon the other on the left. I quickly perceived that they cast hostile glances upon one another; and that their patches were placed in those different situations, as party-signals to distinguish friends from foes. In the middle boxes, between these two opposite bodies, were several ladies who patched indifferently on both sides of their faces, and seemed to sit there with no other intention but to see the opera.

It transpired that those on the right hand were Whigs, and those on the left were Tories. Now, whether this was true party loyalty or just a fashionable offshoot of politics is hard to tell. However, if we recall the impression the sensational Sacheverell made on the female Tories, they certainly followed party lines. When the ladies were not adoring or reviling the superstar cleric, what were they reading?

Despite Steele's claim that he was keen to attract female readers, *The Tatler* is a very general publication. We need to look to other writers for something truly focused on women as readers. The leader in the field was John Dunton, who produced a variety of titles. It would be fair to say that Dunton was the first bookseller who saw the potential of the market for women's reading.

Dunton could claim to have lived an extraordinary life. There were surely not too many of his contemporaries who could say they had crossed the Atlantic and hawked books to the students at a very new university called Harvard. Equally unique and certainly more bizarre, he also hid in his house for nearly a year, journeying out just the once, and then dressed as a woman. This last came about because he made himself responsible for the debts of his sister-in-law, whose creditors were keen to recoup. He could also lay claim to an impressive number of firsts in the print trade, including the first real attempt at capturing the women's sector with *The Ladies Dictionary, Being a General Entertainment for the Fair-Sex*. Tacked below the title was the justifiable boast that here was 'A Work Never attempted before in English'. After bruiting his 'Project of Composing a Dictionary for the use of the fair sex', Dunton offers his sincere hopes that it would be met with a 'Courteous Reception'.

Beauty tips are a staple topic in women's magazines, and it seems it was no different three centuries ago. *The Ladies Dictionary* devotes pages to 'Beautifying, Reasons and Arguments for its lawfulness and that it is not discommendable in itself ... Arts to restore or preserve a fair and lovely Complexion have been question'd and cavell'd with by the austeerer sort whether they are not only unfit to be practised but even sinful.' Admittedly the discussion is less about product than about the sin of pride, with the rather alarming quote from a Puritan that 'we cannot be servants of the lord if we are industrious in seeking to please men'. The editor comes out in acceptance of make-up, with the conclusion that 'the Harlot beautifies her face to attract lascivious wandring eyes, and the virtuous lady to gain and keep the love of a chast husband'. In all, the *Dictionary* is an interesting and harmless window into seventeenth-century living.

Dunton's other venture into this new and exciting sales opportunity was the *Athenian Mercury*, which was as much question-and-answer column as it was newspaper. It must have answered a need, however, as it ran for six years at a time when regular publications were few and far between. It might have been the extraordinary range of readers' questions, ranging from queries on a bee's humming to questions on 'Divinity, Poetry, Metaphysicks, Physicks, Mathematicks, History, Love, Politicks, Oeconomicks' and 'Visions and Revelations'. The *Athenian Mercury* was among the most popular of the newspapers and periodicals read in London's coffee houses. It closed on 14 June 1697, after the death of Dunton's wife. It had a longer shelf life than most, with various collected and abridged editions between 1703 and 1728 under the title *Athenian Oracle*. Dunton himself described the first volume as being 'the new Philosophic and Miscellaneous *Oracle*; which will be purely a Philosophic Miscellany' while 'the Second Volume shall come abroad under the title of "*Athenae Redivivae*; or, *the Divine Oracle*"; and to be a Directory for Tender Consciences, and contain all the uncommon cases proposed to the Athenian Society by persons under trouble of mind ... Our Third Volume is to be made public under the title of "*Athenae Redivivae*; or, *the Secret Oracle*"; which is to answer the nicer Questions which were privately sent to the Athenian Society.'

Despite the popularity of Dunton's efforts, works aimed at women were still scarce. Nevertheless, fierce rivalries burned among the few titles with any pretence to being woman-friendly. One periodical, the *British Apollo*, was particularly aggressive, and was antagonistic towards rivals even though each one had its own particular style. The *Apollo* was an example of a newspaper written by and for men, which, if the letters are to be believed, apparently managed to attract a female readership. The banner claims it contains 'Curious Amusements for the INGENIOUS' and is 'Perform'd by a Society of GENTLEMEN', but there are a fair number of questions from women generally about being badly treated by men. For example, in issue six in March 1708 a lady called Oliva writes to enquire 'how we may distinguish between a real Passion and feign'd one'. The answer is brutal but to the point, and the puzzled Oliva is advised to shed her 'vanity and Affectation' and ignore the 'Impertinent Triflers' who 'sigh for my lady and Ogle her Chamber-maid'. But there is some good advice, particularly the warning against those 'Slovenly Morose Fellows' who only think of their 'prevailing appetite ... To love Oliva and to lie with her is the same thing in their Dialect.'

Another piece is from a man in answer to a letter from a 'pretty witty young lady of eight hundred pounds fortune' who, despite 'many fruitless journeys she has made up to London in quest of a husband', has failed to secure one. The male correspondent appeals to the editors to be introduced as he is 'lying under the same unlucky predicament' and has failed to 'ingage some pretty she' even though he is 'young, in good business' and thinks he deserves 'a wife with so much money'. The editor, having considered the request, gives the young man short shrift, suggesting that he needs to be a better marital prospect if he wants to succeed in getting a rich wife. Another concerns a 'country bred young creature' who has been assured by a young man that he would marry her.

The night before the ceremony 'nothing would keep his base hands from under my Petticoats, offering such things as my Modesty will not allow me to repeat'. The horrified young lady fled and now asks the *Apollo* whether she could legally refuse to marry him. The answer is equivocal, suggesting that she wait a little and watch his behaviour while admitting that there was no shortage of men who are 'so inflamed with love' that they are willing to marry 'if they cannot obtain their Satisfaction in the way of Libertines'.

The questions are generally about romantic and marital relations and do not reflect well on male suitors, but one rather unusual question might have raised a few eyebrows since it involved same-sex cohabitation. A woman writes in to say that her friend is pressing for them to live together so that 'there is only wanting convenient opportunities for her to be more free in the Expression of her Friendship'. Whether this is a code for a more intimate relationship is unclear. Tactfully, the *Apollo* urges the correspondent to be careful as there needs to be 'an exact Likeness in all Inclinations and Dispositions'.

The next question was sure to raise a few hackles, hopefully male as well as female: 'Are women as capable of learning as men?' The answer is long and rambling – and supremely unsatisfying. It seems absurd in a period boasting such brilliant women as playwright Aphra Behn and traveller Lady Mary Wortley Montague that the letter writer could really believe 'they are cast in too soft a mould, are made of too fine, too delicate a composure to endure the severity of study, the drudgery of contemplation, the fatigue of profound speculations of deep researches'. The reason given is biblical:

Had Eve sprang out of Adams head ... we might indeed be of other sentiments. But since she was taken out of his side to denote her his companion in inferior matters ... Not that there may be some women eminent for learning ... [some women think very quickly] ... our creator has ... afforded us ... companions to divert our vacant hours, to relieve our wearied minds, to supply our wasted vigor, to recruit our exhausted thoughts, and prepare us for our future labours, our succeeding studies.

It must have been unpleasant for the intelligent woman to read this, and in a later edition there is a challenge to the misogynist reply. This in turn is answered by an even more rambling reply, which is rounded off by the extraordinary explanation that women were not created to have power over men as their pregnancies render them periodically incapable. This is an extraordinary opinion to express in 1709, at a time when the country was ruled by a queen who had undergone seventeen mostly tragic pregnancies.

The answers to disappointed women are sympathetic, even though the tone sis patronising. A question on whether women have souls since they are so closely related to geese cannot be taken seriously; even by eighteenth-century standards it was bizarre. Thankfully, the answer was a good one – women indeed had souls, 'since many women would make meer ganders out of such wise querists'. One gentleman offers a query which is, strangely, written in verse:

A fortnight since I pick'd up in the park
A wench when (as you guess) 'twas wond'rous dark
So when in morn from the Nymph I rose
I found her ugly, cold and without a nose
Now to be mortified thus in my prime
D'you think it not atonement for the crime?

The answer from the 'agony aunt' to the very worried client is hardly reassuring. We must take into account that having gone with a prostitute he is quite rightly concerned that he has caught syphilis from his night of passion:

> The sight of her, no lesser faults atones
> But when you find compunction in your bones,
> When the effects have brought you to the plague
> Of no more nose by night than eyes by night
> You may repent prompt by your crazy state
> And yet perhaps you may repent too late.

To modern eyes, the playful format of the query suggests it is not genuine. Nonetheless, it is quite explicit in its warning about sexual activity.

The British Apollo might have patronised its female readers, but there was nothing patronising about its fierce attacks on *The Female Tatler*. This latter publication was a strange creation. It has more in common with today's *Hello!* and *Heat* than its contemporaries, but its quirky nastiness is unique. Its author (probably male) traded under the name of Mrs Crackenhorpe. The avowed intention of Mrs C ('a Lady that knows everything') is 'to prate a little' because she is 'intimate with everybody at first sight' and she 'knows everybody's Actions'. She claimed to be very careful 'not to reflect upon any Person whatsoever, but gently to correct the Vices and Vanities which some of Distinction, as well as others, wilfully commit', so the ethos of this paper is very much in line with the scandalous *New Atalantis*. We could also compare it to the now defunct *News of the World* for its reforming zeal, which provides a good cover for reporting the things the rich folk think they can get away with. There was a malicious undertone to this righteousness, as Mrs C opines that 'we daily hear of unacceptable Whims and extravagant Frolicks, committed by the better sort' and insists that the only way to 'correct great Men's Foibles is to ridicule 'em'. The effect is of a combination of cruel caricature and campaigning tabloid. It is a poisonous but effective recipe.

The Female Tatler is focused on people who are clearly well known to their contemporaries, like the errant Arabella Ticklepulse, who is reported to have left her husband, Doctor Ticklepulse, for the third time. Interesting as the foibles of Londoners might be, politics is never far from the page in this period. Even Mrs C is questioned as to her political allegiance. She replies that while 'Faction is even carry'd to Diversions: we have our party plays and our party operas, and I wish those who are so obstinately empty when they go to Blackheath to see the Palatines, to enquire which is the Whigg camp and which the Tory one.' The Palatines were an eighteenth-century equivalent of the displaced refugees who might seek asylum today. Being unlucky enough to be Protestants in German territories conquered by the French in 1709, they were summarily expelled by Louis XIV. They numbered around 13,000, and they were given shelter in tents on the common in Blackheath, south of London. They were eventually shipped out to Ireland and America, but, as is so often the way, some locals rioted against their presence while others provided them with a temporary safe haven. It is refreshing to read the humane response of the editor of *The Female Tatler* to questions of party politics.

However laudable we might find this even-handed approach to the Palatines, *The British Apollo* took great exception to *The Female Tatler*'s success. In fact, it was so successful in the skewering of its targets that the *Apollo* printed a poem detailing the contempt in which it held *The Female Tatler*:

Let Tatling Gossip from conceal'd abode
Spit forth her venom like an angry Toad
Apollo's offspring soar aloft too high
To be concern'd at Fish-wife ribaldry ...

Pursue thy scandal, feeble spight disclose
Slander only does thyself expose.

Far from being above the *Female Tatler*, the *Apollo*'s editorial team are clearly incensed enough to add further barbs to their attack, exposing the author of the 'abuses and lies' and claiming Mrs C is in fact an attorney with the name of B— who 'rambles around in Female Disguise' and 'lives upon scandal, as toads do on poison'; despite this, he is somehow 'so dull' that he is to be pitied.

The two publications were certainly in competition, and the attacks the *Apollo* directed at Mrs C in September 1709 alone would lead one to believe that there was genuine animosity. There are insults like 'ridiculous', 'silly wretch', and 'the most unthinking Scribler that ever writ'; indeed, every issue in that month seems to carry something unpleasant about the rival. Whether or not the *Apollo* had a hand in the downfall of *The Female Tatler*, it certainly looked forward to celebrating Mrs C's farewell.

They did not have to wait too long, as it soon became clear that the glitterati did not appreciate having their follies exposed, even with heavily disguised names. The strain of anonymising scandal and ensuring there was a grain of truth in the stories may have become too much for the original author. The person supposedly represented by 'Mrs Deputy Bustle' in *The Female Tatler*'s stories protested that Mrs C had mistaken her for someone else and that the scandal attached to her name was false. By issue 52 Mrs C's enemies had got to her, and she gave notice that she had 'resigned her pretensions of writing the female Tatler to a society of modest ladies, who in their turn will oblige the public with whatever they shall meet with, that will be diverting, innocent or instructive'. And with that, she was gone.

When Mrs C's successors pointed out that they were no longer a scandal sheet but offered genteel fare, not everybody was pleased.

They reported one disgruntled reader as writing in to say that 'scandal was the rise of your paper so whenever that fails it will sink.' Why be timid and print childish stories when real vices could be reported, enabling editors to metaphorically lash the culprits? 'Nothing,' the reader continues, 'can be a greater diversion than to see others handsomely exposed; railing at vices and follies of the age in general is insignificant ... we want you to point at the persons that are guilty of 'em.' All this was signed 'Thomas Love-truth'. Without the satire and sheer chutzpah of singling out the people who were behaving badly, the whole thing became too insipid for the public taste. It closed in March 1710, less than a year after it had begun.

We can't tell whether Mrs C enjoyed the notoriety, but one suspects they quite liked being called 'a Doxey' and a 'Mauking above and the Nizey below'. Although obscure, this insult is well aimed – a doxey is a prostitute, a mauking is a loose woman and nizey means foolish. Other comments included doubts that Mrs C was a gentlewoman: 'her scurrilous reflections on others, before they made one on her, shew her more fit to be carted than coached'. For a well-born and well-connected lady this would have been more than extremely unflattering; it would have been outrageous. All of this must have been amusing to the person behind Mrs C, who, as the *Apollo* suspected, is in fact likely to have been a man named Thomas Baker. Not everybody was horrified to be included, as at least one correspondent liked to be seen as a bit of a cad: 'Lord Plausible said, Let it be never so Scurrilous, no Body can be offended at what a Lady writes, and shou'd you, Madam, stamp me the greatest Rake and Libertine in the Kingdom, so far from being disurb'd at it, I should think myself highly honoured that you are pleased to take notice of me at all.'

There were other periodicals which at least made an attempt at targeting women. *The Ladies Diary*, which began in 1704, claimed to have been designed 'for the diversion and use of the fair sex'. As well as the kind of things normally found in an almanack, such as information about the tides and sunset times, special attention was paid to things that would specifically interest and be useful to women running a household and worrying about educating their children. It was to be packed with 'virtue and religion; the jovial, with innocent amusements and pleasant adventures' and 'something exalted to exercise their wit', and the patronising promise of 'some subjects adapted to their level'. It was all 'innocent, modest, instructive, and agreeable'. Indeed, it has to be said that for a few years the *Diary* was true to its word. In 1706 there was a 'Brief Chronology of Famous Women' all the way from Eve through Boadicea and Lady Godiva to Elizabeth I. This was seemingly intended to inspire women to emulate these icons of female bravery and English integrity. There are inspiring stories of queens from Antiquity, concluding with 'our present Queen Anne, whose reign has been attended with so many amazing instances of success that almost surpasses human belief'. There could be no safer way to please the readership than to praise the 'Great and Glorious Queen Anne'.

As you would expect, the *Diary* also included the usual list of cures for ailments, from fixing 'the Hickop' by putting your fingers in your ears to ridding a child of jaundice by giving them a concoction of rhubarb, currants and nutmeg. Equally, there is a homemade treatment for gallstones consisting of pills made of borax and oil of turpentine, which does not sound particularly effective. The remedy recommended for whitlows is bizarre, suggesting applying ground snails on the offending area in a poultice.

This was indeed a 'magazine' for ladies, with instructions on keeping children healthy and educated, a few pleasant stories, some very difficult riddles, and reviews of books on education.

For some reason, it also contained the dates of the current royal heads of state in Europe. It was an anodyne, informative publication. Alas, this format lasted just a few years before it reverted to being a magazine providing algebraic puzzles. While the very gifted Ada Lovelace might have found these challenges a breeze, it is possible that they were too much for the average lady of the day, whose education was unlikely to have extended so far.

This becomes clear when we look at the *Ladies Diary* in its collected volume, which goes from 1704 to 1773. It was apparently aimed at the female part of the population (or at least those who could afford an education and the price of the journal) and specialised in mathematical questions and poetical enigmas. The plan for the new undertaking was made clear in the preface:

[This is] designed on purpose for the diversion and use of the fair sex, which shall contain (besides those things common to other almanacks) something to suit all conditions, qualities, and humours. The ladies may here find their essences, perfumes, and unguents; the waiting-woman and servants, excellent directions in cookery, pastry, and confectionary; the married shall have medicines for their relief, and instructions for the advancement of their families; the virgin directions for love and marriage; the serious be accommodated with instances of vertue and religion.

This sounds marvellous, even though the first page starts with the statement that 'man was made lord over all things' and woman was afterwards created as a 'correspondent to his affections'. On the other hand, in contrast to advice given in the little handbooks, he comments in his rules and directions for love and Marriage: 'NEVER marry a vicious man in hopes of reclaiming of him afterwards; for those who are habituated to any manner of debauchery or vice, if you think to reclaim by fair means, or by foul, you will find yourself fatally mistaken.' This is probably a sensible comment for all ages.

Even more to the point is a comment bewailing the fate of the eligible young woman: 'But before I proceed, I cannot but take notice of the hardship the fair virgin is reduced to, in that she may not court the man she loves, but only accept in marriage one of those who happens to court her, whereas the men may address themselves to whom they please; this, I must confess, is very unequal.' From its inception to 1712, the magazine attempted to offer new ideas for female entertainment, including some very pedestrian poetry and long-winded romantic fiction. After this, however, it was back to the elaborate riddles and mathematical puzzles. It is worth noting that although it is called the *Ladies Diary*, the riddles and algebra questions are all set by men. In fact, while one might feel encouraged that answers appear to come from 'Emilia' and 'Mrs Misterton', these are the only two females who ventured to send in solutions, making this ladies' diary predominately masculine.

We can also look at another curious and strangely eclectic publication that was supposedly targeted at women. This is the similarly named *Ladies Diary or the Woman's Almanack for the Year of our Lord 1710*, which was nearer to a women's magazine than some of the others mentioned. It contained some intriguing little 'Geographical Paradoxes', such as 'There are also some places on the earth in which it is neither Day nor Night at certain time of the year for the space of 24 hours'. The general thrust of this almanac is markedly different to others in its estimation of the female intellect. Ladies are invited to submit 'aenigmas, arithmetical questions or other subjects [and] are desired always to send their explications with them; and if they, or any others, who find out solutions of any of the aenigmas or questions have a desire to have their names printed upon notice given, it shall be done accordingly'.

But there was a warning – if the contributors didn't pay the postage, their letters would be returned. Of course, what is extraordinary given the comments by less enlightened gentlemen is that women appeared to have the intellect to submit and then actually solve these arithmetical questions.

That takes care of the first half of the *Women's Almanac*. We are on safer ground with the rather more romantic second half. The publication now concerned itself with love, which is 'not only the Spring of the Passions, but … is all the Passions in one'. There is a puzzling claim that 'without love there would be no science in the world', and there are some quite charming ladylike riddles. These varied in difficulty, and in the best tradition of customer feedback twenty issues of the almanac were offered to the first lady who sent in the correct answers.

The concluding section of this strange little text is the end of a story of 'the Unfortunate Lover', continued from the last diary. It is an amusing tale which seems to involve falling into moats, sitting on wet feathers and finally sitting on a close-stool. Most of its content might not have been thought of as suitable for the delicate sensibilities of the fair sex; it appears to be a little more risqué than other magazines allow, so it stands out as unusual.

Another attempt at producing a magazine expressly for the female market was the *Visiter*, which appeared in June 1723 and was intentionally apolitical. The purpose of the publication was to improve the lot of those living a 'Domestick Life'. The editor had boldly made women 'his most precious care'. He was not going to sermonise and tell them what to wear or do; he simply wanted to entertain them. If the fair readers wanted to write to him, he would happily print their letters. He followed through on this offer in the second issue – or at least he published what he claimed were readers' letters. The first one, signed 'Emilia', is so extravagant in its praise that a cynic might wonder whether the journalist himself might have had a hand in it. It certainly made the point that everybody should read about his 'greater genius', 'good nature' and 'good sense', gushing that 'I had rather give sixpence for a paper of your sort than one stuff'd with nothing but Politicks'.

In the second issue, a truly novel comment is made on the subject of education. We have seen women compared to geese, and doubts raised about their capacity for profound speculation. In a bold comment in the *Visiter*, the author admits that their capacity for literary criticism is perhaps not as keen as that of their male counterparts. This appears to be a conventional assessment of women's limited capacity, but the writer then points out that the fairer sex do not have much in the way of education, which is described as inhuman. They go so far as to suggest that if there were a female Oxford or Cambridge they 'would not produce as many blockheads' as those male universities do. There is an audacious suggestion that women can not only make puddings but also conduct intelligent conversations with their guests; they could be clever and at the same time manage a household well. To modern eyes this might be considered patronising, but in 1723 it was quite a bold statement.

The *Visiter* is an attractive read. We should note particularly the comment about a woman's ability to sniff out pretentiousness. As they say, 'A gentleman who can explain this [Latin phrase] verbatim to a lady may justly be looked upon as a master of that language; so those who to the profoundest ignorance in letters join the greatest pretensions to skill in them, will dare no longer to stop the mouth of a woman of ... superior natural sense, tho the different manner of their education may have given him opportunity to pretend undiscovered to the knowledge of what he might be the greatest stranger to.'

While it is necessary to point out the discrepancies between the aforementioned publications as regards female intelligence, the *Visiter* is a little inconsistent on the controversial subject of gossip. In the best tradition of glamour magazines, the *Visiter* contains some reports that would have been sensational at the time. For example, the granddaughter of William Penn, Puritan and founder of Pennsylvania, has been baptised in an Anglican church. Given the rifts in the Protestant world, for the non-Anglican reader this was an example of disgraceful behaviour. There is the announcement that Lady Russell has died, leaving a fortune of £5,000 to the Duke of Bedford. And although we do not know the identity of the culprit, there is an outrageous story of a widow who had made a great display of grief at her late husband's funeral – having married her fourth husband the night before. An unavoidable bit of scandal was to be found in Captain 'Bluff's' letter decrying the habits of young ladies who swarm 'like Butterflies' around the soldiers encamped in London. The good captain begs the *Visiter* to point out to the readers that as a fifty-year-old man he hasn't been bothered by women for a good ten years and now he is pestered by 'pert young baggages' who want to drink 'champaigne' with him in his camp. There is a veiled warning that they will have the pay for this in a 'coin that will pass currant' – that is, the soldiers paying for the ladies' entertainment will want the ladies to 'entertain' them. He could be more explicit, but he is clearly toning his language down. We don't know the identities of the ladies in question, but if they had any standing in the social order then other, more salacious papers would expose them – or at least refer to them by easily recognisable pseudonyms.

In the roundup of writing suitable for women we should return to Richard Steele's *Tatler*, with which we started this chapter. Steele was patronising enough to write in the preface of the first issue, 'I resolve also to have something which may be of entertainment to the fair sex, in honour of whom I have invented the title of the paper.' The second issue contains a little story about a lovelorn nobleman who is pining for a lady he sees by chance. It is not clear if this was meant for the female reader, but 'The Medicine – a Tale for the Ladies' certainly is. It centres on a young couple who have a few marital difficulties. He drinks, she scolds. There is a happy ending after they are given a bottle containing a magic potion which cures their faults. And to no one's surprise, when they finally run out of the potion it is revealed that it was simply water and they had solved their issues just by behaving with more kindness to one another. The publication also included gossip about the great beauties of the age. Unfortunately, their identities are hidden by their code names and it is difficult to work out who they were from this remove.

An innovation arrives in issue 10 of *The Tatler* when Isaac Bickerstaff introduces his half-sister 'Jenny' to give it a feminine touch and possibly to introduce a female name onto the editorial list, even though it was in fact Steele in disguise. The first declaration from Jenny was a criticism of some men's picture of the perfect wife, who has no life of her own outside of her husband's company. While it was by no means revolutionary, there are some quirky ideas which are interesting. One of these is that all men should come with references from previous girlfriends. As Jenny so wisely suggested, a householder wouldn't take on a footman without credentials but women quite happily take on the 'most notorious offender' as a husband. A woman, she says, 'is to the last degree reproachable for being deceived and [a man] suffers no loss of credit for being a deceiver'. These are sobering thoughts, and it is possible that Steele invented Jenny to say the things he couldn't say as a man. It is certainly noticeable that Steele was involved in a string of periodicals that focused on women.

Other periodicals appeared as the eighteenth century progressed and the rough edges of the Restoration were polished off. There was *Town Talk*, a series of letters to a lady in the country.

The *Tea Table*, which the British Library ascribes to Eliza Heywood, is a series of anecdotes of a most anodyne nature. These are coupled with comments on people who are initialled but whose identities are not obvious to the modern reader. Towards the end of the period in focus comes the *Female Spectator* in 1744. This magazine, issued monthly, was edited by the same Eliza Heywood, who had a reputation for reporting on the kind of scandals which were so beloved of the early years of the eighteenth century and which had got the unreformed *Female Tatler* into such trouble. She was an actress turned author, and, having tried her hand at theatre criticism, she had an eye for trends. She struck gold with her entry into the world of women's magazines.

Female readers were ready for a monthly essay where there was no chance of your private moral slip-ups being exposed. The *Female Spectator* consisted of stories which were used as vehicles for romantic fiction which contained sound advice, generally in the behaviour of ladies and young women. For instance, Ms Heywood suggests that it 'betrays a great want of policy, as well as an unjust austerity, to seclude a young lady, and shut her up from all [social] intercourse with men, for fear she should find one among them who might happen to please her too well. Chance may in a moment destroy all that the utmost care can do; and I say a woman is in far less danger of losing her heart, when every day surrounded with a variety of gay objects, than when by some accident she falls into the conversation of a single-one.' For the purposes of the improving story, that man will be a bad apple. Or, horror, they might be swept off their feet by a servant. This was literal in the case of the suggestively named Eagaretta, who 'condescended to marry the greasy foot man that ran before her chair' because he was 'the only man her over-careful father permitted her to speak to'.

Sometimes, even marrying a gentleman could be fraught with danger. A cad will find you and with the help of a wicked go-between you will be tricked 'into everlasting ruin'. Delicate and innocent young ladies are warned by reading of Seomanthe's plight. She was a young lady who was due to come into a 'large fortune on the day of her marriage', but she was preyed upon by a wicked woman who spotted her and by various wiles introduced her to a bounder 'who was so far a gentleman as to be bred to no business, and whose whole estate was laid out on his back, in hopes of appearing charming in the eyes of some monied woman'. The upshot of this wicked pair's machinations was predictably a Mills and Boone bodice ripper without the happy ending. The innocent girl eloped with him by escaping through a window one night:

> Early in the morning they were married, and it is possible passed some days in the usual transports of a bridal state. But when their place of abode was discovered by the friends and kindred of Seomanthe, who, distracted at her elopement, had searched the whole town, in how wretched a manner was she found! The villain had drawn her whole fortune out of the Bank, robbed her of all her jewels, and the best of her apparel, had shipped everything off, and was himself embarked she knew not to what place. The people of the house where they lodged, perceiving him, whom they expected to have been their paymaster, gone, seized on the few trifles he had left behind, as satisfaction for their rent, and were going to turn the unfortunate Seomanthe out of doors.

Poor Seomanthe was rescued by some friends, but was left living on their charity with no notion of where her errant husband had gone. Young ladies with fortunes were told to beware of handsome young men with no visible means of support.

Compared to the *Female Tatler*, the *Female Spectator* is a bit of a killjoy. It doesn't approve of public masques where you have to buy tickets for there is no vetting of the guests, where the young innocent will meet 'the most abandoned rake, or low-breed fellow'. Another little anecdote describes the horror that might be found: 'A witty gentleman ... told me, he never was so much diverted in his life as one night, when he saw the greatest prude in the nation, after having been accosted with some very odd expressions, by one, who doubtless mistook her for another, run, as if to shield herself from his importunities, to a certain fille-de-joye, to whom he had given a ticket, and cry out, "O Madam, did you hear the filthy Creature?"' The editor, taking on a prudish tone, says it was 'punishment for her appearing in a place so little conformable to the austerity she professed in other things'.

Months later, the editor is still discussing the pros and cons of public entertainment in the pleasure gardens. By this time she is wavering:

But the misfortune is, that whatever is done by persons of quality presently becomes the mode, which everyone is ambitious of apeing, let it suit ever so ill with their circumstances: it is not the fine prospect that Ranelagh is happy in, the pleasant walks, the magnificent amphitheatre, nor the melodious sounds that issue from the orchestra, that make the assembly there so numerous; but the vanity everyone has of joining company, as it were, with their superiors; — of having it in their power to boast, when they come home, of the notice taken of them by such a lord, or such a great lady; to descant upon their dresses, their behaviour and pretend to discover who likes who; what fine new married lady coquets it with her husband's intimate; what duke regards his wife with no more than an enforced complaisance; and whether the fortune, or person, of the young heiress, is the object of her obsequious follower's flame.

The thought of the lower classes intermingling with the glitterati is anathema to the genteel editor. On the other hand, if they didn't mix then where would they find the scandals which fuel the periodical business?

And so the *Female Spectator* rolled on. It obviously hit the spot for the public, but it is dull after the earlier scandal sheets. Thereafter, ladies' magazines became increasingly respectable. The *Ladies Curiosity* or *Weekly Apollo*, for instance, was obsessed with marriage and all that could go wrong. These included a wife who married for love but has no love for her husband and tells her spouse so every day, and a husband who says he married for love but actually married for money. One of these stories ends brutally, with a curious reversal of what would typically be expected in this period. The conclusion to a story of a male gold-digger is that he raped his wife and was then hanged. At least, the argument goes, the woman was free of him. The alternative is that he remains in the household, but the likelihood here is that he will abuse her daily – 'the crime is renewed and she is made unhappy for the rest of her life'.

The theme of love and marriage is particularly strong in the second issue of the *Ladies Curiosity*, which includes 'Matrimonial whoredom' (marrying for money), 'Of Constancy in Love', 'A Case in Love Stated, and resolved', 'A wife of Quality', 'Of Marriage and Divorce', 'The Properest Time for a Woman to Marry' and 'the Different Sorts of Lovers'. This is relieved by diversions in 'Taste in Plays, Of Education, Vain Pursuits, Good Manners', love poetry and some love songs (with music). Also included in the magazine is a piece on 'Reasons for unhappy marriages'. There is even a space for readers' letters. The questions put to the editor include one asking whether to marry a respectable and comfortable young tradesman or a devoted old man who is very rich. That decision is being forced, with the girl's guardian coming under pressure from the geriatric suitor. The advice is equivocal; the call of money is very strong. However, one can sympathise with the editor's comments on divorce:

> In the next place let us try how 'tis with marriage. The grand inconvenience of marriage is to being obliged to live with one man or one woman till death parts, tho' they hate and despise one another heartily. To remedy this evil, there is one way, i.e. to suffer some alterations in our laws about marriage; and make divorces, in all just cases, more easy and less expensive than at present: for, tho' 'tis said a man shall not put away his wife but in one case, it is not said, That a man and his wife shall not part, when they freely, fully, and upon the maturest deliberation, consent. There may be moral incapacities, which as effectually destroy the end of marriage, as natural. If divorces were permitted in all reasonable cases we should soon find an end put to the wretched state of old batchelors, who are miserable in themselves and useless to the world; cut off from society; solitary wanderers; coffee-house drones; sour splenetick fellows, who languish out life, and find no relief but in the idle chat of a soaking club: without the lasting and solid pleasures of husband, wife and children, who, by a long train of mutual good offices, are most delightfully endeared to one another.

It is difficult to see how anyone could argue with such good advice. And so the ladies magazine develops throughout the ensuing years. The essays are joined by fashion commentary and yet more suggestions on the appropriate behaviour of ladies, including running their households and managing their servants. We can only wonder how many people missed the joys of scandal until the paparazzi appeared several hundred years later.

6

ADVERTISING

As today, the cover price on early publications was insufficient to cover their costs. The newspapers needed extra revenue, and so the advertising industry was born. The publishers sold space for everything, from adverts for syphilis cures to notices about runaway servants. Extravagant claims were made with no advertising authority to regulate them. Some of the advertisements are dull to modern eyes, consisting of volumes of sermons, but as a whole they offer an insight into how the readership lived and how they spent their time and their money. For anyone interested in social history, these adverts are an invaluable guide. Some of the advertising is frightening, and with no notion of a Trades Description Act or rigorous testing for medicines the acres of space filled by spurious products are likely to have killed more people than they cured. This chapter discusses what the people at the time were worrying about and thinking of buying, and how they spent their leisure hours. It's a journey through hope and despair.

Perhaps we should begin with the most important element of the topic, at least for the proprietor: the financial benefits of carrying paid-for advertising. We have discussed the pitfalls of printing newspapers and the trouble printers, publishers and booksellers could get themselves into. With that in mind, if the aim was simply to turn a profit and have a much simpler life then the best thing to do was to buck the trend, ignore politics and concentrate on profitable advertising. The number of advertisements evident in the records, despite the tax slapped on them in 1712, shows that newspaper publishers appreciated this fact, although it was some time before a publication dedicated to advertising appeared.

The Daily Advertiser was an early entry into the field of pure advertising, opening up its doors to advertisers on 3 February 1730. It is difficult to ascertain who published and printed this paper, but the proprietor was obviously well clued up on marketing. They had worked out that the first rule of selling something is to let people know it is available. Their first action was therefore to declare that 'this paper will be given Gratis to all Coffee-Houses Four Days successively, and afterwards Printed every Day, Sundays excepted'. The next rule of marketing is to describe to people what is on offer and make it look attractive. Thus the front page of the brand-new publication established that 'this Paper is intended to consist wholly of Advertisements, together with the Prices of Stocks, Course of Exchange, and Names and Descriptions of Persons becoming Bankrupts'. Of course, it is also very important that the product is easy to find, so the proprietors pinned up copies of the day's issue on walls in all the places where their target market might see it. So if you were doing business in the Royal Exchange, near the Bank of England, East India House or Westminster Hall, you would see *The Daily Advertiser*.

A further innovation was to place the advertisements in some kind of order: a column for house purchases, a column for books, and so on. It was clear that some thought had gone into the layout. A further, extremely clever innovation was the column for undelivered letters. The explanation appears altruistic:

'And as it frequently happens that letters as well Inland as Foreign, are directed to persons unknown and for want of proper descriptions remain undelivered to the prejudice of his Majesty's Revenue of Postage and injury to that few persons to whom they belong, to prevent which inconveniences for the future as far as it may be authentic lists of such letters will be daily printed in this paper to the end those whom it shall concern may apply at the General Post Office.' The coffee-houses 'Where Advertisements are taken in' were named. Overall the strategy was successful, and the circulation rose to around to 2,000 copies daily.

Most newspapers followed the more traditional pattern of news followed by advertisements, and some of these promised life-changing experiences and opportunities. As is often the case, these offers could prove suspect under closer scrutiny. A golden opening to a better life appears to be the invitation to 'settle upon the healthful island of St Hellena'. Those seventeenth-century readers wishing to make a new start – in the place where Napoleon would meet his end – needed to look no further than the advertising column of their *Parliamentary Intelligencer*. Providing they made their way to the offices of the East India Company before 20 November 1660, they could take up the tantalising offer of free passage to this rocky outcrop in the Atlantic. When they got there they would receive free accommodation, and although it was not mentioned they would also be given a packet of land. They may have been disappointed when they arrived; like so much marketing material with foreign travel included, the offering needed a large pinch of salt. Even with the free boat ride and the land, the East India Company were having great difficulty in recruiting people to live and work there. One of the most remote islands in the world, Saint Helena was not the paradise the Company promised.

For those preferring a shorter journey, there was always a trip to the theatre. For readers looking for a good night out, at the Theatre

Royal in Drury Lane there was *The Sea Voyage*; this sounds like a treat, with 'entertainments of singing' and 'several comick dances'. On the other hand, some people might prefer to stay at home with a cookery book. *The Court and Country Cook* would give them instructions on preserving fruits among other things, and might prove a very useful reference for the kitchen. Every now and then a little bit of humanity peeps through the rather plain text; there is the rather sad tale of a faithful servant of the king who leaves gaol at the Restoration with his little pack containing all his clothes, no doubt he was looking forward to re-joining the royal household with all its glitz and glamour. Tragically, he set his bundle down for a few moments and some ne'er-do-well stole it. As a consolation, it is reported that the king offered a reward for the bag's recovery.

On the other hand, trawling through the advertisements does lead to the conclusion that some members of the royal household were doomed to be unlucky. Charles II's queen, Catherine of Braganza, was in some ways a tragic figure, childless and trapped in a court with an openly philandering husband. Her Catholic faith isolated her. Without a child, much of her maternal affection was lavished on her little dogs. So we must have some sympathy for the unfortunate queen when her precious Pers went missing. She placed a high price on the dog's return, with a reward of two guineas offered for the return of the pooch.

The popular belief is that classified advertisements were originally on the front page, but during this period they were at the back. They didn't migrate to the front until later in the century. However, whatever the position of the advertising the one thing that preoccupied the readers was their health. With very little scientific knowledge, the nation's physical well-being was in a sorry state in the 1690s and 1700s, so it was only to be expected that a very high percentage of the adverts deal with health. The result of this instance of hope over experience was an increase in profits for the newspaper proprietors, and there are acres of newsprint devoted to the most alarming 'cures'. To say that the claims made by the physicians, pharmacists and quacks are extravagant and even downright fabrications is an understatement.

Taking a survey of the over-the-counter medication is an eye-opener. We will start with an umbrella word: 'consumption'. This would apply to the condition of anyone unfortunate enough to suffer from of any sort of chest complaint such as asthma or disorders of the lung. The choice of cures was dazzling. Readers were assured that any or all of these conditions would be infallibly cured by the Great Chemical Elixir. The claims for this wonder drug are certainly bold: 'it at once strikes, and absolutely eradicates the first Principle or cause of consumptions'.

There is little or no order in the advertising columns and cures for this and every other condition that you can think of, and quite a few that don't bear repeating sit cheek by fevered jowl next to advertisements for houses, clothes and lost things. Although categorisation was lacking in the original columns, we need to impose some order so that we might more easily explore what is an extraordinary collection of windows into a world that has long gone.

Despite the jumbled positioning of the advertisements, they are well targeted and even without the benefit of marketing diplomas or agencies these businesses certainly knew their market. They lacked the jingles, focus groups and bright colours of a modern sales campaign, but the people behind the products really knew their customers. They had no compunction about breaching any ethical rules regarding the veracity of their claims.

First we can look at the process of placing an advertisement into the papers, and the costs involved. It became slightly more expensive in 1712, when the government slapped the aforementioned tax on advertising. This one-shilling tax was brought in at the same time as the Stamp Tax, and provided a revenue stream for the government. The Stamp Tax was levied depending on the size and number of sheets of paper in a publication, and its real purpose was to discourage the worrying proliferation of newspapers and act as a limiter to unruly journalists. If the number of advertisements is a measure of the effectiveness of this tax, it must have disappointed the ministry but gladdened the hearts of the men tasked with filling the Treasury coffers.

The actual placing of the advertising was rather like putting a classified ad in the local paper without the convenience of the internet or a telephone. There was a variety of ways to deliver the copy. The individual or their servant took it in person to the printer, or there were drop-off points at designated coffee-houses, bookshops and other outlets. So for instance, *The Tatler* was sold by John Morphew and the advertisements could be taken directly to him. Advertising in *The Spectato*r gives you the option of taking the adverts to the printer, S. Buckley, but also to a rather unlikely Charles Lillie, perfumer. In 1738, *The London Daily Post* had organised a network and advised the potential advertiser that they would only take adverts of 'moderate length', which would cost 2*s* each. For delivery there was the choice of John Shakleburgh, bookseller; The Sun; Mrs Chapman; The Kings Arms Tavern; Mr Amy's Pamphlet shop; Mr Fisher, bookseller; and The Rose.

So there were plenty of places around London which acted as agents to the newspapers. One interesting point that is worth remembering is that apart from reading materials this is one of the few areas of the print world which appeared to be free of politics, although the newspapers would likely choose to advertise books and pamphlets which aligned with their avowed loyalties. Of course, disease does not differentiate between political parties and the adverts for medicine were aimed at everyone. Naturally, the expense of the advertisement and the likelihood of the reader being able to afford the goods being offered leads us to the conclusion that the marketers targeted the well-off with their books and luxury items. Disposable income is a universal concept, so while the average labourer might dream of buying that coach and horses with a little place in the country they are unlikely to be able to afford more than the newspaper itself. Lottery tickets and results were also announced here, giving an aspirational element to the advertising.

The first category of cure-alls that strikes the modern reader is shocking and fascinating at the same time. We are about to enter the murkier side of Early Modern life. It is an unavoidable fact that an unnervingly high proportion of Englishmen and women in this period suffered from the 'Secret disease'. Such ailments were known by a variety of names, some of which are not at all polite; the very habit of calling them 'secret' would suggest a degree of discretion. Against that the number of clinicians offering sure-fire cures indicates that a huge percentage of the country had managed to infect themselves and each other. Sadly, the only weapons against these sexually transmitted diseases were the offerings of some of the biggest charlatans ever seen. The statistics are sobering. There were enough people worried about it for one historian to calculate that at least 300 books and pamphlets were published between 1600 and 1800 on the subject. And the help was plentiful but useless. There were hundreds of products claiming to alleviate the sufferings of the infected patients.

We will just look at a selection of what was on offer. Dr Cam is ready with The Admirable Electuary, which 'infallibly cures all degrees and symptoms'. Two pots should be enough, and the good doctor claimed that it was a quick, pleasant and easy remedy. As a footnote, he warns patients not to buy their medicines from toyshops or booksellers. If the patient was unsure about Dr Cam, there were plenty of other quacks to go to. Why not try the 'doctor in physic [who] cures all the degrees and indispositions in venereal persons and by a most easie safe and expeditious method.

He likewise gives his advice in all diseases and prescribes a cure.'
If the unfortunate sufferer has tried Dr Cam and the 'doctor in
physic' and they didn't work, there was always Wright's Diuretick
or cleansing tincture which, intriguingly, frees the body of 'relicks
of the venereal disease after ill managed cures'.

To modern eyes, the least promising medical intervention was
something called the Anodyne Neck Lace, which claimed to effect
a cure just by wearing it. One testimonial claimed that although
the patient had suffered from the 'secret disease to that height that
I was told by several able men that I should never be cured', this
piece of jewellery worked. It cost 5s and appeared in adverts in
many papers, although it was just a string of beads. As an added
incentive to purchase it came with free gifts, mostly pamphlets.
People probably clung to these strange quack cures in desperation,
even though their contemporaries pointed out quite sensibly that
'there is another branch of pretenders to this art [of medicine]
who, without either horse or pickle herring, lie snug in a garret,
and send down notice to the world of their extraordinary parts
and abilities by printed bills and advertisements'. It is unclear what
part the pickle herring plays, but the sentiment is clear.

Even by late in the eighteenth century, when one would think
that people would have realised what a waste of time and money
the necklace was, one distinguished physician complained that
mothers were still putting it around their children's necks to
guard against death by teething. The advertisement appealed to
a mother's most basic instincts: 'What mother can forgive herself,
who suffers her child to die without an *anodyne necklace*!' It seems
extraordinary that a simple string of beads which started off as an
ineffectual cure for venereal disease has widened its remit to curing
a threatened fatal attack of teething.

Perhaps the most remarkable aspect of seventeenth- and
eighteenth-century medicine is its extraordinary claim to efficiency.

1. Thomas Rowlandson's representation of a Grub Street poet. (Courtesy of Yale Center for British Art)

2. After James II left the throne, William III became joint sovereign with James' daughter Mary I. During William's reign, the Licensing Act lapsed. (Courtesy of the Rijksmuseum)

3. Louis XIV was the arch enemy of the English during the decades around the turn of the seventeenth century, providing material for British newspapers. (Courtesy of the Rijksmuseum)

4. Samuel Pepys, diarist, observer and collector of ballads. (Courtesy of Yale Center for British Art)

Right: 5. Grub Street 1746: Rocque's map of London outside the walls of the City of London. Milton Street is now inside the City.

Below: 6. Hogarth's *Distrest Poet* is a depiction of a Grub Street hack's poverty-stricken living conditions while writing anything that will earn him some money. (Courtesy of the Metropolitan Museum of Art)

THE DISTREST POET.

Above left: 7. Another example of the squalor associated with the poorer end of Grub Street, this time the exteriors.

Above right: 8. Richard Steele, founder of *The Guardian* and co-founder of *The Spectator*. (Courtesy of Yale Center for British Art)

Left: 9. Joseph Addison, co-founder with Steele of *The Spectator*. (Courtesy of the Wellcome Collection)

10. The front page of
The Spectator. Among other
things, it made some effort to
improve behaviour of society.
(Courtesy of the British Library)

11. A typical advertisement
for medical treatments; this
is from one J. Russel, 'oculist
and physician', and dates to the
late 1600s. (Courtesy of the
Wellcome Collection)

12. A 1754 engraving of Old South Sea House, the headquarters of the South Sea Company. The newspapers played an intrinsic role in building the 'Bubble' up and then helping in its decline. (Courtesy of Harvard University)

13. Ranelagh Gardens, popular with every rank of person for a good night out but also notorious for liaisons. (Courtesy of Yale Center for British Art)

14. A typical
representation of
Charles I from the
pamphleteers of the
English Civil Wars.

15. The pillory,
a typical form of
punishment for
transgressing by
publication.

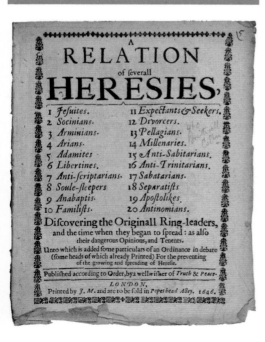

Above left: 16. *The Daily Courant.* This publication paved the way in the newspaper industry.

Above right: 17. *The Medley*, set up by Arthur Maynwaring, aide to the Duchess of Marlborough and staunch anti-Tory, explicitly to discredit Swift's and Manley's *The Examiner*. (Courtesy of the Folger Shakespeare Library)

Left: 18. *A list of heresies.* The antagonism between the various versions of Protestantism was fierce. (Courtesy of the Folger Shakespeare Library)

THe TRYALS of several WITCHES lately Executed in *New-England*, with many Remarkable *Curiosities* therein Occurring. By *Cotton Mather*. Published by the Special Command of his EXCELLENCY the Governour of *New-England*. First Printed in *Boston*, and now Reprinted in *London* for *John Dunton* at the *Raven* in the *Poultrey*.

Above: 19. An advertisement from the *Athenian Gazette* about witchcraft in New England. (Courtesy of the Folger Shakespeare Library)

Right: 20. Delarivier Manley's *New Atalantis*, 1709. Manley's contribution to the origins of the press were significant, particularly for a woman. (Courtesy of the Folger Shakespeare Library)

SECRET
MEMOIRS
AND
MANNERS
Of several
Persons of Quality,
O F
Both SEXES.
FROM THE
New ATALANTIS,
A N
Island in the *Mediteranean*.

Written Originally in ITALIAM.

The Second Edition.

LONDON:
Printed for *John Morphew* near *Stationer's-Hall*, and *J. Woodward* in St. *Christopher's* Church-yard, in *Thread-needle-street*. 1709.

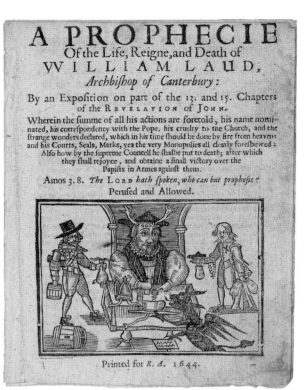

21. *A prophecie of the life ... and death of William Laud ... a final victory over the Papists.* Laud was possibly the most loathed cleric of the seventeenth century. (Courtesy of the Folger Shakespeare Library)

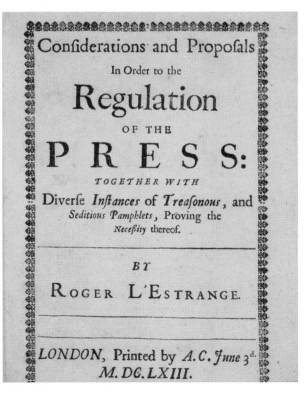

22. Sir Roger l'Estrange's ideas for controlling the press, from 1663. (Courtesy of the Folger Shakespeare Library)

23. It was during Anne's reign that an author's copyright began to be asserted. (Courtesy of the Yale Center for British Art)

24. William Cavendish, 1st Duke of Newcastle, who did not believe that the lower orders needed to learn to read. (Courtesy of the Yale Center for British Art)

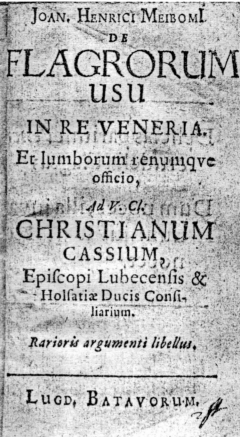

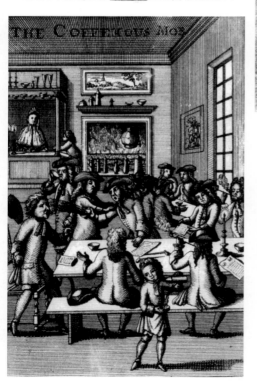

Above left: 25. A bookseller at an auction around 1700. It appears that a doctor's library is being sold off.

Above right: 26. A treatise on the use of flogging in medicine and venery. Curll published this in English in 1718.

Left: 27. 'The Coffeehouse mob' from Ned Ward's satirical poem *Vulgus Brittanicus* (1710).

Right: 28. Alexander Pope, who recalled his letters to improve his literary legacy. (Courtesy of the Yale Centre for British Art)

Below right: 29. Hogarth's depiction of Pope as 'Pope Alexander', which was originally included in his 'The Distrest Poet' but was removed before the official release. It is unclear whether it mocks Pope or his opponents.

Below: 30. A cartoon of Alexander Pope punishing Curll for reproducing his letters without permission. (Courtesy of the Yale Centre for British Art)

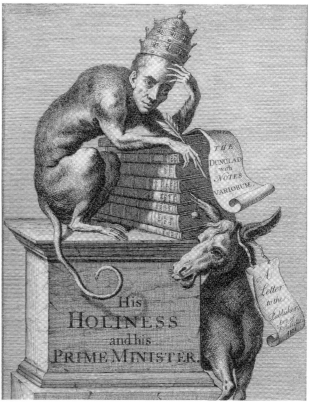

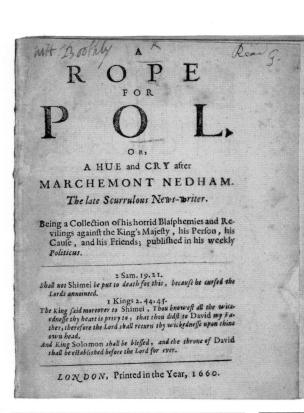

A ROPE FOR POL.

OR,

A HUE and CRY after

MARCHEMONT NEDHAM.

The late Scurrulous News-writer.

Being a Collection of his horrid Blasphemies and Revilings against the King's Majesty, his Person, his Cause, and his Friends; published in his weekly *Politicus*.

2 Sam. 19. 21.
Shall not Shimei be put to death for this, because he cursed the Lords annointed.

1 Kings 2. 44, 45.
The King said moreover to Shimei, Thou knowest all the wickednesse thy heart is privy to, that thou didst to David my Father, therefore the Lord shall return thy wickednesse upon thine own head.
And King Solomon shall be blessed, and the throne of David shall be established before the Lord for ever.

LONDON, Printed in the Year, 1660.

Left: 31. Nedham's *A Rope for Pol.* (Courtesy of the Folger Shakespeare Library)

Below left: 32. An early example of the *couranto*: *Pigges corantoe, or Newes from the North.* (Courtesy of the Folger Shakespeare Library)

Below: 33. *Good newes to Christendome.* An early example of a newssheet depicting blood raining on Rome, indicating that the 'Great Turke' was being called to become a Christian. Printed in 1620. (Courtesy of the Folger Shakespeare Library)

PIGGES CORANTOE,

OR

NEVVES FROM the North.

LONDON,
Printed for *L. C.* and *M. W.*
1642.

Good Newes to Christendome.

Sent to a Venetian in Ligorne, from a Merchant in ALEXANDRIA.

Discouering a wonderfull and strange Apparition, visibly seene for many dayes togæther in Arabia, ouer the place, where the supposed Tombe of MAHOMET (the Turkish Prophet) is inclosed: By which the learned Arabians prognosticate the Reducing & Calling of the great Turke to Christianitie. With many other notable Accidents; But the most remarkable is the miraculous rayning of Bloud about ROME.

Done out of the Italian.

LONDON,
Printed for NATHANIEL BUTTER. 1620.

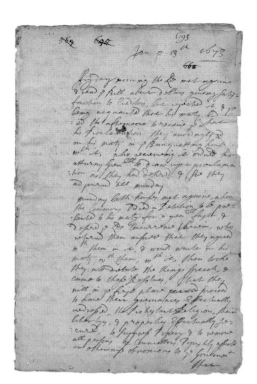

Right: 34. An example of a newsletter from the late seventeenth century. (Courtesy of the Folger Shakespeare Library)

Below: 35. A representation of Defoe in the pillory for having written *The Shortest Way with the Dissenters*. (Courtesy of the Wellcome Collection)

By the King.

A PROCLAMATION

To Reftrain the Spreading of Falfe News, and Licentious talking of Matters
OF

State and Government.

CHARLES R.

God fave the King.

LONDON,
Printed by the Aſſigns of *John Bill* and *Chriſtopher Barker*, Printers
to the Kings moſt Excellent Majeſty. 1674.

Above left: 36. Jonathan Swift, High Tory satirist and one of Harley's most effective writers. Disappointed in his career progression in England, Swift took up the post of Dean of St Patrick's Cathedral in Dublin. (Courtesy of Yale Center for British Art)

Above right: 37. Robert Harley, Earl of Oxford, possibly the first English statesman to realise the power of the press. (Courtesy of the Rijksmuseum)

Left: 38. A proclamation to restrain the spreading of false news and licentious discussion of matters of state and government from 1674. (Courtesy of the Folger Shakespeare Library)

It would appear that one pill often cures all. The miraculous 'Royal Bitter Tincture' is a case in point. It is claimed to cure 'all disorders in the stomach and blood' and in addition 'it gives immediate ease in the Gripes and Cholick, Wind, Vapeurs, and Headache'. It is effective against the 'scurvy, jaundice, flux, vomiting, worms, and leprosy'. It also cites a variety of diseases which are obscure but clearly troublesome. To put this into perspective, when searching an archive of historical newspapers, between 1700 and 1740 the phrase 'venereal disease' yields 900 advertisements. Even without looking at them in detail, these advertisements say something about the world of the late Stuarts and early Hanoverians. The population of England at this time was around five million and with the level of clinical ignorance the numbers who were suffering from incurable diseases must have been significant. Even more notable is the fact that the advertisements which promised so much were published week after week indicating the high level of trust in medicines which we know to have been useless. Or perhaps it was desperation.

There are other things which needed to be cured which we might recognise today. For instance, a trip to the dentist is still a less than attractive prospect for many of us. If you looked up a physician of forty years' practice in Whalebone Court you would find a 'most excellent Gargarism or mouth water which will make black or yellow teeth as white as snow ... and it will also cure the scurvy and all other diseases incident in the mouth, teeth and gums'. An alternative option might be the 'Unparalleled Powder for cleaning the teeth which has given great satisfaction'. According to the advertisement this has an unmatched success rate for a variety of conditions. With one use it makes 'the teeth as white as ivory, tho never so black or yellow and effectively preserves them from rotting or decaying'. And if it was gum problems that were worrying the patient, just like its rival product above, this one cures scurvy, prevents 'deductions and kills worms at the roots of the teeth'. Just for good measure, it also fastens loose teeth. The matter of worms was a truly inventive scam – the 'practitioner' poked around in the gums and then produced by sleight of hand some silkworm eggs from the client's mouth.

If the citizen who has so far tried the cures for a variety of illnesses needs more help, the next condition to tackle would be their sight. It is always important to choose an optician or oculist with a known approval rating. In the 1700s, the myopic Londoner might well have visited Mr Brinsden, oculist and surgeon, because he boasted a remarkable and impressive testimonial list. The number of people he has cured is phenomenal. He claims to have wrought his skills on people who were suffering with the most difficult of diseases of the eye. Even more laudable was his claim that he only did it for the good of mankind, although he does not mention if his services come free of charge. However, we must marvel at the case of John Willott, who was once blind and could now read small print. There were also Mrs Baxter, Thomas Batty and the Reverend Mr Garner's wife, who were cured of an obstruction of the optic nerve. William Chamber and Mrs Corbit were no longer blind. Finishing the list of happily cured patients is the son of Jane Evans who was born blind. We have no details of how Mr Brinsden achieved these miraculous results. Other practitioners were equally mysterious, and I doubt that many people want to hear how the expert who removes cataracts did it without the benefit of modern techniques.

With the teeth in good shape and 20/20 vision restored, the next aspect of personal appearance to attend to might be your crowning glory in the eighteenth century: the periwig. At Mr Allcraft's toyshop there was available a product which would make the wig 'nice'. It would also have the simultaneous benefit of strengthening the brain, reviving the spirits and making the heart cheerful –

claims which even the most expensive shampoo can hardly make these days.

If the patient was still not happy at this point, he or she could go to Dr Pitt. This learned doctor promised to expose 'The Craft and Frauds of Physick', with the further assurance that he would supply the 'very best medicines' at the lowest prices. As an added bonus, he would reveal how 'the costly preparations now in greatest esteem' should be condemned, along with an explanation of how the 'frequent use of physic' will prove 'defective to health'. He also provided 'instructions to prevent being cheated and destroyed by the prevailing practice'. As a finishing touch to this section, there is the additional assurance that there is no need to panic if the patient has been bitten by a mad animal. 'An Easy Short and Certain Method' to alleviate such a situation is available. It is also 'published by Authority', which must have come as a relief, even though there is no indication exactly whose authority is being quoted.

We should assume by now that the reader is feeling well and that his wig has been refreshed, so he might be on the lookout for something new for his wardrobe. There were some good bargains to be had, at least according to the advertising. There was an opportunity to visit the Old Silk Gown Ware House, where a fresh parcel of silk gowns had lately been made up to be sold at a cheaper price than in any other shop or warehouse. Each gown was advertised as priced individually, so that anyone who bought a silk dress would be reassured that they were paying no more than they should. If the customer had the means to make up the garments themselves, such as gowns, petticoats or headdresses, or had the services of a dressmaker, there were rolls of silk in all sorts of colours. At the same shop they had scarves and aprons, all ready-made. The ladies were well catered for, but an equal number of retail outlets could cater for the gentlemen, including plenty of advertisements for fabrics for clerical gowns. Finally, the exotically named *Magazin de Robbe de Chambre* had a stock of gowns for men and women, of garden satins, rich flowered silks and fine calicoes at knock-down prices. They were cheap, the advertisement stated, because they were bankrupt stock, something which appears very frequently in the adverts. Perhaps the most intriguing element of these advertisements for clothing was the emphasis on the lowest prices and the wide variety of ready-made articles of clothing available.

It was not just retail opportunities which filled the advertising columns. There were other issues which appeared in these columns, some of which might look strange to modern eyes. One recurring theme is that of the runaway wife. This concern is explained by William Blackstone, whose learned work on English common law explains the abandoned husband's worries succinctly. The fear is that he will be landed with her spending spree because 'by marriage, the husband and wife are one person in law: that is, the very being or legal existence of the woman is suspended during the marriage, or at least is incorporated and consolidated into that of the husband: under whose wing, protection, and cover, she performs everything'. Put simply, she does not exist as an independent entity, so any debts she incurs are by definition his.

The lists of wives whose husbands nervously disclaim their responsibility gives a sorry picture of some marriages in the period. We might not be surprised to learn that Henry Forster, whose wife Ann Forster, alias Warren, of Wapping, Stepney in London, 'hath eloped from her husband and habitation and hath contracted diverse debts'. However, we might be surprised that he is advertising the fact. The husbands in these cases were for the most part exercising a damage limitation exercise. Henry, for instance, warned duped shopkeepers that 'whoever treats with her must expect that her said husband will be no way chargeable and whoever has any bills papers or effects in their hands that they do not pay from them at their perils.' Sometimes the runaway wife was accused of involvement in more serious activities. The following statement, which appears as a privately placed item in the classified column, shows something that looks like a well-planned conspiracy.

... whereas a sentence of divorce has passed against Frances Deeye at the suit of John Deeye her husband in the High Court of Delegates ... upon a pretence of a fact of adultery suggested or be sworn against here by one Margaret Collins a person of a very lewd and dissolute life and conversation and who now stands indicted for perjury in that very cause together with Joseph Goodale [and] a proctor in Doctors Commons who also stands indicted for knowingly, maliciously fraudulently and deceitfully framing, drawing, writing signing and under his hand as a notary public attesting a certain false writing as if the said Margaret Collins had been sworn a witness in the said cause who in truth had never been sworn nor taken any oath to give her testimony in the said cause, the bills of indictment being found against them by the Grand Jury at Guildhall ... If any person therefore shall so far discover the author or printer of the said advertisement as affects them by legal and due proof provided they are of good substance Joseph Goodale of Doctors Commons ... promise for the discovery of the author 10 guineas and a further five guineas upon proof to be made as aforesaid.

From this it appears that the husband of the unfortunate Frances conspired with the other characters in this scenario to gain a divorce from his innocent wife by perjury. In a time when divorce was difficult and expensive, one can only feel sympathy for the wife in this case, traduced so publicly in a classified column.

Reading through the advertisements there are many which show, unsurprisingly, that marriage was no guarantee of happiness and that some women would take their destinies into their own hands. These were days when divorce was only for the very rich. On the basis of the two or three lines in these advertisements we clearly can't comment on the justification of their departure from the marital home, but they risked their reputations in doing so and it has to be said that in some of the abandoned husbands' declarations it is not clear which they missed more, the wife or the goods she took with her.

Just to give a further flavour of these examples of marital breakdown, we can have a look at some of the adverts which put couples' problems on public display. Since women had very few if any rights, it is unsurprising that there are no announcements from wives concerning absent husbands. However, some examples of runaway wives make for interesting reading. In 1702, Teresa Moor eloped, taking 'diverse goods'. Tradesmen are instructed 'not to entertain her' nor 'entrust her with any money or goods for the said Thomas her husband will not pay the same'. It is difficult to tell whether Anne Vincent in 1707 is in a better place; her husband would have her back but refused to pay her debts. The level of detail in this case even touches on the wife's mode of transport, as Mr Vincent is adamant that he will not pay her coach fare and was prepared to sue anyone who gave her passage. Her description isn't too flattering either. She is apparently a 'middle sized woman about 55, pretty thick in the body', with only two or three teeth on her lower jaw and none in her upper jaw.

The list of runaway wives is long. Mr Parsons won't pay Jane Parsons' extensive debts, Elizabeth Percy is now living with Henry Goodwin and has taken his name, and the enterprising Anne Huff ran away a year ago after ransacking Mr Huff's house, taking away goods of considerable value; Mr Huff refused to pay her debts. Unusually, Elizabeth Littleton took two bundles of clothes with her and went to live with the Hon. Gilbert Vane as his nurse. The list goes on. There are some husbands who were willing to take back their wayward spouses. For instance, Elizabeth Beale left by advice of 'evil persons, taking divers goods and linen'. If she came back, she would be kindly received and want for nothing suitable for the wife of Mr Beale – but he still wouldn't pay her debts. Jane Mitchell refused to live with her husband but was currently cohabiting with several infamous men. She took £500 worth of goods and still 'endeavours to ruin him by running into debt'. There were some husbands for whom, without knowing the full story, there might be some sympathy. Joan Heartly took 'goods having confederated with evil persons' and 'caused [Mr Heartly] to be cast into prison by feigned and illegal actions and still continues to contrive his ruin. He has provided all proper and entertainment' and 'will gladly receive her again despite what has passed'. So it goes on, although Mary Serle is better off; at least she has an independent annuity and has sufficient to maintain herself.

Some of the advertisements have little stories attached. Spare a thought for John Winch, who had a bit of a surprise when he got home from a two-year stint in the Royal Navy and found his wife 'very big with a bastard child'. Finally, Bethia Colcock left with no provocation from her husband and took 'his daughter and £600 in gold and plate and all his household including linen and his clothes and all the deeds and writings of their estate leaving not so much as a bed to lie upon'. It is hardly surprising that he couldn't find her anywhere, but if she returned in twenty days he would receive her kindly, willing as he was to forgive and forget. Despite this assurance, one cannot help wondering what kind of reception Bethia would really receive. And here's a sad little ending to these tales of unhappy families: in 1718, a female infant about a month old was dropped in Black Lion Court. 'If any person will give notice of the parents or true settlement of the Child so as the parish of St Michael may be discharged of the child. Her name was Frances Busby, written on a piece of paper left in the basket.'

We can leave some of this unhappiness behind us and look at something a little more hopeful. There were plenty of individuals ready to put themselves forward for work centuries ago. Take 'A person who writes a very good hand, understands vulgar and decimal arithmetic and accoumpts and has skills which might come in useful for bricklayers, carpenters, masons, joiners plaisters and glaciers [glaziers]'. This accomplished individual 'is desirous to serve any person of quality or gentleman as steward, either in town or country'. He also has references, and any interested employer is urged to go to the specified coffee-house where he is available for an interview.

Finding a job is a major concern for anyone who does not have a private income, and although there were some job adverts littered through these classified ads they are few and far between. One man's attempt to help what we might call the middle classes and would at that time be referred to as the middling ranks appeared in a curious but highly respected publication called *A Collection for Improvement of Agriculture and Trade*. This title ran from 1692 to 1703 and was written and edited by an apothecary named John Houghton. This concerned gentleman was a member of the Royal Society and was on a mission to bring together expertise from a range of correspondents in the worlds of science and agriculture. He believed they could then truly add to the body of knowledge. The publication eventually morphed into a kind of agency, and as well as sound agricultural advice it carried advertising for various products and vacancies. It became a kind of mixture between *New Scientist* and the recruitment pages of *The Guardian* or *The Times*. For instance, where else would you find notes on the administering and efficacy of Bloom's Horse-Balls in treating equine ailments directly above an equally interesting advertisement from a 'single gentleman' who has a house only 12 miles from London and wishes to share it with a couple or another single gentleman?

Then comes an advertisement for what can only be described as an early form of employment/estate agency: 'Whoever will buy or hire, sell or lease houses, lodgings, or estates and or will put out apprentices, wants servants or will go to service, will take or go to board, will put to school or want scholars, or will have anything else, enquired for, that is honourable for me to do, it may be entered in my books for half a crown each, and its probable I may help them.'

There is evidence in an edition of 1694 that the editor was as true as his word. Heading up a page, he lists professions such as physician, surgeon, lawyer, scholar, gardener and 'woodmonger' and where they could be found. Mr Page, the surgeon, can be found in Aldgate while Mr Benfield in Hoxton could satisfy any gardening needs. There was something for all ages, including an advertisement from someone looking for a 'lusty fellow to be an apprentice to an anchor-smith' with no need for money to pay for the apprenticeship. A final word on this is a delightful advert to be seen in the same paper: 'A Sober Gentleman of six years standing in the University and of good family not unskilled in the French Language and in all cases full qualified to be a tutor to a young gentleman either at home or to travel abroad desires such an employment. If any Security be needful it may be had to be thousand pound.' The last sentence is intriguing. The idea of an applicant putting up money as surety for a job is an interesting concept, although if the tutor was responsible for the well-being of the son and heir then a nervous parent might require this reassurance.

But there was another side to the employment market which was not so straightforward: many column inches were taken up by employers advertising that their staff had disappeared. Presumably these individuals were apprenticed in some way, and it is a shame there is little chance of hearing their side of the story. We may not be surprised that the army, particularly in the middle of a nation-consuming war, would not take kindly to their soldiers deserting. One wonders what happened to the rogue who ran away from Captain John Armstrong's company, or to the man who decided while in Lieutenant-Colonel Philip Tolbert's company that war was not for him.

It is not quite so easy to see why an employer would spend the 2s advertising fee to get a maidservant back, but there was a reason. Covenanted servants were people who had entered into a contract with their employer to stay for a certain number of years. One example comes in a quite threatening advertisement concerning a William Powel who was a covenanted servant to the Rector of Llangellock in Breconshire. In addition to the note that giving information on the runaway to the rector's London agent will earn a reward of 10s, there is a warning that if the man is found to have been taken into service, his new employer will be prosecuted. Such adverts usually describe the missing person, and William is described as a short, thin young man of ruddy complexion with black hair, and Londoners are advised to keep their eyes open for he was last seen at the house of Benjamin Price.

There are worse examples. One raises the troubling question of how it was possible to sign up an eight-year-old who then felt the need to escape from his master. William Tink, the lad in question, is described as thick and 'quaddy' with 'his hair cut off his head if not since grown ... he hath also a full face, thick lips and a frowning countenance'. And finally, for English missing persons we should spare a thought for the two boys who ran away from their parents. Their ages were 'about' fifteen and eight. The elder is hard of hearing and the younger is red-headed. It's a curiously cold statement. We are told that returning the boys or offering information as to their whereabouts will earn a reward.

As well as these strange examples of the ways in which servants were bound to their employers, we are constantly reminded that the riches of eighteenth-century England owed much to the slave trade. It is easy to assume that although England was enriched by the trade, actual slavery was on on the other side of the world, and it is disturbing to think that civilised Englishmen were pursuing runaway slaves in the Home Counties, indeed in London itself. So when Arnold Pigeon's 'negro', named Africa, ran away, Pigeon offered 20s reward for his return, which was exactly the same sum as the reward for a 'flea-bitten' nag which strayed from a field and was advertised in the same paper. A 'negro woman' is worth a reward of 40s. The list goes on: a lad of eighteen is again worth 20s. The language used for both the covenanted servants and the black 'employees' is very much that of owners and possessions.

So far we have covered a reasonable spread of advertising. We have seen the dubious cures and treatments available from the doctor, the dentist and the optician. We have read about servants who are absent and wives who have run away with their husband's property or some lewd fellow (in some cases both). And there are still scores of interesting items in the classified advertisements.

One thing that strikes home while looking through these columns is how extraordinarily careless our forebears seem to have been. Almost every newspaper carries an anguished cry that something has been lost. There's a rose diamond lost in a Hackney coach, which begs the question of why someone would not take more care of such valuable property. But the lost-and-found category has an eclectic mix of items. In fact, in one issue of 1708 there are pleas for a lost banknote for £50 and also a fallow-coloured greyhound. An expensive loss in a coach was a gold seal tied to a silk purse which contained some money. Very generously (or perhaps realistically), the owner is taking no notice of the cash. It is truly a mystery how Sir Richard Hoar managed to lose 'six pairs of stays, one with diamond buckles, a night gown, a red velvet cap and a calico gown'. He is phlegmatic about his chances of recovery of the clothing and is resigned to only getting the diamonds back 'no questions asked'. Good luck with that. One would hope that coach passengers would be rather more careful about weapons, and that the pistol in a blue velvet bag and a silver-hilted sword do not find their way into the wrong hands. But by far the greatest losses are among the dog-owning population, which leads one to believe that dogs were either a valuable commodity or their owners were particularly careless with open doors and gates.

The pet theme, if not exactly overwhelming, does throw up some quite odd lost 'products'. For instance, there seems to be a trend for canaries and other more exotic birds such as scarlet nightingales and blue sparrows alongside pheasants and Muscovy ducks. For those owners who retain these feathered friends, there are books to help look after them when they are sick. Perhaps the oddest advertisement for pets is that in the *London Gazette* in February 1685 for two elephants, a male and a female, for sale by the candle. This was a common form of auction at this time. An inch of candle being lighted, he who made the bid as the candle gave its expiring wink was declared the buyer; sometimes a pin is stuck in a candle, and the last bidder before the pin falls out is the winner. Curiously, there is no indication of where the elephants have come from, and it must have been quite tricky to keep them in London. It can only be hoped that the eventual owners were more careful than those discussed above.

Perhaps the most unusual theft noted in the columns was that of a Jewish Sefer Torah, the sacred manuscript used in synagogues during the services. The Jewish population in London was tiny, just a few hundred souls, and there was just one temple in Bevis

Marks. For the worshippers this was a serious loss, although the manuscript itself had very little monetary value to anyone outside the congregation. The size of the item, up to 24 inches wide and possibly 112 feet long when unfurled, made it unwieldy. With its silk cover and silver adornments, which also disappeared, the object was never going to be easy to fence. It is likely that the thieves had their eye on the silver, which could be melted down. But for the synagogue itself, the handwritten scroll was infinitely more valuable. The reward was 20 guineas.

Possibly the greatest proportion of advertisements concerned books. The phrase 'this day is published' is repeated ad infinitum, and the choice of reading material gives an insight into the literary tastes of the age. These works are a million miles from the attractively packaged books on sale today; even the titles are intimidating. As we have already noted, the novel was in its infancy and there was very little that was not educational, spiritual, political or practical. In fact for some literary critics Daniel Defoe 'invented' the novel as we know it. He started writing them after his stint in *The Review,* and *Robinson Crusoe* appeared in 1719.

To give a flavour of the reading material on offer there is a proliferation of sermons and essays on religion, books on grammar, not forgetting the transactions of the Royal Society There are also bound volumes of newspapers, yet more sermons, and lighter items such as *A Miscellany of Poems by a Lady.* For the very educated there were such publications as a poem *To a Bencher of the Inner Temple*, written entirely in Latin. Although these texts might seem daunting to the modern reader it is clear that there was an identified market for these learned volumes. No bookseller or printer would bother to produce such books to lie on the shelf. There were also books which were less straight-laced on sale but they were not advertised.

Some idea of the breadth of choice can be seen from a list of books for sale on one day in February 1701 in the *Post Boy. A True List of the Knights, Citizens and Burgesses of this Present Parliament* really is a close-written list of the members of Parliament. There was also *The Freeholders plea against stock jobbing elections of Parliament men.* This starts off with a remarkably modern comment: 'Of all the nations in the world, we may say, without detracting from the character of our native country that England has, for some ages past, been the most distracted with divisions and parties among themselves.' And it is arguable whether as the pamphleteer says, we are 'harder to be govern'd in time of Peace than War'. This little thirty-page piece is remarkably prescient. It talks of the motivation behind the election of MPs – why would people spend so much (and it quotes sums of up to eleven thousand pounds) and spend six months at a time away from their home, all for nothing? It is, the pamphleteer points out, because they are influencing the stock markets while they are in Westminster. This wise commentator also predicts the need for the Great Reform Bill of over one hundred years later by pointing out rotten boroughs and unrepresented expanding towns. He or she ends with the thought that if you use 'clandestine methods to get elected' you must have 'clandestine design' to carry on while you are there.

Then there is *The court at Kensington, a poem on the most celebrated beauties there*, a rather more frivolous piece of ephemera. This is seven pages of what can only be described as boot-licking of the most abject kind. It begins with a nod to the 'beaut'ous forms' but it is really dedicated to extolling William III describing him as 'So awful, so Majestic William stood, form'd like a man with the lustre of a god, unequall'd great, beyond example good, his every smile fresh beams of joy dispence.' A quick modern description of William gives the lie to this sycophantic verse. He was not 'an imposing or impressive figure

… diminutively short … not conventionally handsome … pale and thin'. Thankfully the piece does not include illustrations. The poem goes go on to praise various female courtiers without a key so it is difficult to identify them. Interestingly there is no price and it is anonymous. Alongside this is *Mr Atterbury's book of the rights and powers and privileges of an English convocation considered.* This is most likely to be an answer to a book by the High Church activist William Atterbury, who campaigned to bring the Anglican Church back into the political arena. Needless to say it was a book for those who took such things very seriously, which seems to have been a high percentage of the literate adult population. It is more of a worthy pamphlet than a book; by early eighteenth century standards it's probably the equivalent of the sound bite as it is a mere thirty-four closely printed pages and feeds the obsession with affairs of state. Equally polemical is *A Brief Enquiry into the Ground, Authority and Rights of Ecclesiastical Synods: upon the Principles of Scripture and Right Reason.* This might appeal because at a modest sixpence it is half the price of the book which will be published 'on Thursday'. However dull the non-specialist might find these works now, they were grist to the political mill three hundred years ago. There is also available a law text book, *The practice of the courts of the Kings Bench and common pleas.* There is not much to say about this as it is aimed at students who were no doubt presumed to need it. The *Systema Horticulture or The art of gardening in three books* is a must have for aspirational gardeners although I am not sure if the reader would actually do the hard work rather than use the services of a labourer. It is very comprehensive and 'treateth of' soil, walks, arbours, springs, fountains, grottos, statues, raising, planting and improving florists (meaning experts in flowers), the kitchen garden, and it is useful for 'every sort of land, as well for use and profit, as for ornament and delight'. This is apparently the fourth edition so it must have been as popular as it is detailed. And to finish it off there is an advert for 'a library or parcel of books in any language whatsoever to dispose of may have the full value of them if they bring or send a catalogue ... he will give a gratuity to anyone who helps him to a library'. This might be someone who has great deal of shelving to fill and possibly has no intention of reading any of the volumes.

It is common sense that someone who purchases books would have to have somewhere to put them. So we will have a look at the property section, although no such division existed in the columns. There were some bizarre offerings. While one might expect an opportunity to negotiate fixtures and fittings when purchasing a property it is rare to find one complete with the pans and coppers and everything else you need for soap boiling. In 1705 on Snow Hill in the city of London this was available. For the prospective brewer there was a property in the Strand which might suit the purchaser. Regretfully this brewhouse was available as a result of the unfortunate Mr Bones, victualler, going bankrupt.

It would probably be better for your health to escape London's grime and go to fresh and leafy Hillingdon for a very good brick house. Since London was of course very much smaller in the eighteenth century the prospective home owner could choose to live in Upper Street in Islington in a house where the back door opened onto fields. This house came complete with 'two dove cots, a large aviary' and a fountain. It sounds delightful, particularly as it includes the furniture. If Islington sounds attractive but the owner wanted to build something to their own taste, there was nine acres of land.

So, once again the reader has somewhere to live and even make soap or brew beer. The problems of the secret disease, eye problems, teeth and have been addressed. The garden is immaculate and there is a lovely new gown to wear. Nothing has been lost recently. The reader's wife does not appear to have eloped with anyone. What is left in the world of early modern advertising?

There is of course the theatre. This was a huge part of the life of the Londoner. The bare facts are that with the King came the kind of entertainment that the people had missed over the years of the Interregnum. The changes to the theatre when it returned were radical and one might wonder whether Shakespeare himself would have recognised it. They had roofs, stages and proscenium arches. The stage manager could change scenery. It was all very exciting. But what was probably the most exciting thing (at least for the rakes who hung around the stage) was that women were now allowed to appear in public as actresses. If we remember back to Charles I's wife, she appeared in masques as Court. But now the commercial theatres embraced the concept of women playing women. We probably all know about Nell Gwynne, Charles II's orange-selling mistress who told people she was the 'Protestant Whore' to distinguish herself from Charles' French mistress, but there were plenty of other nubile young actresses appearing on the newly relaunched theatres. And of course newspapers were ready and willing from the outset to accept advertising for the varied offerings.

The earliest one I could find was from 1663, which is more of a review and play-script advertisement combined. It extols the *Slighted Maid* which 'was acted with great applause at the Theatre in Little Lincolns-Inn-Fields' and the play script could be bought from Tho. Dring. This appeared in *Mercurius Publicus* in April 1663. A little further on in 1691, they are still hybrid advertisements for the printed play, such as Dryden's Dramatic Opera, *King Arthur*, printed for Jacob Tonson. Performed at Queens Theatre, alas we do not know whether it was applauded or not. At last in 1701 we have some idea of an 'excellent comedy, called the *Jew of Venice*, which appears to have been admirably acted.

But these snippets were hardly advertisements. However, by 1702 the canny theatrical entrepreneurs eventually realised that to entice an audience to a play it was a good idea to tell them about the play *before* it opened. And so when there was a benefit performance of the comedy, *Love Makes a Man,* the advert reveals the main casting, and also news of 'pretty entertainments' which would be announced on the day of the performance. It also appears that the date of the play has been changed at the request of several 'persons of Quality'. And intriguingly, if the audience went behind the scenes, they were to give their money directly to Mr Pinkeman.

By 1704 we have two advertisements for plays, one beneath the other. Theatre managers have become more adept at promotion. From the wording of the advertisement the whole entertainment was a bit of a jumble. The benefit for Mrs Oldfield is announced as being 'At the Desire of several Persons of Quality'. As she was the mistress of the Duchess of Marlborough's secretary, we can speculate who these very important people were. The performance is at the Theatre Royal, Drury Lane, and there are a couple of short plays plus some music by the late Henry Purcell, plus dancing. While this does sound like a delightful evening out, if it didn't take the public's fancy there was a slightly less elaborate show on at the New Theatre, which not only included the play but also gave you the opportunity to watch the Scotch Dancers.

But the play was obviously the thing. It was a hugely popular entertainment. And given that there was still a small number of theatres in London it is amazing how many advertisements there were. There is a point to be made here though. While the *Mousetrap* and Andrew Lloyd Webber musicals run for years today, the plays in the early eighteenth century generally had at the most runs of just a few days. So the turn-round was very quick. A meticulous scholar in the thirties undertook the onerous task of looking through all the play notices in the available newspapers from 1700–1703. He found 155 and some of them are strikingly different from anything seen on the stage today. Here is a flavour of what was available (and what happened).

For instance, in the *London Post* of 12 December 1700 they report that when the 'new Play called, *Love Makes a Man; or, The Fop's Good Luck,* was acted at the Theatre Royal in Drury Lane' there was uproar when the 'French Scaramouch Dance betwixt the second and third Acts [sent] a certain Person' into a bit of a frenzy and he 'went in a Frolick, Incognito, up into the upper Gallery, and so pelted the Dancers with Oranges, that they were forced to quit the Stage, and the Playhouse was all in an Uproar.' The audience in the stalls apparently took over at that point and seeing who was acting in such an alarming way, seemed to have yelled to the people in the gallery to send him over the balcony down into the pit. Rather than be flung headlong into a very angry mob he ran down the stairs. But somebody with a bit of foresight sent for the Constable who 'secured' and sent him to the Gatehouse.

In another but much more sober report in the *London Post* of June 1701, we learn that 'the Play called the *Tempest* [it doesn't say whether it was Shakespeare's play] was acted at the *Old Playhouse*; and that called *Love for Love* at the New'. So there were two plays being produced simultaneously, 'both for the benefit of the poor English Slaves'. The performances raised the grand sum of £250. The *Post* of the same day also announced, 'It being put on the Playhouse Bills on Friday last, That each Company were to Act that day, and the whole Profits to go to'ards the Redemption of the English now in Slavery at Machanisso in Barbary. We are credibly informed, That pursuant thereunto the Treasurers of the Theatre Royal in Drury Lane, did on Saturday last pay into the hands of the Church Wardens of St Martin's the sum of £20 out of the Receipts of the Play acted by that Company, towards the Relief of those our Natives from Slavery, which good example 'tis hoped may move others to be speedy and generous in their Charity for the same purpose. What the other Company gave I do not yet hear.' It appears from this that theatre-land turned out in force to support these slaves.

Samuel Pepys records in his diary that he spent an evening talking to Englishmen who had been enslaved in North Africa. The slave traders made raids on the Cornish and Devon coastal villages and kidnapped men, women and children. Fishermen were also vulnerable. A charity was set up in 1646 to buy the slaves back. But it took until 1816 to finally destroy the trade.

This was all very worthy but for some people it just wasn't exciting enough. So alongside the play and a musical evening in July 1701 at Mrs Campion's benefit they brought in 'Vaulting on the Horse' by the famous Mr Evans, lately come into England. His trick was to lie on the horse with 'his body extended on one hand in which Posture he drinks several glasses of Wine with the other, and from that throws himself a Summerset over the horse's head to the Admiration of all that see him'. And if this is really not enough to get a Londoner out of the house there is one last treat that could be had at the theatre: 'the Famous Mr Clynch being now in Town will for this once at the desire of several Persons of Quality, perform his Imitation of an Organ with 3 Voices, the double Curtell, and the Bells, the Hunts-man with his Horn and Pack of Dogs. All which he performs with his mouth on the open stage, being what no man beside himself could ever yet attain to.'

So there we have it. Anything you might want to buy is in the classified section. There was a dark side, with details for cock fights, which took place before the races in Norwich and the ones that were held in London were for large amounts of prize money. As has been said of newspapers today, all human life and its desires and needs are there in the classifieds.

7

WAYWARD TEXTS AND
WAYWARD PRINTERS

In this chapter we consider the mechanics of the book trade and some of the more curious ephemera. We start with anonymous poems and pamphlets, which, despite their lowly status, were an important element in the world of print. Printing is obviously the most fundamental of the processes. Without printers there is no industry and even the most talented writers needed their publishers and booksellers. And with the vagaries and ever-changing legal challenges of the seventeenth and eighteenth centuries these producers were even more important. Without the internet, self-publishing or social media, the channels of communication were limited and the creative spark needed the practical skills of the printers and booksellers to put the words in front of the reader. Sometimes publishers and booksellers did not simply act as a channel of communication. In some cases these backroom boys and girls offered shelter to writers who had been targeted by the politicians. Some of them were larger than life characters in their own right. We have two really interesting examples to give a flavour of printers' activities, both of whom in their different ways ran very close to the legal wind. To be more explicit, in both cases and in their own ways they ignored or flouted the legal system either for personal gain or for ideological reasons. One was continually at odds with the authorities through dubious practices and the other rose to become a significant political activist in his own right.

But firstly we have to return to the importance of the publisher, printer and bookseller. What did they do as what might be called 'midwives' to the immature but extremely active press? If we start at the bottom and work our way up we can see the spread and influence of these very important people. If we recall some of the detail from our earlier chapters, the responsibility and therefore the liability reached a long way down when it came to prosecutions for anything the government wanted to suppress. Booksellers, publishers and printers were an intrinsic part of the history of the press, particularly in the early years when the roles were fluid. Even more importantly, when the law breathed down the necks of the producers of scandalous publications it often looked upon each individual as equally culpable. In the UK news media traditionally support one of the two major parties, or they claim no bias. In the early eighteenth century, it was the sole purpose of some newspapers to fight the political war of words. Publications separated along party political lines far more rigidly than today. Because of these intense party affiliations and the cat and mouse game played with the asuthorities, printing became an exciting if sometimes precarious occupation. For very different reasons the printer and publisher featured in this chapter illustrate just how close to the wind they sailed and how they survived.

The less flamboyant character, John Barber the Tory printer's full story will be featured later in the chapter as he was a central figure in Harley's propaganda machine, but before that we will look at the bookseller and publisher who often handled his output. Much of Swift's work was published by John Morphew, an important but sometimes shadowy figure in the trade. He also handled the sales of the output of many Tory writers, but as a canny businessman he tried to stay out of trouble and worked for both Whigs and the Tories. He doesn't always get the credit for this, but he was an unsung hero in at least one important aspect of the early newspaper industry. Financially shrewd, he was one of the first to realise the value of advertising revenue. Very early in his career he came to the conclusion that advertising was a service that could prove lucrative. He was prompted to this breakthrough, apparently, after William III lost his dog in 1699 and ordered a classified advertisement seeking information on his 'smooth, black dog, less than a greyhound', and requesting that intelligence concerning the animal might be returned to 'his Majesty's back stairs'. If the King needed a classified advertisement to find his pet surely the rest of the world would too, and they would pay for it. According to one researcher the price of these first advertisements was set at about one shilling for eight lines, but Morphew, seeing a need which could be fulfilled with ease and at a profit, increased the amount. He reasoned that it was for the public good that trade should be encouraged and therefore it was only right that everyone should benefit, particularly the communication channel and the publisher. As a result he put the price up to tuppence per line and invented the rate card.

Despite Morphew's desire to stay below the parapet his experience as a bookseller in the fervid political atmosphere demonstrated that the quietest and most business-like men of the trade could easily end up in court. His strenuous efforts not to get involved in the cut and thrust of politics and his claims always to have merely sold the offending items rather than support them were not convincing for politicians looking for people to punish. He found himself implicated in at least two of the notable cases of the period. One of his worst years was 1709 when he found himself in trouble twice. The Whig ministry had already taken him up for publishing two Tory newspapers, *The General Postscript* and the *Rehearsal Revived,* when he found himself in further difficulties. It was also the year when Delarivier Manley's outrageously popular scandal fiction *New Atalantis* came out and its attacks on the Marlboroughs and the other major Whigs really upset them. Morphew was the bookseller and this of course meant he was included in the brouhaha and general round-up of offenders. Later on he found himself in the thick of it again as the publisher of the *Public Spirit of the Whigs.* Thankfully for Morphew the two newspapers ceased publication immediately and his involvement in the *New Atalantis* prosecution came to nothing. *The Public Spirit of the Whigs* involves another one of our featured characters and we will come to it later in the chapter but it is enough to say now that it was set up by the ministry. Any attempts by Morphew to stay out of the limelight were thwarted by his association with the senior Tories and at the end of Queen Anne's reign he became ensnared in another case. The Whig ministry which took over just before the arrival of the Hanoverians and George I pursued the long-running Tory *Post Boy.* Following a random process to find someone to prosecute they selected a piece written by Daniel Defoe. They also targeted the widowed printer Lucy Beardwell and of course Defoe 'for bringing a scandalous and seditious Paragraph to be inserted in ye Postboy of 19th August 1714'. Reading the account of this case it becomes obvious that actually pinning down the culprits was tricky. The people involved all denied knowing anything about the origins of the offending paper. Mrs Beardwell couldn't say for sure that she had printed it, and anyway, if she had, she couldn't remember who had given it to her and, also, she had lost the manuscript. Another associate said that all he ever did for the *Post Boy* was translate foreign news bulletins. Four more people who had received copies couldn't identify the issue used as evidence. The case against Defoe as the author was impossible to prove. Though Morphew admitted to being the publisher of the paper, he protested that he did not know the author or the proprietor. Even Abel Boyer, who was the publisher, claimed to know nothing. So the attempted prosecution fell apart, principally because acting as a team the responsible parties ran rings round the authorities. Thereafter, with the Tories in opposition and the new Whig ministry acting as regents for the absent George I, Morphew tried to resurrect the Tory *Examiner* and other Tory papers. But the moment had passed and Morphew slid into the background, only re-appearing to be arrested for his publication of another *Post Boy* which upset the Whigs by discussing Anglo-Swedish relations, or rather Anglo-Swedish Jacobite activities. Morphew presents us with an example of how even the most careful of high-profile publishers who worked for both sides of the political divide could not avoid arrest by the ever vigilant Government Messengers. The nervous paranoia of the new political parties prompted the hounding of any potential troublemakers in order to root them out and destroy them, although it has to be said they weren't always successful.

But before we look at our next characters there is an important section of the market to look at. At the bottom of the print pile was the most populist of publications, the ballad. It was often printed without the inconvenience of licensing by the rough end of the printing trade. The ballads were read and sung anywhere that was available to the hawker and if there was a convenient place they were pinned up for all to see. They were produced by the lower orders of printers who did not have the luxury of well-known authors whose name on a frontispiece would be enough to guarantee sales. Nor did they enjoy the patronage of politicians to provide them with regular income from subsidised political newspapers. Given that they had to look for profit where they could find it, inevitably they were not too fussy about any political divisions or persuasions. They simply followed the money and printed anything that would sell. These ballads, of variable quality, were very popular as well as being populist. Pepys, who had a collection, records reading a ridiculous example on his way home on a very cold evening. He notes that it is 'made in praise of the Duke of Albemarle, to the tune of St. George, the tune being printed, too; and I observe that people have great encouragement to make ballads of him of this kind'. The Duke of Albemarle Pepys refers to was George Monck, said by some to have engineered the Restoration. Pepys also comments on the low standard of music of the balladeers. The truth appears to be that they were equally indifferent to the politics and the tune, so the accompaniment was chosen by how it matched the words rather than any significance the melody might carry.

As always in this period it does not do to lay down hard and fast rules about anything to do with the world of print. So ignoring the musical shortcomings of these ballads or single sheet pamphlets it is clear from some examples just how partisan they could be. Once again the great English public were prepared to spend their hard-earned money on the blatant propaganda that suited their politics. One suggestion is that the partisan stance taken by some of the pamphlets should be read as ironic and that the coffee house rang with laughter at the over-blown sentiments. Since we are not able to go back in time to listen to the reaction, we can only judge them by the reaction of the authorities. The Whig ministry of 1716 didn't seem to appreciate irony and took the proliferation of cheap pamphlets and ballads very seriously. While we are used to the Defoes, Swifts and Steeles of the world being pursued and sometimes caught by the authorities, they now also went after people such as perfumers, peruke makers and publicans because they acted as distribution points. What did they object to? Perhaps it would be useful here to give some examples of the breadth of the opinions expressed in these cheap and sometimes cheerful little pieces of ephemera sold on street corners. One contemporary argued that 'The medling with Hawkers and Ballad-Singers may be thought a Trifle; but it ceases to be so, when we consider that the Crying and Singing such Stuff, as vile as it is, makes the Government familiar, and consequently contemptible to the People, warms the Minds of the Rabble, who are more capable of Action than Speculation, and are animated by Noise and nonsense'. The writer (possibly Defoe) goes on to remind the authorities that when the Sacheverell case was at its height, 'There was just such a Cry of Sedition when the Doctor [Sacheverell] was condemned. The Ministers despis'd it so long, that they were themselves despised by it. Some of them saw their Error at last, but 'twas too late. The Mob were prepar'd for Violence, and they were hooted and bawled out of their Ministry. The greatest Mischief arises from the small Papers, and their being noised about the Streets: 'tis the quickest and surest Way Sedition has to take. Pamphlets work slowly, and the Operation of one Pamphlet is often spoil'd by that of another. Besides, the Publishers of 'em are to be come at, and the Printer and Publisher being as much accountable for the Offence they give as the Author, the State will know how to find out and chastise the Offender. Their Liberty therefore ought not to be abridged, but those that abuse it to be punish'd. If there is not due and speedy Care taken in these Matters, the Faction will most certainly grow upon the Government.' So there we have condemnation of the cheap output of the balladeers.

The general public did not help the ministry when the authorities finally arrested and punished the printers and others whom they held responsible. In another incident the 'rabble' certainly showed that they liked to take control and often caused mayhem doing it. The mob may have been motivated by politics or they may have simply liked a good open-air fight, but when the Tory printer William Hurt produced a single sheet poem called *The British Embassadress's Speech to the French King* in July 1713, which suggests that the Queen has gone too far in the ongoing treaties with France, Harley's moderate Tory ministry decided that this wasn't helping the peace process and promptly brought the unfortunate printer in front of the Queen's Bench, where he was sentenced to two separate hours in the pillory. Interestingly there are two conflicting reports of William's times in the stocks. One correspondent wrote 'Mr. Hurt the Printer ... stood in the Pillory last Saturday at Westminster ... was very handsomely dressed, drank her majesty's health and the house of Hanover's in a glass of sack and has not so much as an egg or bit of dirt thrown at him.' The other report, in *The Political State of Great Britain* makes the two sessions sound a lot more unpleasant with the printer's friends fighting off an attempt to stone him to death and a brawl which ended up with 'eleven or twelve persons ... laid sprawling on the ground sorely wounded with cudgels'. The whole episode ended safely for the unfortunate but brave Mr Hurt who was carried into a nearby tavern. It is significant in the context of the press simply because it shows that everyone involved in these publications was liable. The treatment of William Hurt shows even more plainly how close to physical harm a printer could find himself.

As we are looking at the production side of the print industry we should now consider its size in terms of circulation. It is nearly impossible to calculate accurately the print runs and readership of these publications. Readership is also difficult to calculate because we simply have no way of calculating the number of people who saw the newspapers and pamphlets. The Stamp Act of 1712 should provide a handy method of calculating approximately how many copies of each paper might have been printed. But the word approximately is appropriate because even using the official figures for stamped paper still leaves a margin of error. The Stamp

Tax has been mentioned before but now is a good time to explain it a little further. In an attempt to curb the press and bring it to order the Tories put a tax on the paper used to print newspapers. It was illegal to print papers on unstamped paper so the principle was that anything that appeared that hadn't been recorded was therefore ripe for destruction and anyone associated with it was liable for prosecution. It is complicated and unnecessary to be too detailed about paper sizes and the different ways a printer might use the sheets, but generally there was a tax of one half-penny per newspaper. From the number of sheets purchased by each printer a calculation of how much paper was used can be made. However there is a caveat. We do not always know if the printer stockpiled paper or printed more than one newspaper. As with any of the facts and figures concerning these publications, the likely lack of control, human error and overall vagueness means that the numbers are only guidelines. Circulation figures were small compared to nowadays but the population was tiny and the newspapers may have been read by many different people, particularly if they were in coffee houses being passed around where customer numbers would give a more useful estimate of the impact. Defoe's *Review* for instance seems to have sold a mere 125 to 500 per issue. This hardly mattered as it was heavily subsidised by Harley and it was taken seriously despite its meagre circulation. It is unfortunate that the figures for some of the other well-known titles such as Swift's *Examiner* are not recorded since they were published prior to the Stamp Tax, but in 1712, after the great satirist had given up his editor's chair, it was apparently selling well over a thousand copies. If circulation figures are to be trusted Whig papers did marginally better, at least it seems Steele's *Spectator* did, at two thousand to two thousand two hundred daily, which sounds very healthy. The Tory *Post Boy* reached the heights of three thousand and its Tory stablemate the *Evening Post* managed an impressive four thousand. Overall the weekly total of all newspapers including the regional ones was somewhere between 26,000 and 63,000, an admittedly huge margin for error. The highest figure that I can find is not surprisingly the official government newspaper, the *London Gazette,* which regularly topped 8,000 with a print run of up to 11,000 copies. Calculating the profits of these newspapers is even trickier but they were not huge, particularly if we remember that a good number of the brave printers and publishers faced fines from the ministry if they offended in any way. What I can say is that there is an estimate for the *Gazette* of a profit of £1,786 over 135 issues.

We also need to remember that the cover prices which were not high were supplemented by the advertising, which could run to a tidy sum. As we saw in the last chapter the government also looked to make some money out of the commercial side of newsprint by slapping a one shilling tax on advertisements. So the newspaper business was probably not lucrative but we shouldn't forget to factor in the rest of the printing and publishing business that was undertaken. The printers did not simply produce the newspapers; they took on plenty of work besides.

Before we come to our high-profile printers it would be useful to look at a printer whose career was run of the mill but who was caught up and it appears ruined in the web of press spies. Those spies were working for Harley when he was Secretary of State. Harley encouraged writers to further his Tory ambitions but also understood the necessity of repressing the ministry's critics. Here is also the story of a printer turned informer, which perfectly demonstrates how nasty the whole business of printing could become. The name of the poacher turned gamekeeper was Robert Clare, whose fellow printers turned against him when they realised he was sneakily reporting their misdemeanours to the authorities. It seems he kept his hand in as a printer by working on the *London*

Gazette but his real job was to spy on his fellow printers. And he was very good at it, reporting on sixty-three publications. His messages to Harley in his reports are quite chilling and are a clear illustration of the effort the ministry were putting into suppressing the more rebellious members of the trade. But some care needs to be taken because these were politicians who were the puppet masters of the press spies and sometimes they wanted to be seen to be doing the job rather than doing anything that might harm their own prospects. For instance, in the case of a particularly contentious Tory pamphlet called *The Memorial of the Church of England* there was some doubt as to how much Harley actually wanted a successful prosecution. The Whig Lord Chancellor, William Lord Cowper, doubted how serious he was. He wrote in his diary 'Went over those Sec[retary] Harley had already examined. He extream bad at it; if not designedly, to hinder the Discovery: manag'd neither with Cunning nor Gravity, to imprint any Awe on those examined; by which, I believe, he spoil'd the thing on his former Examinations'.

As Harley's Rottweiler snoop, Clare was under pressure to deliver the goods. He was told that he 'was not Sharp enough in [his] Quest' but protested that he had done his best: 'Tho' I have diligently enquir'd into the Authors and Printers of them, yet I could get no Information … I hope next Week to be more certain and full. I could heartily wish I had a Power to visit every Printing-house in Town, which I endeavour to do every Day … I shall stick at no Trouble, so I can but give Your Honour Satisfaction.' Eventually pursuing his target with relentless enthusiasm, he tracked the printer down to Wales. 'Upon farther Enquiry after Mr. Edwards, I am inform'd he is with his Mother (or some other Relation) in Flintshire in Wales. The Person that gave me this Information told me, he could not get out of ye Person that told him, the particular Name of ye Place or Town in ye said shire. However, I know 'em both; and if Your Honour thinks convenient to have 'em before Your Honour to be farther Examin'd, I will endeavour to secure them as you shall be pleas'd to direct.'

The correspondence between Clare and Harley reveals a level of activity which to modern eyes is wholly out of keeping with the severity of the crime. The actual pamphlet which caused all the trouble is not identified but the spy clearly thought it worth flagging up as dangerous and the authorities seemed to agree. Whatever the content, the papers were 'cry'd about the streets' by the printer, a Mr Bradford. Having procured a Warrant, Clare and the Messenger, who was responsible for apprehending printers, went to Bradford's house where they were denied entry and threatened with a pistol. The report goes on that not being able to get in the two went to find a constable to help. The three of them were then joined by a further two watchmen who guarded the house while Clare went off to get instructions. They were told to go back the next day, which they did and since they couldn't arrest Bradford they did the next best thing, which was to attempt to arrest his wife. The description of her is not flattering. She was apparently 'known to be an ill Woman, and is the chief Orderer and Director in everything she undertakes; keeping her Husband, as a Prisoner, to protect her in her ill Practices, which are known to be many and very prejudicial'. They obtained another warrant and went to serve it. Again they were barred entry so they climbed in through the shop window and in Clare's own words 'after a small Scuffle, seiz'd Mrs. Bradford, and search'd the House throughout for the Papers, but could find none of them'. She had been tipped off which had 'no doubt, made her secure all things worthy our Notice out of the way'. If we can say one thing about Mr Clare it is that he was certainly tenacious.

The attentions of Clare and Harley's network of spies were directed towards the printing of political pamphlets considered seditious. There were other ways of upsetting the authorities and our next character managed to offend across the board. We are now looking at a publisher who among other things catered for readers who wanted a change from politics, although he printed political material. He made his reputation partly by pandering to a demand for the more sensational publications of dubious moral content. He was well known and quite blatant in his nefarious ways, although he might have been wiser to have hidden his name better. He was perhaps the most notorious of the printers of this period. He was Edmund Curll, called variously 'unspeakable' or 'abominable' by his contemporaries. Jonathan Swift described him as 'one thorough book-selling Rogue. [No-one] is better qualified to vex an author, than all his contemporary scriblers in Critick or Satire, not only by stolen Copies of what was incorrect or unfit for the publick ... I had a long design on the ears of that Curl[l] ... but the rogue would never allow me a fair stroke at them, though my penknife was ready and sharp.' Swift, who was not certainly not shy of pointing out his contemporaries' errors, was only one of the many people who would gladly see the insufferable bookseller and general nuisance punished. Whether you took the high ground against either moral turpitude or business malpractice, you would still find Curll at the bottom of your hill. He was basically an opportunist willing to publish anything that would sell. It made very little difference to this 'rogue' whether or not it was respectable or even his to print. With something that amounted to a talent for being disliked he managed to upset many of the writers of the period including, alongside Swift, the brilliant Alexander Pope, creator of some of the most wounding poetry of the age. Pope was clearly someone who did not suffer any slights to his dignity or his reputation. The poet and the publisher were like oil and water and seemed to be made to be at odds. Curll probably did not have any real qualms about his treatment of the super-sensitive

Pope but the poet was supremely jealous of his literary legacy and he had become an inveterate enemy of Curll.

The practice that caused the most problems between Curll and the writers was his incurable habit of printing things that didn't belong to him. Queen Anne's Act, giving new rights of ownership to authors, was irrelevant to him. One of his ways of getting around these minor legal niceties was by sometimes printing things under a writer's name that they hadn't written and didn't know anything about.

He should have known better than to use Pope's name in his nefarious practices. Of all the authors around in this age of great writers, Pope was arguably the most concerned about his name and how he would be remembered by posterity. He was so precious about what went out that he recalled his correspondence and edited the letters to improve them and make sure there was nothing that would detract from his legacy to English literature. So the publisher and the author found themselves in a war of words, and worse. Curll as the embodiment of the proverbial bad penny kept turning up to get himself into trouble. But he also didn't seem to care much about the consequences of his villainous actions. His bad behaviour and the subsequent punishments pursued him from the schoolyard to the Kings Bench. And it has to be said it was not always his own fault. There was at least one occasion where the drubbing he received could be regarded by some as more than a little excessive. Although well documented, it is difficult to believe. It was a brilliantly orchestrated attack and while one should never condone violence, he could have seen it coming. It was as farcical as anything Gilbert and Sullivan's Lord High Executioner could have dreamed up and perhaps in Curll's case the punishment fitted the crime.

The story starts when a worthy and well-regarded gentleman died. To honour his passing the boys of Westminster School decided to mark the occasion with a small ceremony. They gave him a good and appropriate memorial, with the Captain of the school making a farewell oration. To mark the solemnity of the occasion and to celebrate the deceased's scholarship, the piece was composed entirely in Latin. A modern view of the marketing potential of a Latin eulogy to a dead schoolmaster would not be marked by enthusiasm and a fat marketing budget. Even in the early eighteenth century it is difficult to believe that it had the hallmarks of an overnight best-seller. However, Curll must have thought differently and having somehow got possession of the text and probably without asking for permission and certainly without being given it, he published the piece. Shortly after, the boys apparently invited him to visit the school. No doubt expecting to receive something, if only an acknowledgement of his publicising it, he accepted the invitation. Alas, their gratitude was expressed in rather rough terms. They had a blanket ready for him, and when he arrived the boys bundled him into it and carried him into the school yard and he was given a thorough beating and forced to ask forgiveness for his trespass. His habit of printing works without the authors' permission was already well known and well established, so a note of satisfaction was more than evident when a pamphlet appeared with a long poem attacking his piracy. The boys may have been set onto this merry jape by some other, older, antagonists and the episode clearly amused Alexander Pope, who wrote with glee to a friend that the publisher had been whipped. Pope on one occasion decided that, like the schoolboys, he would attack Curll physically. He was a little more subtle than the lads at Westminster but I think just as cruel. He invited Curll for a drink and slipped an emetic into his glass which gave the poor man a bad dose of vomiting. So while many of his contemporaries looked upon Curll as a creature who had crawled out from under a stone and who should be returned there as soon as possible, even given the raw edge to the early 1700s, perhaps this animosity may have been taken too far.

Having said that, Curll could at least claim both the attention and a fair amount of negativity from three of the greatest writers of his time. We have seen what the mighty Swift and Pope thought of him and the third writer was another titan of the page. Defoe also took various swipes at him under the guise of his editorship of *Mist's Weekly Journal*. Curll's habit of publishing slightly pornographic books which had the veneer of medical treatises was considered so disgusting by Defoe that he referred to Curll in the following terms 'his tongue is an echo of all the beastly language his shop is filled with and filthiness drivels in the very tone of his voice.' Not one to take anything lying down Curll published his answers to Defoe's diatribes. The first one defended his books on impotency, onanism, virginity and whether eunuchs should marry. First he went through his arguments (it has to be said with extraordinary dullness) as to why they are not 'bawdy' and in fact 'treat only of matters of the greatest importance to Society ... and are directly calculated for antidotes against debauchery and unnatural lewdness'. After this justification the piece goes on to declare that as he is not going to stop printing his books there is little point in attacking him. Defoe took no notice and continued to disapprove of Curll for many years but to no avail. Without doubt he was one of the most unpopular booksellers of all time.

In addition to his habit of stealing other people's work he was in fact active in the pornographic area of the publishing industry and he was also, like his contemporaries, printing material with a political edge. For Curll this was not ideology. If there was anything likely to find a ready market, Curll would inevitably be in there. With his usual disregard for the conventions or even the law he found himself in trouble in this as well. Upsetting authors is not a good idea but upsetting the authorities is even less to be recommended. Curll, with his self-destruct instincts, also fell foul of the most powerful of antagonists he could have chosen, Parliament itself. He had a bookshop in the city, like all the good men of his trade but he found himself in Westminster in front of the authorities rather too often. As so many printers did before and after him he succumbed to the temptation of printing Parliamentary proceedings without permission and in 1716 the Lords ordered 'Sarah Popping, and John Pemberton and Edmund Curll, Booksellers, to be brought to the Bar of this House, in order to be examined touching the printed Paper, intituled, "An Account of the Trial of the Earl of Winton," on account whereof the said Persons are now in Custody'. The first two were discharged without fees on account of their claim of not really being aware of what Curll was asking them to do. The Lords later called Curll's printer to come before them. They ordered 'That the Gentleman Usher of the Black Rod, his Deputy or Deputies, do forthwith attach the Body of the said Daniel Bridge, for his Contempt and Breach of the Orders and Privileges of this House, in printing the said Paper, and keep him in safe Custody until further Order; and this shall be a sufficient Warrant in that Behalf'. But Bridge and Curll were well aware of what they had done and when they were presented to the House they fell to their knees and expressed 'their Ignorance of the said Order, and their hearty Sorrow for their Offence', and praying, 'in regard they have Families, which must inevitably be ruined unless this House have Compassion on them, that they may be discharged from their Confinement'. They clearly made a good case for themselves, 'The House being moved, that Edmund Curll and Daniel Bridge, in Custody of the Black Rod … may be brought to the Bar, in order to their Discharge', and they were released from custody and received a reprimand from the Lord Chancellor. Unlike their 'innocent' colleagues, however, they had to pay their fees.

Curll's talent for upsetting the legal authorities also showed originality and versatility. He holds the dubious honour of becoming the first person in English law to be found guilty of publishing pornography. The actual terminology used for the material was that it was obscene and was likely to corrupt people. The novelty of the offense caused a minor debate with one judge starting the trial off with a puzzled expression pointing out that 'I own this is a great offence; but I know of no law by which we can punish it. Common law is common usage, and where there is no law there can be no transgression. At common law, drunkenness, or cursing and swearing, were not punishable ... This is but a general solicitation of chastity, and not indictable to be punishable at common law, as an offence against the peace, intending to weaken the bonds of civil society, virtue, and morality.'

The only idea they could come up with carried an interesting punishment. In 1728 Curll found himself in the pillory. He had published a naughty little book called *The Nun in Her Smock*, the contents of which can be imagined. In fact one of the judges in a curious volte-face said later that it had some merit in that it showed the corrupt ways of the Popish religion; the book was clearly to his taste. However, Curll was only partly convicted and punished because of this publication. He had also published memoirs of a spy who had been granted a warrant by Good Queen Anne. This, I suspect, was the more serious offence. These memoirs were of a highly sensitive nature and were deemed scandalous and seditious by the judges on the King's Bench. This particular brush with the law ended in a two-fold punishment. He was fined for the publication of the nun déshabillée but put in the stocks for the political works.

There is no doubt the judges wished Curll to spend an hour being humiliated in the pillory. And he could have done without the fine of £40. But ever the entrepreneur he spent the hour usefully telling the gathered crowd (through printed sheets) that he was up there for defending the memory of Queen Anne. As a public relations exercise it sounds as though he had flooded the area of Charing Cross where the pillory stood with pamphlets declaring his innocence and the crowd loved him. Not only was he not pelted in time-honoured fashion, but when he was released they carried him off in triumph to a local hostelry to celebrate. The record of trials at the Kings Bench reports it somewhat tartly: 'And the defendant was afterwards set in the pillory, as he well deserved. This Edmund Curll stood in the pillory at Charing-Cross, but was not pelted, or used ill; for being an artful, cunning (though wicked) fellow, he had contrived to have printed papers dispersed all about Charing-Cross, telling the people, he stood there for vindicating the memory of queen Anne; which had such an effect on the mob, that it would have been dangerous even to have spoken against him: and when he was taken down out of the pillory, the mob carried him off, as it were in triumph, to a neighbouring tavern'.

This had not been his first only venture into the murky world of off-colour literature. He published a translation of what purported to be a serious discussion of problems of the marital bed. It was titled *A Treatise on the use of Flogging*. A description of the frontispiece says it all: It showed 'A woman beating a man with his breeches down in front of a mirror, while he gazed over his shoulder at a girl clad in a smock with her hand at her breasts'. The text does not live up to the erotic promise of the illustration. But it may have been a clever marketing ploy: once the customers had discovered that the text did not live up to the title they would be too embarrassed to complain. Attempting to clamber up onto the moral high ground, the preface points out that 'The Fault is not in the Subject Matter but in the Inclination of the reader.' So it's what is in the reader's mind that makes the book naughty. Curll's intention was a purely medical one.

Curll was nothing if not cheeky. He clearly knew a lot about the legal pitfalls of the print trade – although he didn't seem that good at escaping prosecution. With an extraordinary show of brass neck he went to the Treasury suggesting ways in which they could enforce the Stamp Act. As poacher turned gamekeeper he pointed out to them that there was no efficient way of applying the Act and that he would put himself up as an ideal candidate for the job of chief sneak. He also reminded them that there was no law which dealt with the actual size of the newspaper or the number of lines in specific advertisements. And in an appeal to their more practical side he suggested that if there were an Act of Parliament which addressed these issues 'it would tend to the advancement of Her Majesty's revenue'. They also liked the idea of setting Curll onto the balladeers who were liable to payment of the appropriate duties, but too often 'we receive information of their being printed and published contrary to law.' Clearly the treasury wanted to get the offenders prosecuted so they ordered Curll to act as a consultant and sent the appropriate staff to 'take his direction how to discover the offenders for the future'. They considered him 'well qualified for the services aforesaid, and do not think it necessary to put the Government to the expense of an inspector of newspapers and advertisements'. Though it appears that Curll made a representation to Robert Walpole proposing the appointment of an inspector to be the ears and eyes of the Treasury, which he claimed would increase the tax revenue by £10,000 a year.

We have one thing to thank Curll for. One of his major achievements according to one biographer was to produce a large number of books which were more affordable and in doing so help create a new, cheaper end of the book trade. Curll was certainly a major figure in the print industry for almost all of the first half of the eighteenth century. It is true to say that his version of freedom of the press was not so much political as personal. It almost doesn't matter whether he thought in terms of anything other than the financial gains to be had from publishing racy books. His actions make him a pioneer in defying the law to give the readers what they wanted.

We must leave Curll to his trips to the King's Bench and the inveterate hatred of three of the most famous satirists of all time. The next example of a significant figure in the printing business in the period was a contemporary of Curll but was successful financially and in his own terms, politically. This was a printer who worked with the most important people in government. In fact, he was so successful that two biographies appeared on his death in 1741. One was by Curll and not particularly flattering and the other makes it immediately clear that the subject is 'a Favourite of Fortune'.

As can be imagined the world of print and politics was very small in the first few decades of the eighteenth century. If it wasn't the case that everybody knew everybody else, I would venture that among the printers and politicians there was a great number of relationships, as friends, competitors or business partners or probably a mixture of all three. And while Curll was known by the great and the good and not necessarily liked, one of his 'victims', another printer, enjoyed the acknowledgement of the highest echelons of the Tory hierarchy and their writers. This one rose through the City of London ranks to become Lord Mayor. Equally importantly he made a lot of money. And if you look at the life of this second printer, you think he must have been blessed by a guardian angel, because he seems to have been the original Teflon man.

His name was John Barber and like Curll was dragged before Parliament on several occasions. All of these attempts at prosecution were unsuccessful. This may have been because he had friends in high places or because he managed to cover his back successfully. Most probably it was a mixture of the two.

He started his career off in the usual way as an apprentice and struck out on his own in 1700. By 1705 his affinity to the Tory party brought him into contact with one of his most successful authors, and his subsequent mistress, the very clever Delarivier Manley whom we have met before. Her professional life is inextricably wound up with Barber's so we will give her a potted biography here, particularly as she becomes embroiled in a dispute with Curll. He was known for his cavalier attitudes to other people's work and it turns out, also to other people's lives. Manley was an interesting woman quite apart from her bold entry into the world of professional journalism and her blatant and scandalous novels. She had lived with Barbara Castlemaine for six months as a good luck charm at the gaming table. She had been the toast of the theatrical town at the end of the seventeenth century counting the aristocracy among her supporters. To cap all this she had been married to a bigamous cousin who also happened to be a Member of Parliament. The bigamy was not her fault since she claimed she was duped into thinking that the first wife was dead. But she must have known what she was doing when she became the mistress of the infamous Warden (Governor) of the Fleet Prison. She possibly had two children by him and also got mixed up in a case of disputed inheritance, which ended up with Manley and her lover badly out of pocket. This very complex and high-profile court case involved both her current lover and her bigamous husband as lawyers for the two opposing parties.

All this activity and being thrown into the Tower for a few days accused of seditious libel made her an interesting subject for a biography. So her life story would have been eagerly awaited by her many fans and (Whig) enemies if and when she chose to write it. Our friend Curll, could not hang around until Manley decided to put her autobiographical pen to paper so he threatened her that he had already commissioned a less than flattering version of her life story. She could stop him publishing it as an unauthorised biography by providing something of her own. Bearing in mind that her story was colourful enough without any of the printer's sensational additions she put pen to paper and in a few weeks Curll had a best-seller on his hands.

The next example of how a printer might make a mark on the world also had a connection with Manley although a more intimate one. Her final boyfriend, John Barber, a 'humble' printer according to both his biographers, was indebted to Manley for launching his career. Her connections were widespread and she moved in some of the highest circles. And as noted above, her first forays into writing had brought her into contact with the biggest stars in the Tory firmament. One of them was Henry St John, later Lord Bolingbroke, Harley's second in command (and thereafter rival for the leadership of the Tories). According to both of Barber's biographers it was she who introduced him to the top echelons of the Tories when they held the reins of power and it was through her that he found himself in the exalted company of a London literary club: the Society of Brothers. The inauguration of this exclusive group took place in June 1711 and was designed as an informal dining circle. Initiated by St John, and then organised by Swift it was made up of Tory wits and gentlemen with the declared purpose to reward 'deserving persons with our interest and recommendation'. In this ambition it was inspired by its rival Kit Kat club which was formed for Whig men of letters. The founder members were the great and the good of the Tory party. Even Abigail Masham, the Tory favourite of Queen Anne who had replaced the volatile Duchess of Marlborough, was represented by her husband, Lord Masham and her brother, Jack Hill. Other luminaries included Robert Harley's son and John Arbuthnot, the Royal Physician and author of the *John Bull* satire. The Society was therefore clearly one of influence and power, and Manley's friend John Barber 'constantly' attended its dinners.

In this way the printer Barber was at the heart of the Tory inner circle. Curll the printer who had not a political bone in his body made the most of Barber's cosy relationship with these very important people. With his usual instinct for commercial advantage he claimed that when Manley and Barber started their relationship she moved in with him as his mistress. She, with uncharacteristic modesty, claimed it was merely to oversee her work. Posterity has to make a judgement on this but Curll certainly saw the partnership as an opportunity to capitalise on Barber's colourful career and that of his lodger/lover.

In his cobbled together biography of his fellow printer he described Barber's treatment of his mistress in the following terms: 'Here opens a Scene of the blackest ingratitude to his best Friend Mrs. Manley, through whose Interest all those Persons who contributed to make his Fortune were owing, besides the large Sums he acquired from her Writings.' She on the other hand seems to have been permanently short of cash in this stage of her career, using Barber to plead her case: 'Mr Barber was order'd to bring me from a number of Great men who were call'd The Society of Rewarding of merit. I had hopes that my poor endeavours to do service might have given me some mark of [the Earl of Peterborough's] favour; particularly I was assured that my Lord Masham and Sr. William Windham, two of the Society, were commissioned by the rest to desire in their names, that your Lordships would send me an hundred pound, with assurances at the same time of their farther Favour. I have been likewise informed, that your Lordship agreed to their request, and that my Lord Harley ingaged to put you in mind of it.'

We will never know whether Barber's business flourished on the back of Manley's success or his natural ability, aided and abetted by his support of the Tories. What is more remarkable is his inexorable rise in the political world after the Tories had been banished into the wilderness on the Whig's triumphant return with

George I. Barber had been one of the lynchpins of the party in their glory years. Jonathan Swift, as we have seen, also wrote on behalf of Robert Harley and the Tories. In his correspondence he refers to Barber several times as he enjoys working dinners with him. He 'dined with the printer' as they produced a 'pamphlet [which] makes a world of noise, and will do a great deal of good'. He recalls putting a very significant piece of business Barber's way: 'I have this morning got the *Gazette* for Ben Tooke [another well-known printer] and one Barber a printer; it will be about three hundred pounds a year between them.' Swift even spent evenings socialising with Barber, possibly indulging in some innocent card games and enjoying a little harmless gambling.

It was a shame that the pamphlets and books that Barber printed were not equally harmless, and in the tradition of printers of his age he found himself in trouble. The first time was when he printed Manley's scandal fiction. The pair were arrested but escaped prosecution by the claim that all the juicy gossip was old and well-known so what was the problem? Manley had also used the device of pseudonyms with keys published separately so that if the reader couldn't guess the victim's identity there was a handy guide in circulation.

The second time Barber came under scrutiny was at the end of Queen Anne's reign. The Tory Ministry gave Barber a pamphlet to print. It was Swift's highly contentious *The Public Spirit of the Whigs,* which was intended to answer Richard Steele's *Crisis.* Unfortunately, as Curll's biography succinctly puts it: 'there happened to be one Passage in it, highly injurious to the Scots, and severely reflecting on their whole Nation.' Ministerial panic followed immediately as they were reluctant for it to be known that they had commissioned this inflammatory piece of work. Unfortunately, although they had commissioned Swift he was not inclined to take orders and so he had written and sent off the pamphlet without having it cleared. So when the 'exceptionable Part ... appeared in public' the Scots Lords were up in arms, complained that they had been insulted and 'insisted on having the Author and Printer punished with the greatest Severity'. They were furious particularly as the Queen had, as we have seen, right from the beginning of her reign, expressed her concerns about the danger of too much free speech: 'I think it might have been for the Public Service to have had some further Laws for restraining the great Licence, which is assumed, of Publishing and Spreading scandalous Pamphlets and libels ...'

The Lords were eager to remind the Queen that they were doing their best: 'We have begun our Endeavours to suppress seditious Papers ... by applying ourselves to discover the Author, Printer, and Publisher of a Pamphlet, intituled, 'The Publick Spirit of the Whigs' which we conceive to be a false, malicious, and factious Libel, highly dishonourable and scandalous to Your Subjects of Scotland, tending to the Destruction of the Constitution, and (by making false and unjust Reflections upon the Union and the Steps and Motives to it) most injurious to Your Majesty.'

This was a bit tricky for Harley et al as they had commissioned the wretched pamphlet and now had to claim they had nothing to do with it. In the confusion Barber was sent for to find a solution, and they needed it fast. How on earth were they going to extricate themselves out of the situation they had got themselves into? They used the printer as a scapegoat. This seemed to satisfy the Lords who no doubt relished the thought of stringing up Harley. This is meant metaphorically of course but there were still probably some people who would have liked to do it in reality. This, however, is where the ministry and their conspirator the printer worked together as a well-oiled machine. It was fortunate that sections were printed separately and spliced together for publication. So 'with great Sagacity' he retrieved all the copies that were waiting in the publisher's premises and, one suspects (although I have no proof) he knew when the State Messengers were going to search for them. Bolingbroke played his part equally impressively and had written an inoffensive section to replace the one which was causing all the trouble. In a remarkably short space of time the offending pages were removed and replaced with the clean ones. A corresponding set of doctored copies which to all intents and purposes looked exactly the same was delivered to the Messengers. The pair managed all this so quickly that when Barber appeared before the Lords accused of publishing, selling and dispersing the Libel and they ordered the piece to be read publicly to him they were bitterly disappointed. They simply could not find the particular page that had caused all the trouble; it had vanished and had been replaced by 'compliment' rather than 'Invective'. They were even more furious with him as at 'the Time of the printing the said seditious Libel' this renegade printer (as they saw it) was entrusted with printing *The Gazette*, the official government newspaper.

Barber stuck to his story and when examined refused to give any answers which might incriminate him. The report of the proceedings show the Lords as greatly annoyed that 'we have not as yet been able to discover the Author of the said Libel, or who brought the written Copy thereof to be printed.' Despite (or perhaps because of) his refusal to answer questions they offered a reward of £300 'to any Person who shall discover, and make due Proof against, the Author or Authors of the said Libel'. Swift thought the sum paltry and considered it as evidence that there was no real will to find him. The whole affair was swept under the ministerial carpet and the Whigs were left without an author and no way of prosecuting the printer.

This whole incident not surprisingly put Barber in very good stead with Bolingbroke and Oxford. Dr Swift, the author of the whole unfortunate affair was also pleased and between them 'they omitted no Opportunity of doing him eminent Services'. As a very material proof of how pleased they were with him he was given the 'Reversionary Grant of the Employment of King's Printer which was to take place in the Year 1738-9'. Curll goes on to claim that Barber sold the grant on to another printer and made a very considerable profit. By this time Barber was accumulating a fortune. He was one of the people who made a profit out of the South Sea Bubble and according to the second biographer Barber actually made £30,000 by selling his shares at the right time. He had invested nearly all his capital in the scheme that had wrecked so many others. Curll, with perhaps a touch of envy, reported that Barber 'added greatly to his wealth by the South Sea scheme'. Maybe Curll thought that Barber was rising above his station when he treated himself to a country residence and purchased 'an estate' at East Sheen. With his new-found riches he stepped back from the day-to-day operations and appointed a manager to look after his affairs. Even with the manager his business still managed to have a close brush with the law when they printed a 'fine edition' of the works of the lately deceased Duke of Buckingham. This time the Whigs were in the ascendancy and the text apparently cast aspersions on people in high places. Once again, Barber and his employees escaped prosecution, this time because the pamphlet had not actually been published. At this point he becomes too remote from his own printing trade for our purposes, but he continued to prosper, becoming an Alderman and then in 1733, he became the Mayor. He was a High Tory and a Jacobite but he was well respected. But his relevance to this book is his closeness to the people in high places and the way he worked with them to promote the ministry. It was a sign of how much regard government now gave to the printed word, and how they had come to realise that the printer deserved respect.

8

INTO THE PROVINCES:
LIFE OUTSIDE LONDON

London was the great and growing hub of life in the seventeenth and eighteenth century but the provinces were growing richer and more important and it was not long before they were demanding their own publications. It may have begun with dispatches taking the news to the provinces and vicars may have read out the news from the pulpit, but this was not enough to satisfy the increasingly confident country beyond the metropolis. The provincial press as an entity probably began in Norwich, although the earliest issues are missing. The earliest extant copy of a regional newspaper is from 1702 in Bristol, a mixture of sections from other publications. Its main purpose was as a revenue stream for the printer. But the country soon demanded more, and regional newspapers began to appear round the counties. The chapter examines how the early regional press developed.

So far we have looked at London and its magnetic effect on the rest of the country. This does not mean that the population outside the sprawling and growing capital were any less eager to keep up to date with the latest news. And of course the printers and writers were well aware of this and with an eye to business the industry acknowledged and profited from the fact. Despite the London-centric nature of print at the time, everyone, particularly the elite, were well aware of the nation outside the capital. The politicians and their aristocratic backers had their country houses and much of their revenue came from the agriculture on their land. As the century progressed they profited from the industrial revolution as they discovered minerals and began to build a network firstly of toll roads and then of canals.

For the ranks further down the social ladder London was an exciting place to visit either in person or in their imagination. For some it might have been a dream. But many of them were living equally comfortable lives outside the new and fashionable streets in the West End. And although the financial institutions were developing in the City of London there were merchant banks also opening up in the provinces to handle the profits from growing trade. There was life outside London. In a previous chapter we've already seen the shires merited John Houghton establishing a publication which provided an employment exchange and farming advice for the agricultural industry. Even in the London papers there is evidence that rural life was closer to the metropolis than it is now. Only in the most far-fetched scenario today would you find a story which involved cows in central London. And it is difficult to imagine the need for turnstiles at each end of Lincolns Inn Fields to stop the grazing cattle going walk-about in the City. In the eighteenth century this was clearly a possibility as we meet a cow which escaped from its grazing. Bored with grass it decided it would explore the King's Arms inn in Holborn. It was clearly a very discerning beast as according to the *Birmingham Gazette* of 16 November 1741, it 'went upstairs ... into the first gallery; but not liking any Room there, broke several windows then went up the second gallery' and after visiting the rooms there and finding the accommodation equally unpalatable 'it jump'd over the rails upon the shed ... and with her weight broke through the tiling and fell to the ground.'

But while hungry Londoners may have seen themselves as consumers rather than producers, the farmers and landowners viewed the news of what was happening locally and in London as carrying equal weight. Back in the green fields of rural England where industry was beginning to develop they did not see themselves as mere providers. This was the time when the first provincial newspapers, first in Norwich and Bristol and then York, Leeds, and other centres, began to appear.

Towns such as Norwich, Leicester and Colchester were enjoying economic expansion. The citizens of Chester and Middlewich also wanted 'freshest advices'. Newspaper proprietors were equally keen to take advantage of this potential money spinner. Admittedly, regional newspapers grew more slowly than their London counterparts and in the interest of providing sufficient information and comparable development the time scale in this chapter is extended to include the decades towards the end of the eighteenth century.

Perhaps we should look at what one publisher said about his intentions in starting his newspaper. The *Leeds Intelligencer* put out a very grand statement of what his readership might expect from the paper. The aims outlined are interesting once we have battled through the euphuism. He wants his paper to be a communication channel for those with knowledge and experience to share it with the wider world. When we look at the date, 1754, it becomes clear what part the regional newspaper might be able to play in the coming Industrial Revolution. The editor/publisher's plea to knowledgeable readers to throw their opinions into the fray gives insight into the potential of the medium: 'Our expectations of success could hardly be raised too high, if Gentlemen of Sagacity and Penetration, assisted by a special knowledge and experience in the different branches of trade were jointly to apply their attention to this purpose.' It is an invitation for readers to participate in sharing their expertise in this powerful and accessible medium. It is also worth pointing out that the editor pours scorn on some of his rivals. He mocks other 'Newspapers' for reporting the 'continu'd squabbles between the subjects of his Holiness and his most Christian Majesty in France ... incendiaries in Muscovy' or the 'Pretenders to the Throne of Persia'. No, the editor points out, 'Accounts of Occurrences &c. in the neighbourhood whether serious or jocose would be more entertaining to the ... readers in the country than anything ... of the Town.' It's a local paper, he concludes, its purpose is to carry local news.

But it took a little while for this admirable aim to be seen generally. Some of the earliest provincial newspapers were not what we would identify as newspapers at all. The *Stamford Mercury* which began life in 1713 containing little more than a crude woodcut as its banner and a list of goods imported into London. Although it is comforting to know that there was a brisk import trade in port from Lisbon and lemons from Spain alongside anchovies and olives from Leghorn this is not a gossip-filled, thrill-packed newspaper. Carpets from Smyrna might be considered a little more interesting but that is the sum total of the information. It is not a newspaper, it is a loading list. A further issue gives a list of exports, including over two thousand old sheets. There is no indication of where they are going and what anyone would do with them.

Before we turn to the logistics and marketing of these innovative new communication channels we can have a quick peek at a case study from the early regional newspaper industry and see just how complicated the story can be. Taking just one city, York, there appears to have been at least six newspapers that started production during the eighteenth century. The first newspaper was the *York Mercury* (1719), which through a complex web of ownerships became variously the *Original York Journal (1724)*, *Original Mercury, York Journal or Weekly Courant* (1739). By then the latest owner, Thomas Gent, may have run out of titles or simply given in to the competition from the *York Courant* (1724). *The York Gazetteer* popped up in 1740 and disappeared in 1752. There is an interesting and quite sad story concerning John Jackson, the publisher. He was persuaded to give up producing the *Gazetteer* through circumstances as convoluted as some of the news items.

It appears that Jackson's father had been involved in a dubious trial in which he named two men as having robbed him in order to receive reward money. They denied the charge and were acquitted. When his son printed a report of a very similar case in the *Gazetteer* some thirty years later he raked up local memories which affected the old man so much that he never recovered. The newspaper ceased publication shortly afterwards, although whether this was as a result of his son's embarrassment or economics it is difficult to say. Perhaps the most puzzling aspect of these York newspapers, all of which were published between 1719 and 1777, is the number of times they changed their titles. For instance the *York Chronicle* in a five-year period had even more titles than listed above. It was variously called the *York Chronicle and Weekly Advertiser*, *Etherington's York Chronicle*, or the *Northern Flying Post and General Advertiser*. Etherington's finances appeared to have diminished as his number of titles grew and he went bankrupt in January 1777 when his paper was taken over by another printer and renamed yet again.

To go back to the beginning of this chapter we can look at the number of newspapers during the period in question. When Queen Anne came to the throne in 1702 there were two; when George III succeeded in 1760 there were twenty nine. So the simplest arithmetic shows that twenty-seven newspapers were born, though admittedly some died, in the fifty-eight years. Producing a newspaper is not an easy operation, involving writing, printing and distribution and to negotiate a way through this new and complex network of communicating information required a disciplined approach. Since 'discipline' is not the usual word associated with the eighteenth century world of print, it will be an interesting journey and the route takes in their origins, their news content and their distribution networks. And a further question concerns the politics of the publications. Were they as faction-led as their London counterparts? Local elections were hard-fought and were backed by surprisingly high-profile individuals. The Whig Duchess of Marlborough, one of the most influential women in the reign of Queen Anne, interfered in the St Albans elections and the Tory press were very vocal in their outrage. We need to see if this was duplicated elsewhere, perhaps not so close to London because the heated politics of Westminster may not have seemed so relevant farther away from the centre. Judging from at least one newspaper it is safe to assume that politics raised a certain amount of passion in the provinces. We know this because printers were making the same injudicious decisions which landed them in as much trouble as their metropolitan colleagues. One printer in Exeter, Philip Bishop, suffered from printing a Jacobite ballad (he died in 1717 in prison while awaiting his trial). Given the example of his father one would have thought that his son George would have been more careful. This was not the case as he was fined for reprinting Parliamentary debates, which as we know the government didn't take kindly to.

Even Middlesex, no longer a real county and hardly a London suburb, could once be regarded as provincial. Districts which are now integral parts of the capital were once outside London; Swift wrote about walking across the fields in Chelsea and Dickens' heroic little Oliver Twist retired to the green surroundings of Finchley.

Highgate for instance was earmarked as a place to graze sheep to fatten them up for the London market. The *Middlesex Journal* could easily on this basis be regarded as provincial press because its outer reaches such as Uxbridge and Brentford were as much as a day's ride into London. However it may have been its proximity to London which got it mixed up in one of the landmark events in the freedom of the press in Britain. The recurrent bugbear, the printing of House of Commons debates was still forbidden in 1771 when the *Journal* became embroiled in a test case which resulted in defeat for the government restrictions.

The increase in press activity and perhaps the boldness in ignoring the ban on reporting prompted the over-sensitive politicians to put out a warrant for the arrest of the printer, John Wheble, 'as misrepresenting the Speeches, and reflecting on several of the members of this House, in contempt of the order, and in breach of the privilege, of the House'. Wheble's case was quickly taken up by John Wilkes, who at that time was an Alderman of the City of London. Taking advantage of the City's ancient privileges which included the exclusive right to make arrests within its boundaries he took the printer under its protection. If Parliament wanted to bring Whebles to Westminster to answer the charges they would have to rely on him being handed over. Instead of complying with the Commons' request, Wilkes invited a further six printers to take refuge.

Wilkes is known for his membership of the Hellfire Club; he was a libertine, and variously a brilliant polemicist, local magistrate, Member of Parliament, mayor of the City of London and radical politician. As one of the most fascinating, complex and contradictory characters of the eighteenth century he stands out even in a period full of men and women with scandalous private lives who have also made a serious contribution to British history. He was so notorious that the ministers refused to take him on and conceded the point. Parliamentary reporting was no longer prosecuted.

The times were beginning to change in the press's favour and Wilkes' involvement only made the Commons more nervous about trying to stem the tide. Meanwhile in the Commons there were some Members who maintained that it was not the place of authority to defend individual members against libel. The concept that offended Members should tackle cases of libel in their own right rather than through the House was beginning to creep in. There was for the first time an undertone of mutterings that with so many journalists scribbling away the House didn't have time to prosecute them all and equally importantly there would be no time left for running the country. The upshot of this landmark exercise was that the Commons had backed down and another victory was recorded in the progress of press freedom. A further result, and equally important was that Members of Parliament became accountable to their constituents who could now freely read what their representative was doing while he was in Westminster. It was remarkable that it was a provincial newspaper which took centre stage in this struggle to report from the elected seat of power. We can count this as a small victory for a regional paper whose area was in touching distance of the capital.

These are very serious questions so by way of a diversion we can look at what else the provincial newspapers carried. As we have seen before the advertising columns are indicators of what life was like for the citizen. Bearing that in mind how do the goods and services in the country compare to those in London. A look at the advertising columns might give some indication of whether this has a basis in fact. The husbands of town wives are continually disclaiming the debts of their runaway wives. Did their country cousins suffer from the same problem? And there was always the entertainments column. Jane Austen's fictional characters love to dance at the nearby Assembly Rooms. Did they hear the details by word of mouth or by reading the local newspaper? The provinces were not a cultural desert by any means so it will be good to see if there were theatre and concerts available for amusement. All will be revealed in a visit to the advertising columns.

We will leave the lighter and more amusing offerings to the latter end of the chapter and look first at the production, distribution and the demand for these papers. That the country cousins wanted a sight of the news was evident early on in the story of newspapers in general. The London newspapers were certainly expecting business from outside town. The *British Apollo* for instance advertised that 'Any person that has an Estate or Freehold Land about £300 per annum, near the city of York if he will publish it in the Post-Man or in this Paper where he will be treated with about it, either in London or in the City of York he may meet with a Purchaser.' Now it is possible that the land-owner read the advertisement in London but a clue as to the paper's aspirations is a further note buried in the classified column. They clearly expect to receive some communications from elsewhere because, quite sensibly, they refuse to answer questions 'out of the Country' unless the postage is paid.

As all good marketers know, where there is a demand someone will meet it. And even before the London newspapers found their feet there were several provincial publications which made their entry into this void. We have already noted that the first English provincial newspaper was the *Norwich Post*, 1701, with the *Bristol Post Boy* one year later in 1702. A major question to be asked of any business and which cannot be ignored is profit. In the newspaper industry there is no profit if nobody buys what you print and there is no profit if the printer or publisher can't get the newspapers to the readers. So how did the newspaper entrepreneurs distribute their product in the regions? In London the short distances between printer and coffee house or retail outlet, the papers could be sent out easily and quickly. The distances in the country outside the towns were of course longer. Newspaper distributors had no option but to get the news out by road and they were far from reliable or well maintained. Without a good road network and no trains or vans or cars, the printers in town had to rely on horsemen and carriers, which constituted the commercial transport of the day. Even slower were the 'running footmen' whose marathon efforts meant that the news was distributed by foot. The term 'newsagent' was born but they looked very different from those we see today. Printers would use any retail outlet they would find and the agents were given territories and would service the area around their shop. It was similar to the current network of centres where customers can collect the products they have bought over the internet. The outlets were sometimes unlikely and anyone could take on the agency, from milliners to liquor stores, and it was a useful second revenue stream for the shopkeepers. The newspaper proprietors also paid 'newsboys' to walk defined routes delivering to regular newspaper readers. There were even some copies which went back to the capital. The rich country folk who might spend time in both London and at their estates could pay a subscription to receive news of the goings on out of town. Back in the provinces market day gave the hawkers a useful opportunity to shout out their wares, including the local newspaper. These general hawkers who sold whatever they could carry were at the bottom of the sales ladder and would only receive their supply after every other sales channel had been fulfilled.

Now of course comes the thorny question of how many of these early newspapers were actually sold. According to one source, it was very difficult to actually work out the circulation, let alone the readership. Circulation as we know is the number sold, the readership is how many people get to read the paper. The readership of the out-of-date magazines in a GP's waiting room will be considerably more than for the ones which arrive at home and which possibly never even get opened. But a guess can be made. The figures are likely to be in the low thousands and we have to rely on the printers for the statistics. The *Newcastle Weekly* in 1739 proudly boasted some two thousand copies. The numbers are vague and there is an impression that not even the printers really knew how many came off the press. Given that automation probably consisted of an apprentice being told what to do it is not surprising. The economics of the newspaper industry were extremely difficult to calculate and since the printers also produced a variety of work apart from newsprint, exact business models are difficult to work out.

As an afterword, we should probably mention that some of the profit for the less scrupulous or more radical printers went in the fines they were expected to pay when they crossed the line and found themselves in trouble with the law.

This leads us to the political slant of these papers. It has been the *leitmotif* throughout the previous chapters that the English reader was insatiable in his or her thirst for political news. We asked this question a little while ago and it is an important one to consider. How factional were the provincial newspapers? We guess that these papers were eagerly awaited so what did they contain? The only way to find this out is by reading them and there are some interesting touches. In the interests of balance, again a word rarely used in the description of the early modern newspaper industry, it seems at least some of them were prepared to welcome what might be described as party political broadcasts. *Pugh's Hereford Journal* of 4 January 1781 carries electioneering pieces from three candidates for the county seat of Gloucestershire. The campaign had to be put together very quickly after the sudden death of the incumbent MP but the seat had long been contested between several local families. In a long statement George Berkeley inserted alongside his competitors in the classified section he vowed not to be disruptive, a promise not always kept by parliamentary candidates in the eighteenth century. He suggests in the 'manifesto' that if elected he will promote the welfare and interest of the county. The advertisement is extremely light on detail although relatively generous in length. One would like to think that George, a young naval officer from an established Whig family, cut a dashing figure. In fact he didn't win this particular by-election but the politics of the day were such that when the general election came round in 1783 he 'won' the seat unopposed. His rival James Dutton, the Tory candidate, begins his advertisement with a promise that he will conduct himself as conscience dictates, although there is little or no indication of what this means. This was traditionally a safe Tory seat and custom was restored when in the general election Berkeley graciously stood down. This withdrawal was at least partly because the seat was particularly expensive to contest. The cumulative cost of the advertising and the seven months of campaigning is likely to have been a factor in Berkeley's decision.

However, there was a world outside politics and other aspects of life raised their domestic heads above the parapet. Taking just one section of society at random, widows, there are some entertaining, sad and of course very business-like entries. An anecdote from the *Stamford Mercury* of 1712 could only come from a newspaper of this period. The story concerns a lady who seems to have been the subject of a duel fought between an officer and an Irish gentleman who had followed her from London under the pretence of having a fortune of his own. The motivation for the duel is not clear but it appears that the officer introduced the Irishman to the woman who 'did not like him worse for being an Irishman, so that he will rather gain than suffer by the Discovery'. Neither of the gentlemen were mortally wounded. The main complaint was that the officer did not like to see such a wealthy woman slip from his grasp. And we may never know whether it was money or beauty which attracted the Reverend Mr Bradford, vicar of Bishop's Tawton, but we hope his marriage to the young, beautiful and rich widow, unnamed, who lived close by, was a long and happy one. Widows figure prominently in demands for debts to be paid to the estates of their late husbands and short paragraphs appear in every provincial newspaper. The money is to be paid to the grieving widow as in the case of Mary Smith of Peterborough, who promises to sue if the debts are not settled. Mrs Rachael Rhodes of Broad Oak, Yorkshire, used the *Leeds Intelligencer* to sort out her finances after the death of her husband, advertising for both his debtors and creditors to come forward and settle up in either direction.

Editors could have their say in their own publications. There is definitely a feeling of the high moral ground becoming cluttered with worthy editorials as the century progressed. The *Middlewich Journal or General Advertiser* offers an insight into the mind-set of an eighteenth-century editor. The self-congratulatory tone of his 'gratitude', which is the 'brightest ornament of the soul and the most shining Christian Value' is unmistakeable, and is due to the 'Public in general for the Encouragement' offered. However there is something rotten in the town of Middlewich as there are 'those, who for particular Reasons pretend to assert that its continuance will be but of short duration'.

Whatever or whoever was threatening the newspaper was ultimately successful because after two years it folded. And the reason appears to be a mystery because there are no clues. Mr Schofield, whose name appears in the title, however, was apparently aiming at giving value for money, being 'determined to spare no Labour or Expence', although how much effort he put into his work is debatable given the very high proportion of content simply lifted from London newspapers.

The proprietors of these provincial titles certainly regarded themselves as the keepers of the nation's integrity. The first edition of the *Chester Chronicle* in May 1775 makes this point very strongly. John Poole, the editor/publisher declared that he launched the paper because 'It is universally allowed that the freedom of the press is the strongest bulwark to the liberty of every state, wherein the subject hath any share in the legislation.' He then once again appealed to 'the Gentlemen of the neighbourhood [to] suggest any practicable improvement in the execution of this public-spirited work'. The key word here is 'neighbourhood'. Indeed, the editor is keen to 'accelerate the commercial and domestic intelligence of this ancient and respectable city'. He means Chester to remain at the centre of the publication and did not intend to look south to London for inspiration.

Despite these fine words the term 'local' in many papers is stretched to its very limit. Middlewich certainly looks outside its borders for tales of derring-do. It is Chester's close neighbour and the paper cannot resist exciting tales from lands even farther away than that ancient city. How readers must have thrilled at the story of the 'sufferings, and surprizing deliverance of William and Elizabeth Fleming' from the savage 'Indians' in Pennsylvania. They were finally released but the story is not for the fainthearted. It included a murder of a Quaker by an Indian of a particularly bloodthirsty disposition. But it's clearly not entirely the 'savages' who are at fault. Nobody will be surprised that it's the French who are behind their nasty ways. With patriotic outrage the reader learns that 'They came with Orders from the French who supplied them with Ammunition &c. to plunder, burn and destroy every Thing of Value they met with,' not forgetting they are also under instructions to scalp or 'captivate' their unhappy prisoners. In this case this word does not carry its current meaning. There is a frisson of excitement when we are told the central characters are commanded to depart and left cliff-hanging with the classic 'To be continued'. A more hopeful sign came with the good news from New Jersey that as a result of a treaty 'There is not an unfriendly Indian to be seen' and 'all scalping has ceased.'

The wider world must have seemed an exciting place to the inhabitants of Middlewich and its surrounds. The story from Lisbon that the English merchants' stock had gone up in smoke may have disturbed them but they would then be uplifted by the news that 'the Guineas of England ... have prevailed over the French Man's Word'. (The British and the Prussians were at war with the French in the Seven Years War. This time they were wrangling over Silesia). The local news was tame but definitely spooky in comparison. There was excitement generated by labourers in Derby who were employed in digging up some gravel and found ten earthenware pots all containing the bones of small children. It was fortunate that they found all ten of these pots, since the first reaction of the villagers was to find someone to blame for the murder of these infants. There must have been a sigh of relief from some of the more unpopular members of the community when someone with a sensible head on their shoulders pointed out that the Romans buried their infants in this manner and therefore the bones were some fifteen hundred years old. They were very lucky in Middlewich that life was so exciting if the *Plymouth Weekly Journal or General Post* of 1 March 1723 is anything to go by. As far as it appears from this four-page paper (with very large print and spacious leading) literally nothing of any interest locally was worth recording. Even the London news is less than interesting. Lord North and Grey is in perfect health (although he is in the Tower so perhaps that should be credited to his gaolers). He was languishing there as a result of being implicated in a plot to bring back the Stuarts. And that is about the sum of the serious news in the paper. The rest is taken up with a few shipping reports and some gossip that is worth repeating mainly because it puts some of our current trivia on social media to shame in its weirdness.

First there is the barbarity of the French. It was not a surprise to the Georgian reader that a man was found in the street in Paris with a cut to the middle of his body. More amusing but closer to home (not yet Plymouth, there was still no news from the home town) a London woman decided to get married in her shift (underwear) as a way of avoiding paying her former husband's debts (it is not made clear how that would work but obviously she had a plan). This caused a certain amount of hilarity amongst the assembled bystanders but her quick thinking fiancé picked her up bodily and took her across the road and bought her some new clothes and then took her back to the church. Finally (still in London) a woman had a scarf stolen from her neck.

The only reference to anything to do with Plymouth is in the advertising columns where on this particular week some substantial properties are for sale. So in this instance the newspaper is bringing London news to the province but we are no wiser as to anything that happened nearby.

Perhaps Norwich was a much busier town than Plymouth because the *Norwich Gazette* of January 1712, if not exactly full of East Anglian stories, at least gives the place a mention. We have already asked the question – did the provincial papers display the violent factional tendencies as the London ones? Well the answer is in Norwich politics was every bit as central to the press as in the capital. The pioneering *Norwich Post,* founded in 1701, was rooting for the Whigs. Five years later the Tory *Norwich Gazette* was launched. Another Whig paper began in the same year. Norwich was a Whig stronghold but Henry Crossgrove, the proprietor of the *Gazette* could hold his own against his rivals. This state of affairs lasted twelve years as Crossgrove competed with two or three rival Norwich newspapers, but by 1718 the only two left were the *Norwich Gazette* and the *Norwich Mercury*. In a tradition so dear to the London newspapermen these two papers slugged it out in the East Anglian political arena.

True, Crossgrove was on the back foot as an outspoken and openly Jacobite Tory. Like the great newspaper barons of the last century Crossgrove was not shy in using his newspaper to make his opinion of local and national politics absolutely clear. As we have seen so many times freedom of speech was not sacrosanct in eighteenth-century England and Crossgrove found himself coming up against the powers-that-be rather too often. He was twice in line for prosecution for high treason and sedition and both times somehow he managed to wriggle out of the frame.

It did not help that his most hated enemy was the proprietor of the rival *Norwich Mercury*, William Chase. Crossgrove devoted considerable energy to undermining Chase's business and they were both common councillors. Council meetings must have been interesting.

There is no need to go too far to find yet another disgruntled newspaperman and once again a reference to false news pops up. In Ludlow in 1719 there was despair and the honest newspaperman was wringing his hands at the thought of those who were bringing his trade into disrepute. Consider this opening paragraph from the *Ludlow Postman.*

'Newspapers and News-Writers ('tis true) are now-a-days, in this Critical Age, under many scandalous Censures and Reflections of imposing upon the World with Falsehoods; but this I have to say on Behalf of them, that the world is eager of being acquainted with the News as soon as possible; and therefore, we (to please them) are apt to catch hold of Reports which sometimes do not prove true. However, (lest I should be thought to side with Falsehood) I leave that to the Judgement of the wide World, hoping some will give their favourable Opinion; and let them know that I shall Print for my credit, as I hope to meet encouragement; and shall avoid all fraudulent inventions to humour parties and tell the plain Truth on both sides without favour or affection.'

It is a great shame that the *Ludlow Postman* could not survive. With a very limited circulation and therefore minimal advertising it went under only a year after its brave announcement of integrity. The question of false news and biased reporting was a major concern of this feisty little paper. It quoted one correspondent (which we must assume is a genuine reader) who demanded 'that in your reports you express no Regard to Parties, whether High or Low, or Neuter; but that you impartially side [with] Truth'.

But aside from the big questions of the day, the Ludlow newspaper carried some human interest stories which ranged from the bizarre to the genuinely touching. Take the case of the anonymous philanthropist who released thirty-five prisoners from a gaol, paid their debts and then gave them money to help them on their way before setting off in his coach alone. Not so amusing are the reports of the highwaymen who were confronted by three have-a-go Londoners who were killed or wounded in the attempt. And there was no doubt sympathy for the mother of triplets whose children only survived nine days.

There are so many charming tales in this paper that it is tempting to repeat them all. But in the spirit of romance here are two examples. They are two stories which throw a very interesting light on affairs of the heart and marriage and offer a vivid contrast between a couple apparently marrying for love and a cad. The first story involved a particularly popular bride and her musician boyfriend. The bride and groom (aptly named Valentine) celebrated their nuptials with 'uncommon splendour'. Their guests danced away the marriage night at a local inn and made merry until three in the morning, which didn't please the groom (the report does not report who was responsible for paying the drinks bill). He certainly wasn't comfortable when the guests then remembered a local tradition of making themselves at home in the newly-weds' bed and throwing stockings at the groom (aimed at his nose) or each other. The reporter comments that at one time there were more people pelted in the bedroom than 'in the pillory'.

Quite how many of the guests took up residence in the honeymoon suite is really unclear but it was a local tradition, so the groom didn't have much choice in the matter. Given that he was also expected to drink a sticky mixture of eggs, sugar, cinnamon, nutmeg and other spices he may well have had been wondering whether such a big wedding was a good idea. But he seems to have won for himself a particularly sought-after bride, as his rivals for the lady's hand gathered in a good-natured mob outside their house and pinned various wreaths to their door. There was no further comment on the popularity of the lady with her many suitors, but the jolly way the wedding was reported is still a pleasure to read.

This lady was certainly more fortunate than the heiress who was wooed by a trickster with a pretended lottery win. To corroborate the fraud he and his friends hired 'drums and musick' to celebrate his feigned good fortune. However, the thieves fell out and he quarrelled with his associates, one of whom publicised the intended deception in the middle of a coffee house. Undeterred, the perpetrator is reported as having 'native Front' and was 'resolved to carry on his Attack with redoubl'd vigour'. The reaction of the intended bride is not recorded.

The Ludlow editor also encouraged readers' letters which range from the touching to the weird. Some of the questions were quite tricky. He seems to have become the regional agony uncle with heartfelt stories flooding in from the love-sick of Ludlow. Again, there are so many delightful appeals to his good sense from readers who have the most unusual problems that it would be a serious omission not to include an example.

Take the young lady whose former boyfriend might (hypothetically) have climbed into her bedroom one night and fallen very noisily onto the floor, probably waking the household. Should she scream blue murder that she was on the point of being 'ravished', which would save her reputation but have severe and painful consequences for the would-be lover? Alternatively she could lie quietly in her bed while the intruder nursed his sore head. The advice was simple – keep quiet and she might keep her boyfriend, scream and disaster would ensue.

Not so easy is the story of a woman whose first husband had married her bigamously. As was her right she took him to court and he was sentenced to death. In a fit of generosity she pleaded for him to be transported and sometime later had news that he had died. She having remarried, perfectly legally, her first husband resurfaced and asked her to join him to live abroad. Reading between the lines, that was what she wanted to do, so she is was in fact seeking confirmation that the second marriage didn't count. The sternly worded reply was that she was ungrateful to her lawful husband and it was unfair to ask for an answer to what was a clear-cut situation. No doubt the discontented wife found a way to clear her conscience and follow the rogue.

One lovesick swain asked the editor to put in a note in the paper in the hope that a pretty girl ('You can't imagine how handsome she is') will remember the young man who gazed at her at a local schoolboy theatre production. Another girl wanted to invite the boy who looked up at her window every night into her house to warm up by the fire. A really odd request came from a woman who was tired of being a virgin and being laughed at by more giggly females. The question posed concerned whether she should give in to the 'importunities' of the men who prevailed upon her to give in to their advances. The rather ungentlemanly reply was a bit curt. How long had she been a virgin? She claimed twenty-seven years but this was challenged by the less than gallant comment that you can't call yourself a virgin from the day you are born, only after the age of fifteen, the implication being that she was older than she let on.

A doubt soon surfaces that some letters may not have been authentic. For instance, three women are supposed to have written to him suggesting that if he comes across three gentlemen who want good solid wives, who pray every morning and go to bed at 10 pm every night the editor should introduce them. Their only proviso was that any gentleman who enquired must have an estate in good financial order, as they promised to reduce his outgoings by half. Their assumed names were Martha Busie, Deborah Thrifty, and Alice Early. The readers probably made up their own minds whether these letters were spoofs or were genuine. The editor was however, quite careful in his choice of material when it came to more serious matters. In one issue he refused to insert a piece from a Free Thinker which appeared to be attacking another individual. Quite possibly he wanted to stay out of any local feuds, which seems perfectly sensible.

Though some feuds are irresistible as news stories, as in the unfortunate case of Arundel Coke of Bury St Edmunds. (The story features a long way from the East Anglian town in the *Exeter Mercury or Weekly Intelligence* but the journalist obviously could not ignore such a juicy tale.) The report was that Coke assaulted his brother-in-law Edward Cripse after inviting him and his wife for supper. They had just left the house on a visit to a neighbour when a labourer in Coke's pay hit Cripse with a hedging tool. It appears that the assailant had been summoned by a whistle from Coke. The pair left Cripse for dead, the labourer having been encouraged to do the job properly. Unfortunately for Coke but fortunately for the victim, the attempt at murder was not at all efficient and as soon as they had gone the brother-in-law got up and walked to his would-be assassin's home and confronted him. Coke, having been promised a pardon, seems to have claimed a reward offered by turning himself in. The motivation for all this was the reward, but it makes very little sense to admit to a crime for this reason. The whole story was obscure but it probably made good reading for the Exonians, who might well have thanked their lucky stars that such crimes were perpetrated at the other end of the country.

Although we might find these titbits entertaining we still have no clue as to how these provincial readers spent their leisure time. Recreational advertisements appear fairly late in the eighteenth century but when they did appear there was an eclectic mix of amusements available. Bath was one of most popular centres for all things amusing in the eighteenth century and if you cared to venture outside the city you could partake of a Public Breakfast at the Glocester House, Bristol Wells. As well as the breakfast there was 'Musick for Country and Cotillion Dancing … every Monday during the season'. Mr Barton the owner took great pains to invite the Nobility and the Gentry to his Table d'Hote. He also offered suites of rooms to be had at preferential terms. Times, it seems have not changed much and for secure car park we read 'Good stabling for any numbers of horses and Lock up coach houses'.

In 1779 in Liverpool more cultural pursuits were available for the music lover. The recent oratorio, *The Messiah* (at that time it was a mere thirty-five years since its first performance) was being performed in St Peter's Church. For subscribers it would only cost half a guinea to attend this performance and subsequent performances of *Judas Maccabeus* and a new piece called *The Fall of Egypt*. To attend one of these fine musical treats was only five shillings. For something a little lighter there was a *Miscellaneous Concert* at the Theatre Royal in that town. They certainly knew how to enjoy themselves in this thriving port. The Theatre Royal, as seen above, was a venue for concerts. It was only five years old at the time of these advertisements and if the highlighted programmes are to be believed it offered a curious mixture of the serious and the frankly bizarre. At the end of the tragedy *Theodosius* a dance troupe appeared to perform a highland reel. It was the custom of the time to have runs of only a few days so the actors had to change roles for the following day when the fare was *The Duenna*, and another play called the *Touchstone*. On the Monday following they had to be ready to give their all for a comedy called *The Wonder: A Woman Keeps a Secret*.

It would be pleasing to think that the citizens of Liverpool occupied themselves in their leisure time with sacred or other classical music lightened by an outing to the theatre or to a dance. Alas, they had a darker side to their entertainments. Directly below the advertisement for the uplifting tunes of Handel and his fellow composers there is an advertisement for cockfighting. The prize money is astonishing and the numbers of birds shocking. Eighty-two cocks were to be set against each other and the whole bloody episode would carry on for three days. Ten guineas per battle and one hundred guineas for the 'main' battle was offered as prize money, To whet the onlookers' appetite a meal was available at the venue, The Bear's Paw, Wigan.

But while this display of savagery is disappointing there were events which could make people in the East Midlands proud of themselves. In the *Birmingham and Stafford Chronicle* of 21 July 1791 there was a very prominent announcement of the proceedings of the General meeting of the subscribers to promote the abolition of slavery. This well-meaning and worthy group made it their business to send thanks to the politicians who were working so hard to root out the evil practice.

A few years later the *Chester Chronicle* proudly announced the Festival of Music for citizens willing to make the journey to Manchester. This extravaganza ran from Wednesday to Saturday and was a celebration of the opening of the new Assembly Rooms. Beginning with the still beloved *Messiah* the programme moved through to the *Grand Miscellaneous Concert*. But the organisers were aiming to be strict. No money would be taken at the door and ladies were warned that they would have to remove their hats or bonnets and absolutely no feathers were to be worn. The advertisement was apparently not just for the audience; the players were requested to attend a rehearsal on the Monday before. And the whole exhausting celebration included a Grand Ball on the Thursday evening.

Finally there is nothing like a dance to bring people together and what better than to have one in a good cause. This is no doubt what Lady Monson and the Earl of Exeter were thinking when they organised the Lincoln Ball 'for the encouragement of the Lincolnshire Stuff – Manufactory'. The dress code was very strict but perhaps not in the way one would expect. 'Ladies are to be admitted Gratis on their appearing in a Stuff Gown and Petticoat of the colour appointed by the patroness, spun, woven and finished within this county and producing a ticket signed by the weaver and counter signed by James Ibbotson Dyer at Louth, one of which tickets will be delivered with every 18 yards of stuff. No gentlemen but subscribers to be admitted nor any money taken at the door. Gentlemen to appear without any silk or cotton in their dress.' Although the aristocratic organisers were prepared to make an exception for silk stockings. The story behind this is the protection of the wool trade in the face of competition from the new cottons that were becoming ever more popular. The advertisement is a perfect example of the way the regional newspapers could be made to have real significance in the everyday lives of its readers.

We will shortly make a further journey into provincial life in the eighteenth century. But before we do that let's take one last look at the amusements on offer. How could 'Gentlemen, Ladies and others' who presumably had no pretences to gentility resist the invitation to marvel at Signora Violante, 'the famous Italian Rope Dancer'. She was due to grace the Guildhall in Stamford for two weeks 'after her triumphant performances in London before Royalty and Nobility'. Readers were urged to catch her before her return to the capital for an appearance attended by no less a person than His Royal Highness the Prince of Orange.

While we are considering royalty, interest in the outfits worn by the monarch and his family is not new. There was definitely a treat in store for the readers of *The Leeds Intelligencer* on 12 June 1787 with an item by item description of royal dress. The occasion was the Birth Day Ball, an annual event when the rich and the famous all met to show off their finery at court. The description reads like a red carpet review at the Oscars in which each female is meticulously described as she passes along in front of the photographers. Having dismissed the relatively dull George III as wearing half-mourning with black stockings, readers can settle down to watch the parade.

With just the right hint of bitchiness about the Queen, whose costume was 'more admired for its neatness and elegance than any [time] we remember to have seen her majesty' there is enough detail to please the most avid reader of a gossip magazine. Her lemon-coloured train, blue and silver dress and petticoat ornamented with rich embroidery are described exactly, as are the curiously dispersed jewels which completed her outfit.

The report then went on in the same scrupulous detail to include three princesses, a duchess, three countesses and a couple of ladies thrown in for good measure, all of whose outfits are described approvingly as being of 'English manufacture'. Even the coaches they arrived in were up for scrutiny, 'few were new' although several appeared to have fresh coats of paint. All this of course was taking place in London, so readers could enjoy the vicarious pleasure of picturing celebrities in their finest, just as they do today.

The newspapers often found it impossible to resist including stories which were simply too good to leave out despite being well out of the local area. The *Reading Mercury* for instance, which certainly had a serious side, included a story which could go straight to Hollywood to provide the plot for an exciting period drama. A former waiter turned highwayman was pursued for 'more than twenty miles', he on an excellent horse which he had stolen. After an astonishing leap which his pursuers couldn't face he turned and laughed at them saying 'he was sorry he could not have the pleasure of their company any farther'. Having nearly been stopped at the next turnpike he cried out to the toll-keeper 'A race, a race!' who let him through after the highwayman threw down his money. It certainly seems to have taken place on what is now the M4 corridor but it had the most tenuous link to the actual area covered by the paper.

The frivolity sat alongside more weighty matters. The regions had serious business in hand and the newspapers played their part. One thing that is naturally evident in the later issues of the provincial press is the beginning of the Industrial Revolution. When we move to later in the century, by January 1792 the *Leicester Herald* is practically drowning in canals. There were meetings of the subscribers to the intended 'navigable canal from Oakham to Melton Mowbray'; a call for landowners affected by the Union Canal to give in their claims; and a very sharp note regarding the Ashby-de-la-Zouch canal. There was obviously opposition to this particular project as the notice declares that wise heads have 'fully considered the different calculations held forth by the advertisements of the friends and of the opponents to the intended Ashby-de-la-Zouch navigation and particularly the laboured attempts of the opponents to deceive the public'. The notice went on to say that they were prepared to deliver coal from the mines to their customers' doors at a very reasonable price. A little nearer London, and some twenty years earlier, the *Reading Mercury and Oxford Gazette* had an instruction for a survey and estimate of the cost of a new canal between Sonning and Monkey Island in the Thames.

And there were also the embryonic signs of one of the mainstays of today's local newspaper, the column that used to rejoice in the nickname of 'hatch, match and despatch'. The eighteenth-century version is less organised but the notices can be found and they are for the most part evidence of the growing importance of the newspaper to its own geographical area. The *Reading Mercury* of January 1770 marked the death of George Prince, the son of an apothecary, whom the paper describes as a 'sober, dutiful young man, studious and diligent ... a great loss to his afflicted parents'. This is indeed a sad case but his loss would have also been a local tragedy as he was a native of Reading. Equally significant is the report of the grain prices in the Reading area. In those days Reading was purely agricultural and the statistics were highly relevant to the farmers in the vicinity.

The layout of these early papers is occasionally erratic. A good example is *Aris's Birmingham Gazette*, which carries an item on the death of Viscountess Beauchamp sandwiched between the list of circuit judges and the bank stock. There is no hint of who she is, how old she was or anything about her character. By the time the nineteenth century was under way, proper obituary columns began to make their appearance, but in these early days information provision was hit and miss. As in earlier classified columns, there is no attempt to categorise the advertising. As a result items of great importance are sandwiched between equally serious but completely different topics. Items on letting out toll roads will sit next to a treatise of venereal disease and a bizarre retraction from John Birkit, who admits to falsely accusing Stephen Roodhouse of breaking locks. The accusation was apparently made at a time when John was so drunk he could not read the announcement but was offered a guinea for signing it. The juxtaposition of all these items is so haphazard that reading the column becomes a voyage of discovery.

The local papers were providing a vital service for the inhabitants of the towns and villages they served but we need to bear in mind that the populations in these towns were still tiny in comparison to today's figures and bad news is often as eagerly consumed as good. For instance, the *Chelmsford Chronicle or Essex Weekly Advertiser* served a population of 5,500 in 1800. Although it also included the various local villages in its circulation alongside a small number of copies sent to the neighbouring town of Colchester this is a comparatively tiny constituency. Those that didn't actually know each other probably had acquaintances in common. So the embarrassment of seeing your name among the bankrupts must have been excruciating. In such a small town perhaps the *Chronicle* only put into print what everybody already knew. It might not have been news in January 1783 that 'Robert Cooke ... fustian manufacturer' and 'Elizabeth Dent ... widow, dealer and chapwoman' had gone into financial meltdown.

If the regional press meant anything in a time when towns and villages were small, it enabled local news to travel beyond the immediate vicinity. If as we saw above a widow wanted to call in her husband's debts, how else could it be done efficiently other than through the columns of the town newspaper? The alternative was to write a letter to debtors or physically go and find them. Some of the reports cry out for some more detail and sometimes the central figures might not have wanted the local publicity. What could have been the story behind the obviously attractive and interesting Mrs Elizabeth Whiting? As 'late Matron of the General Hospital' in Bath she is celebrating her marriage to a Mr Faulkner in December 1777. But according to the *Reading Mercury* she had just been awarded the enormous sum of 500 guineas at Abingdon Assizes for non-performance of a marriage contract. One can sympathise with the embarrassment of the publicity associated with being jilted but congratulate her on swiftly finding a replacement husband. The strap line under the banner on the front page claims that the newspaper is distributed through Berkshire, Buckinghamshire, Oxfordshire, Wiltshire, Hampshire, Gloucestershire, Hertfordshire, and Middlesex. There was clearly no hiding the fact over such a wide area that her original fiancé had changed his mind.

A further use for the local paper would be to alert those who were not as fortunate as Mrs Whiting that charitable support was available. Widows of clergymen who were employed in the diocese of Winchester could apply to the College of Matrons provided they were over fifty and had an income of less than fifty pounds per annum. Alas, only three vacancies had arisen.

Not all the news was neighbourly. The classified columns of these newspapers are a goldmine of information about the things country folk did to each other. There are stories of enemies such as the dispute between John Purnell and Stephen Hoult. John falsely spread reports that Stephen, a coach-maker, had been declared bankrupt. This naturally 'greatly prejudiced' his 'character, credit, reputation and business'. This was clearly a very serious matter and very nearly went to court, where John would have been prosecuted for spreading these damaging lies. With what seems a laudable generosity, the coach-maker agreed to drop the charges 'being unwilling to distress' John and his family. However, he had no intention of letting his antagonist go scot free. The declaration in the *Reading Mercury* of December

1777 makes it plain that John has confessed to having no grounds for this falsehood. If only we could see the back story to this, which one can speculate was known in the district. What had either of them done to cause such a situation? We are unlikely ever to find out, making close examination of the classified columns both fascinating and frustrating.

So how shall we sum up the regional press in this race through their pages? First of all what distinguishes them from the London papers? There are several things they have in common (much of which is because there was a tendency to lift material from the capital's pages and blatantly reprint it). Until late in the century they were also still being prosecuted for printing Parliamentary reports, and it is a regional newspaper which is used as the catalyst for change. And there are the same kinds of advertisements for footmen, governesses, houses and cures for venereal disease. Sexual behaviour in the provinces was no better than in the capital. There is however a more parochial feel to the classified and some of the news columns. It should be born in mind that three centuries ago Brentford was a quiet village and the M4 corridor was part muddy track and part toll road infested with vicious highwaymen who were nothing like Errol Flynn.

At this point some readers might be wondering what happened to the Scottish, Welsh and Irish press. Scotland in particular was well known as the home of some of the stars of the Enlightenment, so it would follow that there was a serious press. Looking at what is available it appears that despite this identifiable intellectual powerhouse north of the border, the *Edinburgh Echo* like many of its southern counterparts relied on the London papers for its content, with very little space given over to what was happening in the new northern partner in the Union.

The issue of 28 May 1729 for instance devotes three of its four pages to news of events outside the country, with only one column of classified advertising and some reports from circuit judges. The only item of local reporting is a mention of two clerics who are apparently indisposed.

The Scots Magazine in its first issue of 5 January 1739 does not even bother to mention Scotland in its pages, instead giving a breakdown of all the countries in Europe and beyond, including Morocco, Sardinia and Persia. The next issue is devoted to a reproduction of a Tory magazine called the *Craftsman*, which centres on politics and does not mention Scotland. *The Scots Magazine* admittedly is not a newspaper because it appears monthly but it is an indicator of the reading material available at this juncture in the development of the British press.

Across the Irish Sea in Dublin the *Freeman's Journal*, was apparently little more than a mouthpiece for the London government, subsidised by Westminster and containing little about Ireland. The provincial press outside of England appears to have waited until the nineteenth century to flower, which seems a very long time.

Back in England the regional press wa variable in quality and content for most of the eighteenth century but it became increasingly sophisticated. As the Industrial Revolution rolled inexorably on, more and more official notices appeared and shareholders in canals and other entrepreneurial activities were exhorted to attend meetings and take their premiums. The press became inreasingly focussed and looked to London for high politics rather than something to fill the column inches. Titles blossomed and failed, titles changed and as the great cities grew, so did the importance of the local printed word.

9

THE BUBBLE AND THE DANCE

The previous eight chapters have covered a lot of ground but inevitably there is always something that has been missed out, either by accident or because it simply didn't fit in any of the topics under discussion. We will now do a quick round-up of some of the things that have slipped through the net but are worthy of pulling back in. In particular it would be useful to look at how the readers of the newspaper throughout this period might use this expanding communication channel as part of their lives. We have seen that news was paramount and that medicinal or surgical matters figure high on the list of items. But there were also things which might be called special, either because they were significant to the country as a whole and for individuals, or because they were treats.

There was an extraordinary mix of content in the newspapers and other periodicals, including a guide to the available Ladies of the Night. The extra bits included here give an idea of the items we have left out so far. These are not just randomly picked out of the barrel of news. They are items which go some way to defining the people who read the newspapers. The new medium carried, in no particular order, everything from salacious gossip to serious foreign news, lists of appointees and official posts. There were campaign statements from parliamentary candidates, shipping reports, and reports of births, deaths and marriages. Newspapers fuelled stock exchange and lottery mania. In particular, they were an integral part of the madness that became known as the South Sea Bubble.

Whenever there is a mention of greed and the eighteenth century it's almost inevitable when you put the two together it is the notorious South Sea Bubble which is used as an example. For our purposes we need to see if there was as much interest and outrage then as financial scandals engender now. What was the impact on the newspapers from the individuals who had invested (and lost) heavily in the scheme? Given the limitations of the technology the journalists did pretty well, covering the whole episode from saviour of the nation's finances to financial debacle. In fact, it might not be too big a claim that in reviewing the coverage and the tone of the editorials, announcements and advertising we find that the newspapers were implicated in the story. It might not be too far-fetched to say that without the encouragement and condemnation of the journalists, this famous financial disaster might not have made so much money for some people or caused others so much suffering.

It all starts, as so often is the case in this period, with the War of the Spanish Succession. In March 1711 Robert Harley, Tory leader and Lord Treasurer, persuaded Parliament to agree to establish the South Sea Company or to give it is official title *The Governor and Company of the merchants of Great Britain, trading to the South Seas and other parts of America, and for the encouragement of fishing* to raise money to clear unfunded debts racked up by the interminable war. In its simplest terms the new trading company aimed to exploit the potential of Spanish Central and South America. While the war in Spain was underway there were high hopes of profits to be made when it was over. The idea was to consolidate the various loans and then sell them off to the public in the form of shares that would increase in value as Britain won more concessions for trade in the South Sea. Perhaps if the shareholders had known that the first ship of the company wouldn't even set sail until 1717, they might have been a little more cautious. Visions of untold wealth coloured their expectations and turned their rose-tinted spectacles into golden ones. And it was all helped along by the newspapers.

Unfortunately, the final treaties signed in 1713 gave Britain much less opportunity than originally envisaged. However, there were still high hopes and in June 1713 the 'Governor and Company of Merchants of Great Britain trading to the South Seas' rapturously thanked Queen Anne for making a contract with the Spanish King. It would allow them to send ships to the Spanish West Indies and most particularly the 'Assiento, with privileges beyond what any former Assientists ever enjoy'd'. The Assiento was principally concerned in the slave trade and was one of the pillars of the wealth that flowed into Britain in the eighteenth century. It is ironic that the organisation so closely associated with this trade caused misery both to the 'product' and the investors. It is, however, entirely unarguable that it was the investors' greed which caused their downfall, while the 'product' had no choice. The actual fraudulent activity is difficult to pin down, but for our purposes it is what was said rather than what was actually done which is significant.

From the beginning newspapers were part of the marketing and reporting of this extraordinary phenomenon. They certainly helped with the development of the mindset that meant fortunes were to be made and lost. The first mention of the South Sea Company came in September 1711 when the 'managers' of the new company were announced, led by Harley. The information about this opportunity to become wealthy was spread through all the papers, including the advertisement for a pamphlet detailing the 'Design, and advantages of the South Seas Trade with an Answer of all the Objections against it'. The company itself opened for business in late September 1711. By 1712 the elections for officers of the company were taking place. There was money to be made for those investors who had been clever enough to get in early (the really clever ones sold early as well). One of the cleverest was, as we saw earlier, our friend John Barber, printer, Mayor and Jacobite. He is said to have made over £20,000 and as much as £30,000 on what became a fiasco for the less fortunate. As he had the contract for printing the Company's documents it was not surprising he had the opportunity to indulge in what we would now call insider trading.

The marketing was relentless but the trouble really started at the end of 1720 with a proposal to integrate 'a part of [the Company's] Capital Stock in the Bank [of England] and East India Corporation'. A further share issue caused what can only be called a frenzy. And then it went horribly wrong, with the price tumbling from its height of just over one thousand pounds per share. An enquiry revealed bribery and corruption with the Directors of the Company and Members of Parliament implicated.

Robert Harley summed up the mess very succinctly in 1720, trumpeting that the original vision of the South Sea Company had been perverted. It turned into a bubble because its original purpose to 'pay debts' had become a scheme to 'make debts'. His idea had been to 'relieve poor suffering tradesmen' not to 'ease rich men of their spareable money'. One 'Gentleman' in a pamphlet given the title *A Modest Apology occasion'd by the late unhappy turn of affairs with relation to public credit* was expressing what many people were thinking: 'What an infatuation, Lunacy or Phrenzy has for some time possessed the three Kingdoms! It was a Shame and almost a Crime not to be growing Rich ... When Persons of the highest Rank and Distinction so openly and so assiduously ply'd the dirty work of the Exchange-Alley ... it is no Wonder that we saw those of the lower classes ... gaping for mouthfuls of Moonshine.'

The British Library's Burney collection of newspapers from this era has some seven and half thousand mentions of the South Sea Company. There is neither time nor space in our narrative for this avalanche of words so we will simply stop at the significant signposts on the way. In the beginning the optimism is tangible, with the *London Gazette* publishing the regular notices on dividends. By the time we arrive at 28 and 30 October 1721 a Bill is going through the Commons for 'the relief of the unhappy sufferers in the South Sea Company.' With the acid comment that 'the late Sub-Governor and Directors of the South Sea Company, and their officers, and their aiders and abettors, in lending out the Company's money upon stock and subscriptions, without taking sufficient security for repayment thereof, have been guilty of a notorious breach of trust and have thereby occasioned great loss to the Company, for which they ought to make satisfaction out of their own estates.'

Less than two years earlier in January 1720 teasers had been appearing in papers apparently repeating rumours the Company had another great 'scheme' for annuities and ways to go 'a great way towards paying the National Debt'. At one point they had been rivalling the Bank of England in their ambitious plans. By February 1720 their proposals for absorbing some of the National Debt had been approved by the Government. A day did not go past without some mention of the Company in the press. In some instances there were detailed analyses of the figures put out by the Directors. There were also warnings that the schemes were not 'advantageous' but who would believe that when the prospect of becoming rich was dangled in front of them? By March nearly every day in the press there was a pamphlet or a notice which could have been taken as a warning. But, then as now, few investors wanted to think they had been duped or misled.

The *London Journal* of 30 July 1720 filled an entire page with the story of an 'overheard' conversation on the Scheme. It begins with a rant from a character who has missed out on buying into the latest share issue. The complaint hinges not on the mathematics of the proposition but on the lost opportunity to make thousands of pounds. In a poem dedicated to Almighty Money he makes his point in verse:

What makes a homely Woman fair
About five hundred pounds a year
What makes a Virgin of a Whore
About five hundred more
'Tis money guides the world and fate
Makes virtue vice, makes crooked straight
And votes the South-Sea stock a blessing or a cheat

The conclusion is that only those who have missed the opportunity to participate complain. But the author leaves this enigmatic comment, 'What is the Company's Business in this Part of the Case and what ought to be every Man's business may be the subject of another letter'. The opinions, for, against or equivocal, were everywhere. Of course, the main problem was that as the Company increased its share issue more and more people were buying into the scheme, encouraged by the announcements in the press that they could get in on this sure-fire money maker. Investment was further encouraged by the announcement of the marriage of a housekeeper who brought £8,000 of South Sea money to her new husband. Those at the very bottom of the financial heap couldn't possibly invest in this guaranteed profit machine, but this woman had been working for one of the directors. The prospect of making such a huge sum was enough to persuade anyone who had anything to invest, however paltry.

The next curious rumour to appear in the press is the following, which should perhaps have warned shareholders that something was amiss. ''Tis reported that the South Sea Company have made some private offers of a union with the East India Company but they tell us that the latter have absolutely rejected the proposal. What their reason for doing so is not yet altogether publick, unless what is suggested … the inequality of their circumstances.'

The speculative reason is that once the South Sea Company was allowed access to the East India Company the former would simply swallow up the latter. On the other hand (and this also is speculation, though more convincing) the canny East India Company may have looked at the promise of the unsustainable return of a 50% dividend per annum and thought it wise to run a mile. When we compare the growth and future wealth of the East India Company and the deathly path of the South Sea Company, just how wrong the view of the commentator is appears beyond irony.

By the beginning of March 1721 the East India Company might well be congratulating itself on not getting involved with its Caribbean counterpart. It had all gone horribly wrong and there were advertisements for pamphlets condemning the whole tawdry business. The title of one of them says enough: *Reasons for making void and annulling these FRAUDULENT and USURIOUS CONTRACTS into which Multitudes of unhappy persons have been drawn to the utter Ruin of themselves and families by the late Directors of the South Sea Company their Agents and Confederates.* At the same time notices appeared in the papers that there were petitions which had been opened in coffee houses for 'Gentlemen concern'd in asserting their rights by Law against the South Sea Company'. As the crisis grew, so did the reporting in the press of dismissals of officers of the company. Yet more angry pamphlets appeared, censuring the Directors.

There was a change of management in the Company and not surprisingly the old directors were roundly attacked. There was, perhaps for the first time in print, real sympathy for the 'ordinary' man who considered he had been duped by the financiers. The *Post Boy* clearly empathised: 'Tho' many of the Annuitants may be rich, yet many of the Thousands of them are of the meanest sort of Trades, who live by their Labour, and great Numbers of them are also Servants, and all of them have but very small Annuities.' There is also a warning that they would 'turn disaffected' against the Government. As the investigation continued details emerged which would have caused considerable argument in the coffee houses. The anger and frustration must have been tangible when the readers of the *London Journal* learned, ''Tis strongly reported, that a discovery is made of two hundred thousand pounds in the Hands of two great Bankers at Amsterdam belonging to two of the late Directors of the South Sea Company.' The principle of salting away ill-gotten gains into off-shore bank accounts is clearly not new. The blame began to spread to include not just the Directors but also enquiries were to be made 'into the Proceedings of several notorious Change-Alley Gamesters, commonly known by the name of Brokers, who were the Tools and made use of in selling out Stock for the late Directors and others'. Financial misconduct is not new.

April 1721 saw the *Evening Post* printing petitions begging the government to use the confiscated property of the dismissed Directors for the relief of the 'unhappy proprietors' (subscribers and shareholders rather than owners). The pleas from the Gentlemen and Freeholders of Hertford who were the voters begged the Commons in the strongest terms and declared that they were 'amazed to think to what an extravagant height the late directors of the South Sea Company, their Aiders and Confederates had fatally wrought up the credit of their stock, by their wicked arts and Delusions to the injury of the Publick'. In Somerset the voters used the words 'mismanagement, Avarice and fatal contrivances' in their petition. Buckinghamshire described themselves as 'ready to sink under the utmost despair of any redress' although they were confident that the Commons will do something for them.

By May the situation was beginning to look ugly. The *Daily Post* carried an announcement that 'all persons concern'd in the unredeemable Annuities ... are desired to meet at Lloyd's Coffee House ... to assert their right.' At the same time there was some retribution as the property of the disgraced directors was sold off 'for the Relief of the Unhappy Sufferers in the South Sea Company'. There may have been a minor cause for celebration in some households when the following advertisement appeared 'By Order of the Honourable the House of Commons – the particular and inventories of the estates of Charles Joy, Esq., Peter de la Prote Esq., and of William Morley Esq. As also the Particular nd Inventories of James Edmundson, Esq., Joh Turner, Esq., Stephen Child Esq., Richards Houdlitch Esq., Sir John Lambert Bart., Sir John Blunt Bar., Francis Hawes sq., Arthur Ingrams Esq., Roert Chester Esq., late Directors of the South Sea Company and of John Grigsby, Accomptant to the said Company'. According to the *Weekly Journal* the proceeds of these sales were to go 'to the benefit of the said poor Sufferers in the South Sea Company'. Violence seems to have erupted with South Sea Company clerks attacking each other and then brought before a mysterious Parliamentary 'Committee of Secrecy'. Newspapers such as the *Daily Post*, supporting the opposition, could compete with any twenty-first century tabloid in using language which went for the government's jugular. 'It is apparent' the editorial claimed, 'on whom the Hardship falls, and Property is destroy'd ... And since there must be a Suffering, who ought to suffer, or who will be said to suffer.' There was talk of 'Fraud and Injustice' and having the property of one 'taken from him by Force and without his Consent and given to others'. The conclusion is that while management were clearly guilty of 'treachery' it is the Lords of the Treasury who appointed them and they must take the ultimate blame. It is at this point that we see the newspapers really entering the arena. They began giving some detail to explain the fraudulent activities of the Directors of the South Sea Company. The *London Journal*, subsidised by the government, tried to put a brave face.

With such a big story the writers now had the stimulus to be innovative in their technique. There looks like there is something akin to a forum in the *Daily Post* of 26 May 1721. A curious advertisement appeared in the government-backed *Daily Post* apparently put in by the shareholders who met at a particular coffee house. It reported 'They have the greatest Assurance (from the Commons) of Success and Relief against the gross impositions of the South Sea Company ... they cannot entertain the least Apprehensions of being interrupted in the legal Prosecution of their Rights by the common Course of Justice, whatever has been suggested to the contrary.'

At the same time a rather more sceptical *London Journal* had a moment of doubt: 'People begin to say now, that the other two millions payable by the South Sea Company to the Publick will be remitted but what grounds they have for such a report we cannot determine.' Other reports were more surprising, such as the note in the *Weekly Journal* that Brabant in what is now Belgium was unwilling to extradite the former Cashier of the Company to face charges in Britain because he had not committed the crime of rebellion. Fraud apparently did not rate very highly on the crimes and misdemeanours scale in this particular part of the world. The newspapers who had talked up the Company at its inception now could not get enough of the punishments meted out to the Directors, particularly if, like the *Post Boy*, they represented the opposition. The glee with which they announced to their readers that they had 'heard that the late Directors of the South Sea Company, their aiders and abettors will be disqualify'd for ever for holding any Places of Profit or Trust either Civil or Ministry or sitting in Parliament.' This nugget of good news was picked up in several publications, including the *Daily Journal,* the *Weekly Journal* and the *Daily Post*. In fact the news came in thick and fast about the South Sea Company's doings, including a new agreement with Spain. There was also a claim agreed with Spain for one and a half million sterling in compensation for damage in the West Indies to the Company's goods. And there must have been a round of applause somewhere when they read tucked in behind this positive news a very welcome comment that the Spanish King was retreating from his demand for Gibraltar.

The pamphleteers, either out of a sense of duty, for political advantage, or simply to make some money, had a field day. Never far behind and often in front of the howling pack when taking advantage of volatile situations, they did not disappoint. The financial crisis of 1721 was an inspiration to both sensational and more measured pieces. There were serious publications such as the very worthily named *Proposals for Restoring Credit, for making the Bank of England more Useful and Profitable, for relieving the Sufferers of the South Sea Company*. And of course when it came to critiquing authority, the satirists were not slow to produce their barbs with some relish. *The Westminster Bubble* in 1722 created a dialogue between an *Old Bridge and a New*. The poetic allegory describes how a bridge with very little foundation is thrown up next to an old but sturdy bridge. There isn't much subtlety in the verses as the old bridge berates the upstart and finally the tide turns and the new bridge is turned back up the River Thames while the old stone built one stands firm. But of course there is little need for much subtlety when there is an angry mob baying for blood. And so the newspapers reinforce this anger as the extent of the financial disaster unfolds.

Newspapers, then as now, love a scandal and it must have been music to the *Post Boy's* ears when they heard that 'A certain Englishman unknown is come to lodge at an Inn in the Square of Spain; who is guess'd to be Mr Knight, late Cashier of the South Sea Company but he goes by another Name, if it is he and keeps incognito.' If it is the suspect perhaps he is hoping that Spain will have the same attitude to extradition as Brabant. Of course, the more blame that can be spread around the better, so they were there to expose John Aisble, one of the disgraced originators of the scheme and 'late Chancellor of the Exchequer … and a member of the House of Commons in breach of the great trust … and with a view to his own profit has combin'd with the Directors of the South Sea Company in their pernicious practices.' When Aisble defended himself against the charges of 'most dangerous and infamous corruption' the papers were ready to print his speech in full.

By February 1722 the disgraced directors appear to be wandering round Europe, no doubt seeking anonymity. This was not going to happen, at least not as long as the London newspapers could make some mileage out of their distress. The *London Journal* goes to town on the news of 'Mr Robert Knight, late cashier of the South Sea Company [who] has been at Rome and met with a cold reception there, both from the Pope and the Pretender, whose protection he was so far from obtaining that he has been order'd to depart the Ecclesiastical Territories; and 'tis said he is accordingly gone; but where is not yet known. Thus loaded with guilt may the abandon'd wretch wander from place to place and find no asylum and at last be made so sensible of his crimes as to open that scene of mischief to his injur'd country, wherein he had so great a part.' This was a gift to the papers. What could make better copy than a wandering soul, so heavy with crime that the country's worst enemies, the Catholic Church and the detested Jacobite Pretender, would not give him shelter?

There is so much material on the Bubble that it clearly took up much of the public's time reading about it. The newspapers followed every twist and turn in the story, from the first enthusiastic endorsement to the pursuit of the guilty parties. It has been said that this explosion of print about the South Sea Company (it did not earn the name of 'Bubble' until later in the century) should be read as a symptom of other ills that the early Georgians saw as pernicious.

This becomes a really interesting point when we look at the press and its role in society. Newspapers, radio, television, and the internet have been fulfilling the same function for hundreds of years. What you read/see on these channels of communication is the *zeitgeist* of the day. The 1720s were limited to the printed word but writers used it not just to report news (false or otherwise) but also to make their opinions clear on the ills of society.

Sir Richard Steele, the Whig essayist, playwright and MP who had found himself expelled from the Commons for what he considered speaking the truth, slammed into the South Sea Company in 1720. Steele used the expertise of a backbencher called Hutcheson to analyse the maths but he used his own powerful prose to point out that 'a hundred pound in the South-Sea Stock is not a good Hundred Pound.' His analogy for the workings of the Company made the situation crystal clear for those who wished to see it: 'The Managers of a Company with a vast Capital and acting without Trading under a notion of being Traders, are only so many People about a Pot full of English Beef; they skim off the Fat for themselves, while those who were to have their Proportion in the Meat as it was bought, must be contented with the lean Offals, for want of being in Favour with the Providers or in Fee with the Cooks.'

Steele wrote this at the end of March in the unlikely vehicle of his periodical *The Theatre*, but produced other pieces giving his opinion on the whole sorry business, which was that the 'Publick is loaded with Debts and the generality of people extreamly necessitous, while Private Persons to the Disadvantage of the whole community are immoderately rich and every day growing riche by artificial rumours, whereby self-interested men affect the hopes and fears of the people for their own Gain, tho' to the apparent hazard of their Country.' The interesting point about all this is that there were others who pointed out, in print, the shortcomings of investing in a trading company that didn't seem to trade very much. So the print industry, newspapers, pamphlets, periodicals, talked the scheme up in the beginning but then talked it down when they began to doubt its validity some time before it actually crashed.

We can now turn to some of the other curiosities of the first hundred years of the British press. The South Sea Company has provided an atmosphere of gloom so let's go somewhere where we can escape into other worlds, some amusing, some tragic and nearly always with a romantic theme.

There are a couple of intriguing notices which give a picture of life in eighteenth-century London. First there is a two-line advertisement in the *London Evening Post* in November 1728 announcing that the 'Wild Boy came to Town from Hertfordshire last Saturday and has been this Week at Lincoln's Inn Fields Playhouse.' This is a curious story and gives some insight into the curious mindset of readers. Peter the wild boy was found in the woods in 1725 near Hanover. Abandoned and unable to speak, he was presented to George I as a curiosity and brought to England where he was exhibited to the gentry, apparently at the theatre in Lincolns Inn

Fields. Although this seems barbaric nowadays he was well looked after and died at over 70 years of age in Hertfordshire, where he is buried.

The next episode, which shows the violent side of the streets of Hanoverian London, concerns a brawl that turned very ugly. The coachman to the owner of the Covent Garden Playhouse, having picked up a woman decided to have his way with her in the Prince of Wales' coach, which was conveniently standing by while His Royal Highness enjoyed the performance. This in itself is an extraordinary thought; but things get even more bizarre. The man guarding the vehicle obviously objected very strongly to the misuse of the royal property and for his pains was hit over the head with a whip. A mob immediately gathered to watch the fun and participate, which would have easily been prevented if a passing constable, for reasons that are not at all clear, had not joined the fray on the side of the mob, who stoned and pelted the guards while they tried to protect the coach. The only person who seems to have been arrested was the constable's servant after an enthusiastic dive into the fight. Was he arrested by his own master? No mention is made in the report of the state of the coach after this debacle or the reaction of the Prince of Wales when returned. We do not know what happened to the woman who had been picked up. Clearly if she had any sense she would have exited the scene pretty quickly.

Here is another example of bad behaviour which looks a little startling to a modern audience. Whereas 'Immersion theatre' in which the audience is an intrinsic element of the performance is a fashionable modern theatrical practice, some Georgians seem to have taken such participation a little further, in a typically unrestrained manner. This clearly upset the management at the Theatre Royal in Drury Lane, who stated categorically in their play notice in the *London Daily Post* in 1738 that 'the audience having been lately very much disgusted at the Performance being interrupted by persons crowding upon the stage, it is humbly hoped none will take it ill that they cannot be admitted behind scenes for the future.'

The theatre was an important part of the London scene, as it is now, and to complete this example of how important the newspapers were to the people of this period we can go back to Sir Richard Steele and his aptly named *Theatre*. Steele used it as a mouthpiece as we saw above but he had a more straightforward use for it – to comment on the stage. And it makes interesting reading. His mission was to improve the manners and decorum of his fellow Englishmen and women. So imagine his horror when the French Players came to town and were guilty of such 'moral Turpitude' that he launches into a rant which suggests that the French players are close to pornographic. As always the female members of the audience should be protected from 'what is more filthy than could be seen at a Brothel.' He also comments on the cost, which he considers prohibitive. If Steele were writing this today it would be nearer a blog than a periodical, a running commentary on what he considered the issues of the day.

The newspapers as we have seen were eager to decribe what Royalty wore when they were on parade. But what did the middling folk put on when they went out to enjoy themselves? Once again the advertisements go some way to answering this very important question, but possibly not in the way we might expect. If the anxious guest has been invited to a fancy-dress party and doesn't know what to go, there is help at hand in London's Tavistock Street. Timewell's Warehouse, according to the *Gazetteer* of April 1775 has a 'great variety of Masquerade Dresses'. The masquerade is clearly a favourite with the ladies and gentlemen of the period. In one issue of the *Daily Post* in February 1721 there are three consecutive advertisements for masquerade outfits for sale or hire. If the number of outlets offering these dressing up clothes is anything to go by, most of London's fashionable society must have spent a great of time and effort (not to mention money) on this particular entertainment.

One contemporary pamphleteer certainly did not approve of the masquerade, where dancers, as the name suggests, would be masked so that their identity is hidden. One held in February 1725 was so exciting that it inspired a pamphlet 'dedicated to Men of honour, men of pleasure and men of sense'. In it the author discussed the immoral activities of the young men, particularly in the way they drew young women (often married) into the glamour of the Masquerade (or the opera or playhouse). The men prey upon these 'innocents', but women were not let off the hook. In a rather prissy tone the writer went on to say that 'if a woman is in herself wickedly disposed she may find opportunities enough in this Town to indulge her inclinations even supposing that there were no masquerades.' This could be read as a defence of the Masquerade. If people want to be lewd and immoral they will find the opportunity somewhere in any case.

This was a very different reaction to the opinion expressed by the Grand Jury of Middlesex. They presented the following to the King's Bench for the organiser of masquerades to be prosecuted. They are 'Nuisances to the Public ... Nurseries of Lewdness, Extravagancies, and Immorality ... the Masquerade ... is a Meeting of more pernicious Consequences ... supported by Persons of R A N K and Q U A L I T Y – Where, under various Disguises, Crimes equal to barefaced Impieties are practiced, and great Sums of Money illegally lost ... if not ... prevented [they] will absolutely ruin, his Majesty's best Subjects: ... this fashionable, though wicked Diversion, has hitherto escaped the Notice of his Majesty's Justices of the Peace for this County, who have industriously suppressed many other Houses of Disorder and Debauchery.' And so the Grand Jury in their concern for the morals of these superior members of society request the organiser be arrested and punished as though he were running a brothel.

Alas, the worthy Grand Jury obviously did not succeed since the advertisements for masquerades were prominent in the newspaper classifieds right to the end of the century. In the *Morning Post* in June 1776, for instance, there is a note of a 'Subscription masquerade. Orders are given ... for the company to be admitted in Ranelagh Garden tomorrow the 14th at nine of that evening and the rotundo will be opened for supper at eleven o'clock.' The evening it seems is sold out as immediately beneath this notice there are two pleas for tickets. Just as now there is a healthy secondary market for tickets for popular events. And reading between the lines they can be expensive, as the advertiser declares 'that a moderate price will be given'. One masquerade in June 1774 must have been particularly popular, as there are no less than five classified adverts requesting tickets.

It has to be said that they looked quite jolly if the *Festivale di Campagna* held at Mary-le-bone Gardens was typical. With a Concert to kick off the proceedings the entertainment is promised to be 'novel and various.' With a ballroom, ornamented gardens, refreshments and a cold collation served at twelve o'clock the ticket price of 'one guinea and a half' was a snip. On the other hand, would the discerning gentry prefer Ranelagh Gardens where a firework display was promised? For the really classy people of the *bon ton* who 'were in the country at the last rural masquerade, as well as at the request of many who were in town but had not an opportunity of being present at that so much admired species of entertainment' Mrs Cornelys is going to put on another 'Mask' at Carlisle House. This was so exclusive that the price of the tickets is not mentioned.

This is all very sophisticated but dancing at the beginning of the century as advertised in the *Flying Post* was certainly cheaper and had at least the excuse of giving access to the waters of Lambeth Wells. Moreover, if there was no possibility of getting there, although the purchaser would have missed the entertainment the water was available at only a penny a quart. There was even more dancing and water at Islington, although for this entertainment masques were banned. The newspapers here fulfilled a very important need – what to do when you wanted some fun.

But you could have fun at home – reading in itself was a particularly popular pastime and one which relied heavily on the notices in the newspaper. We can discover a great deal about the mindset of the readers just by looking at what was promoted through the classified columns. Some of it looks terrifyingly serious and some of it looks equally terrifyingly incendiary. As would be expected given that the early eighteenth century took politics very seriously, many of the books on sale did not appear to have much fun in them.

Take the second edition (the first edition was obviously a success) advertised in 1701 of *The Dangers of EUROPE. From the growing Power of FRANCE. With some free thoughts on the remedies. And particularly on the Cure of our divisions at home: In order to* [wage] *a successful war abroad against the French King and His Allies.* Also available 'next Thursday' will be *The True Interest and Political Maxims of the Republick of Holland and Westfriesland, in three parts*, along with *The Electors Right Asserted*. These weighty tomes were published before the death of William III and before the War of the Spanish Succession was underway, although William's abiding preoccupation was curtailing Louis XIV and the Catholic French were regarded as national enemies. Books were relatively expensive, and in the beginning of the century there were no lending libraries. So while books may have circulated between friends, only the rich elite could possibly have afforded to buy them.

Thankfully for those readers whose taste was a little less serious you could pick up a dozen novels at a mere six shillings and also find some plays to keep you amused. We might even be surprised at the range of books being advertised in 1700. There was *The Amours of Edward the 4th*, which sounds like a bodice-ripper that might have caused concern to mothers and guardians if they found their innocent daughters immersed in it. Even at this time the loyalty of readers to particular authors was something the publisher's marketing department (if there had been such a thing) would tap into. The potential reader's interest would be aroused by the reminder this racy title is by the author of *The Turkish Spy*, which reveals the 'intrigues and secrets of the Christian Courts'. In fact there were plenty of novels to be had at various outlets 'at reasonable rates'.

Should the reader tire of novels he or she might turn to the newspapers to hear more about the glitterati of the day. And what could be more glittering than the marriage of the Earl (later Duke) of Marlborough's daughter to the equally high-profile Lord Sunderland in 1700? Even more exotic is the news that the Emperor of Morocco has demanded the hand of the Princess Dowager of Conti in marriage and she had demanded time to think about it. Or would the exciting news that there is a negotiation between the Prince of Brazil for the hand of an unnamed Archduchess thrill the followers of foreign royals?

Sometimes (perhaps if there were no royal weddings that week) it would be someone quite undistinguished who would be featured and we are back to the disorganised announcements. The parents or family of the 'agreeable' young lady, Miss Harvey of Oxford, were presumably pleased to read that a Treaty of Marriage is 'on foot, and will be speedily consummated'. The lucky man was Mr Thomas Palmer of Oxford who might have been very happy to get his hands on her ample fortune. When you read the announcements, which in typical fashion are dumped anywhere in the news sections, it is tempting to think that the finances may be as important, if not more, than the charm of the bride. The terminology is closer to negotiations than to romance. On the same day in 1732 the *Daily Post* tells us of the Treaties of Marriage between Sir Thomas Reynell and his bride-to-be Betty Fowler who is a 'Lady of Great Merit' but more significantly has a ten-thousand-pound fortune. At the same time across in Wales Richard Vaughan is about to marry Miss Nanny, 'a rich heiress'. This concentration on the capital the wife brings with her gives later generations real insight into how the eighteenth-century family was created, at least among those ranks that had money. These we have to remember are public announcements about ordinary but wealthy people. The money the bride brings into the marriage is considered important enough to broadcast. This insistence on the monetary value of a bride brings to mind the comment made by one of the conduct books that women have little say in their choice of husbands.

For readers or listeners, consumers of pamphlets bought on the streets or the serious men discussing the latest political developments in the coffee-houses, the newsprint in whatever form it took was a major element in their lives. At work or play, the press was there – sometimes reporting accurately, sometimes not.

CONCLUSION

The successes of the newborn fourth estate make for impressive reading. Through a tenacious refusal to be suppressed, it had transformed itself from an eclectic mix of royal proclamations and ragged pamphlets to a powerful tool for government and opposition alike. It had proved that it could make a serious contribution to the political, industrial and social life of the nation. Its first century of life saw it multiply from a handful of printed sheets into a wide range of newspapers with identifiable personalities. The individuals who helped this development often did so at a personal cost: writers, printers and booksellers in the seventeenth and eighteenth centuries would often risk physical pain, financial ruin, incarceration or humiliation for disseminating their views. Some suffered immeasurably.

This tiny group of printers, booksellers and journalists punched far above its weight. This we can see in the ferocity with which the Star Chamber, the Messengers and other government-sponsored officials pursued them. It was impossible to truly gag them. Despite every setback, the press and print industry achieved major advances, ranging from the primacy of the writer's claim to authorship to the sanctioning of reports on parliamentary debates. In addition, the press became part of the fabric of life for the British citizenry. In sickness and health, for leisure, work or education, the newspapers carried the information necessary to keep the country going. From a lost royal dog to a runaway wife, from learned tomes to scandal sheets, these beloved works detail the minutiae of everyday living.

Appendix 1

DEFINITIONS AND TIMELINE

Throughout the book there are people and events which may be unfamiliar. There follows a very brief background note which may help to explain some of the less well known but still important points.

1600 – 1650

The first fifty years of the seventeenth century laid the foundations for the troubles that split England into two factions. Initially the division was over religion. In 1603 the first steps towards the creation of the United Kingdom came in with the accession of James I of England who also reigned over Scotland as James VI. James was the son of the Catholic Mary Queen of Scots, executed by Elizabeth I of England having been accused of plotting against her. He was baptised as a Catholic but upon his mother's abdication when he was only a baby he was brought up as a Protestant as the Reformation took hold in Scotland and the Scots increasingly turned away from Roman Catholicism. So when the childless Elizabeth died the English immediately invited

James as the ideal successor to become James I of England while he remained James VI of Scotland. The crowns were united but not the countries. James's son Charles succeeded his father in 1625. We touch on Charles's difficulties with Parliament and his lack of funds so it would be helpful at this point to have a further look at the religious differences which were a large element in the civil war that broke out in the 1640s.

The trouble began with his Scottish subjects who were not minded to follow the Christianity as practised by the King and had their own Kirk. The Kirk had abandoned the hierarchy of bishops and had no intention of bending to Charles' imposition of a new prayer book and this led to a refusal not only to follow the English way of religion but also to dispute Charles' overall authority. A failed attempt to invade his own kingdom of Scotland followed and then the English parliament refused to support him in a further effort against the Scots. The English Parliament increasingly believed that their own authority was being undermined and Catholicism was entering through the back door. They retaliated by taking away Charles' rights to dissolve or convene them and this was a major affront to his power. Papists were banned from London and the power of those who wished to make the Established Church less ritualised became an increasingly vociferous element in the House of Commons. Having famously tried and failed to arrest five MPs while they were actually sitting, the antipathy between the king and the separatist or dissenting members escalated. As we see in the first chapter, words were a significant element in this escalation with over four hundred pamphlets and other ephemera issued by the king. Eventually it was time for Charles to defend his rapidly diminishing authority with action and war inevitably broke out.

Who were these 'separatists' or 'dissenters'? The Established Church in England accommodated much of the argument for and against further reforms of English Protestantism during the reign of James I. It was Charles' high-handed turn to the high church Arminians which set the ball rolling for the eventual hostilities. With growing anger at the treatment of the high church favoured by Charles, the nonconformists, the dissenters and the puritans were essentially running the country as the dominant force in the Commons. The Short Parliament of 1640 lasted only two months. The Long Parliament, which assembled in November 1640 and lasted until 1653, took matters into their own hands. On the religious front when it became clear that the Puritans, Congregationalists and Presbyterians were making no headway in toning down the pomp and spectacle of Charles's church they stripped out images and crucifixes from churches. This is how Professor John Coffey describes the internal wranglings that overtook the House of Commons. One probably has to read it twice: 'Puritan reformers became bitterly divided ... a small minority (the Dissenting Brethren) objected to elements of Presbyterianism, and argued in favour of Congregationalism – self-governing churches made up of the godly rather than the whole parish. Outside Westminster ... radical Puritanism flourished. Separatists and Baptists established numerous congregations, and acquired notoriety through pamphleteering and preaching. ... England appeared to having its own Radical Reformation. Presbyterian divines demanded the suppression of heresy and schism ... But they were countered by a vigorous campaign for religious toleration, involving radical Puritans ... Tolerationists threw into question some of the fundamental assumptions of the magisterial Reformation tradition. In particular, they started to deny that the magistrate had ... powers in matters of religion ... This would not have mattered had radical Puritans been isolated and denied political support. But by the mid-1640s, an independent coalition had formed that included some powerful Westminster politicians and military commanders (like Oliver Cromwell).'

So the splintered Protestantism of these years embraced an extraordinary array of sects. These ranged from the austere and worthy Quakers whose behaviour generally was exemplary to the Ranters whose behaviour was at the other end of the scale. Their belief was that conventional morality did not apply to them. One of their practices was preaching in the nude. Joining them at the freer end of the radical protestant scale were the Antinomians who believed that God had made all things good, including sin and the Muggletonians who believed that they were the final prophets and it was their duty to prepare the world for Christ's Second Coming.

The Restoration, 1660–1686

This freedom of worship (although it wasn't as free as some would have liked) was abruptly ended with the Restoration of the monarchy. The government started to pass laws putting the Established church back in charge of England at prayer. The Conventicle Acts banned nonconformist meetings of more than five people outside the household, with heavy penalties. The measures included the Act of Uniformity, forcing out any clergy who had not been ordained by a bishop and who did not adhere to the Book of Common Prayer. Nearly two thousand members of the clergy lost their jobs between 1660 and 1662. And just to make sure that they did not keep any influence over their erstwhile congregations the Five Mile Act prevented sacked dissenter ministers from coming within five miles of their former parish. However, there were Acts of Indulgence and it is wrong to imagine that all dissenters were thrown into prison. At least the authorities had stopped burning them at the stake.

While this antipathy to erring Protestants continued, the English did not forget how much they disliked Rome. The Popish Plot of 1679 fabricated by Titus Oates fed on this antipathy, he invented a Jesuit plot to murder Charles II and put his Catholic brother on the throne. Eventually the plot was discredited but not before several people had been executed. However, the thought of the openly Catholic James, Charles II's brother as heir to the throne was still anathema. The Exclusion Crisis came next and Parliament tried three times unsuccessfully to remove James from the line of succession. For some the Exclusion Crisis was the parent of the two-party system. The Tories believed in the complete eradication of Dissent and the Whigs, while they themselves were for the Established church, were willing to show toleration to the nonconformists. When James did come to the throne in 1685 he passed declarations of indulgence. But James had to go and William of Orange, the husband of James's eldest daughter Mary, was invited to remove him.

The Glorious Revolution and the Last Stuarts

For the last Stuarts, William III and Mary II and Queen Anne, religion became an even more serious matter if that were possible. Politics at home and abroad were focused on two things: the perceived threat to the established Anglican Church from non-conformists and the threat to the nation from the ambitions of Louis XIV. The French king's goal in life seemed to be domination of Europe and the imposition of Catholicism on those counties that had turned their backs on the old faith and embraced Protestantism. We have referred frequently to the War of the Spanish Succession (1701–1714) in which France took on the rest to establish its authority. Now is the time to explain its origins and its outcomes. As is made clear in the name this particular war arose from the disputed succession to the Spanish throne after the death of the childless Charles II, who was the last of the Spanish Habsburgs. In order to sort this out before Charles died the major players signed various treaties which carved up Europe between them. The favoured heir was named as the son of the Elector of

Bavaria. Unfortunately he predeceased Charles and so the process of finding a successor began again. The Spanish territories were to be carved up between Spain and Italy. This new distribution did not please either the Spanish or the Holy Roman Emperor. By this time, Charles the King of Spain decided that he would bequeath the crown to the grandson of Louis XIV, keeping all the various possessions intact. In 1700 the Charles died and Louis, anxious to ensure that France kept hold of the inheritance, invaded the Spanish Netherlands. This prompted the Dutch Republic alongside England and other states throughout Europe to form an alliance to combat France and by 1701 the conflict was under way. The motivation for the individual allies was different but for England it was to maintain the balance of power and curb the ambitions of Louis and France. While Louis was willing to make peace by 1708, the English (or British after the Union with Scotland) refused to do so until Louis had driven his own grandson off the Spanish throne. Clearly he wasn't going to oblige in this and he took up arms again. The war continued with the British and General John Churchill, Duke of Marlborough, kept up his undefeated record. He was sacked by Queen Anne in 1711 and in the next year peace negotiations began. Britain did extremely well out of the treaties, the first one being the Treaty of Utrecht.

The next major event for the British at this time was the urgent need for a successor to Queen Anne, who despite at least 15 pregnancies had not produced an heir. To this was added the complication of the Act of Settlement of 1701, which reserved the succession to a Protestant candidate with a Protestant spouse. These were in rather short supply in Europe, but the eventual heir was declared as Sophia the Electress of Hanover, the granddaughter of James I. Anne just outlived her and the crown went to George, the first Hanoverian.

Appendix 2

A GUIDE TO MONEY IN THE SEVENTEENTH AND EIGHTEENTH CENTURY

Taking 1700 as a point in the period upon which we are concentrating here is a table giving a guide to the purchasing power of money, though such comparisons are notoriously tricky.

1700	2017 equivalent	Approx. wages for skilled tradesman
£100	10700	3 years
150	16,000	4.5 years
200	21,000	6 years
500	53,500	15 years
1000	107,000	30 years
5000	535,000	153 years
10000	1,000,000	304 years
25,000	2,700,000	761 years
50,000	5,400,000	1,522 years
100,000	10,000,000	3,044 years

BIBLIOGRAPHY

Primary Sources
Athenae Redivivae
Athenian Mercury
A Brief Enquiry into the Ground, Authority and Rights of Ecclesiastical Synod
A Collection for Improvement of Agriculture and Trade.
A Looking Glass For Sectaryes Or True Newes From Newberry Being The Relation Of The Newberry Annabaptists
A Modest Proposal for Preventing the Children of Poor People From being a Burthen to Their Parents or Country
A Perfect Diurnall of the Passages in Parliament
A Pleasant Conference upon the Observator and Heraclitus
A Satyr against Injustice
A Short Answer to a Whole Litter of Libels
A strange and lamentable accident that happened lately at Mearl Ashby in Northamptonshire
Birmingham and Stafford Chronicle
Birmingham Gazette
British Apollo
Chester Chronicle
Chronicle and Weekly Advertiser

Considerations and Proposals in Order to the Regulation of the Press

Daily Advertiser

Daily Post

Domestick Intelligence

Duchess of Marlborough's Creed

Dunton's Oracle

English Intelligencer

Etherington's York Chronicle

Exeter Mercury

Faithfull Mercury

Female Spectator

Female Tatler

Flying Post and Medley

Gangraena

General Postscript

Hogs Character of a Projector wherein is desciphered the manner and shape of that vermine

Ladies Curiosity

Ladies Diary

Leeds Intelligencer

Love Tricks

Ludlow Postman

Medley

Mercurius Aulicus

Mercurius Britannicus

Mercurius Civicus

Mercurius Publicus Comprising the Sum and Kingdomes Intelligencer

Middlesex Journal

Middlewich Journal

Mist's Weekly Journal

More Warning yet, being a true relation of a strange and most dreadful apparition which was seen in the air by several persons at Hull

Mr Atterbury's book of the rights and powers and privileges of an English convocation considered

New Atalantis

Newcastle Weekly

Norwich Gazette
Norwich Mercury
Norwich Post
Now's the time to tell the truth
Observator
Old Playhouse
Original Mercury
Original York Journal
Oxford Gazette
Perfect Diurnall of all the proceedings of the English and Scotch Armies
Plymouth Weekly Journal
Post Boy
Post Boy. A True List of the Knights
Proposals for Restoring Credit
Protestant Courant of
Pugh's Hereford Journal
Puritan
Quarles
Reading Mercury
Reasons for making void and annulling these FRAUDULENT and USURIOUS CONTRACTS
Rehearsal Revived
Review
Stamford Mercury
Statesman
Supplement
Systema Horticulture
Tatler
Tea Table
The Theatre
The Accomplished Ladies Rich Closet
The Amours of Edward the 4th
The Art of Political Lying
The Blacksmith
The court at Kensington
The Coffee Scuffle occasioned by a contest between a learned knight and a painfull pedagogue

Bibliography

The Daily Advertiser

The Dangers of EUROPE. From the growing Power of FRANCE

The Electors Right Asserted

The Examiner

The Flying Post

The Freeholders plea against stock jobbing elections of Parliament men

The Gazette

The Guardian

The Life and Character of John Barber Esq., Late Lord Mayor of London Deceased

Turned out of Court at Last

Weekly Apollo

Whore's Progress

Women, or, a Spie for Pride

York Chronicle

York Courant

York Gazetteer

York Journal or Weekly Courant

York Mercury

The Importance of Dunkirk Considered

The Importance of the Guardian Considered

The Lady's New Year's Gift

The Observations on Sir George Wakeman's Trial

The Observator

The Officer's Address to the Ladies

The Perils of False Brethren

The Petticoat Plotters

The Post Boy

The practice of the courts of the Kings Bench

The Protestant Post Boy

The Spectator

The True Interest and Political Maxims of the Republick of Holland

The Turkish Spy

Town Talk

Secondary Sources
Databases
Google Scholar
The National Dictionary of Biography
The History of Parliament
British History Online

Articles and Books
Abbott, Wilbur C., *The First Newspapermen*

Abbott, Wilbur C, *The Restoration Press*

Asquith, Ivon, *Advertising and Press in the late eighteenth and early nineteenth centuries*

Astbury, Raymond, *The Renewal of the Licensing Act in 1693 and its Lapse in 1695*

Backscheider, Paula R., *No Defense: Defoe in 1703*

Barrès-Baker, M. C., *An Introduction to the Early History of Newspaper Advertising*

Benedict, Barbara M., *Encounters with the Object, Advertisements, Time, and Literary Discourse in the Early Eighteenth Century*

Bialusschewski, Arne, *A True Account of the Design, and Advantages of the South-Sea Trade: Profits, Propaganda, and the Peace Preliminaries of 1711*

Bloom, Edward A., *Neoclassic 'Paper Wars' for a Free Press*

Bös, Birte, *'A full Account of the rise, progress and declension of our Journal', Negotiations of failure in early English newspapers*

Brady, Andrea, *Dying with Honour: Literary Propaganda and the Second English Civil War*

Bricker, Andrew Benjamin, *After the Golden Age: Libel, Caricature, and the Deverbalization of Satire*

Bullard, Paddy, *The Scriblerian Mock-Arts: Pseudo-Technical Satire in Swift and His Contemporaries Butler, Martin, A Case Study in Caroline Theatre: 'Mercurius Britannicus' (1641)*

Butler, Martin, *A case Study in Caroline Political Theatre Braithwaite's Mercurius Britannicus (1641)*

Campbell, Jill, *Domestic Intelligence: Newspaper Advertising and the Eighteenth-Century Novel*

Clark, K. R. P., *Defoe, Dissent, and Early Whig Ideology*

Como, David R., *Print, Censorship, and Ideological Escalation in the English Civil Wars*

Cowan, Brian, *Mr. Spectator and the Coffeehouse Public Sphere*

Cowan, Brian, *The Rise of the Coffeehouse Reconsidered*

Crane, R. S. and F. B. Kaye, *A Census of British Newspapers 1620-1800*

Cressy, David, *Levels of Literacy in England, 1530-1730*

Cust, Richard, *News and Politics in Early Seventeenth Century England*

Dawson, Mark S., *First Impressions: Newspaper Advertisements and Early Modern English Body Imaging, 1651–1750*

Dickie, Simon, *Hilarity and Pitilessness in the Mid-Eighteenth Century: English Jestbook Humor*

Dooley, Brendan, *International News Flows in the Seventeenth Century: Problems and Prospects*

Downie, J. A., *Secret Service Payments to Daniel Defoe, 1710-1714*

Downie, J. A., *Swift and Jacobitism*

Eccles, Mark, *Thomas Gainsford, 'Captain Pamphlet'*

Firth, C. H., *The Royalists under the Protectorate*

Fox, Adam, *Rumour News and Popular Opinion in Elizabethan and Early Stuart England*

Frank, Joseph, *Some Clippings from the Pre-Restoration English Newspaper*

French, J. *Milton, Needham, and 'Mercurius Politicus'*

Friedman, Jerome, *The Battle of the Frogs and Fairford's Flies: Miracles and Popular Journalism during the English Revolution*

Gael, Patricia, *The Origins of the Book Review in England, 1663–1749*

Gardner, Victoria, *Liberty, Licence and Leveson*

Gazzard, Hugh, *An Act to Restrain Abuses of Players (1606)*

Goldgar, Bertrand A., *Pope and the 'Grub-Street Journal'*

Griffin, Robert J., *Anonymity and Authorship*

Hamburger, Philip, *The Development of the Law of Seditious Libel and the Control of the Press*

Hamm Jr, Robert B., *Walker v. Tonson in the Court of Public Opinion 'The counterfeit silly curr':*

Hardacre, P. H., *The Royalists in Exile during the Puritan Revolution, 1642-1660*

Herman, Ruth, *The Business of a Woman: The Political Writings of Delarivier Manley*

Holmes, Clive, Julian Goodare, Richard Cust and Mark Kishlansky, *Charles I: A Case of Mistaken Identity*

Hoppit, Julian, *The Myths of the South Sea Bubble*

Hume, Robert D., *'Satire' in the Reign of Charles I*

Hunt, Tamara L., *Servants, Masters and Seditious Libel in Eighteenth-Century England*

Hyland, P. J. B., *Liberty and Libel: Government during the Succession Crisis in Britain 1712-1716*

Jackson, Clare, *Jonathan Swift's Peace of Utrecht*

Johns, Adrian, *Miscellaneous Methods: Authors, Societies and Journals in Early Modern England*

Joseph, Frank, *Some Clippings from the Pre-Restoration English Newspaper*

Kitchin, George, *Roger L'estrange, A contribution to the history of the press in the seventeenth century*

Klein, Lawrence E., *Coffeehouse Civility, 1660-1714: An Aspect of Post-Courtly Culture in England*

Knights, Mark, *The Tory Interpretation of History in the Rage of Parties*

Kyle, Chris R., *From Broadside to Pamphlet, Print and Parliament in the late 1620s*

Lawler, Chris and Akihito Suzuki, *The Diseases of the Self: Representing Consumption 1700-1830*

Lincoln, Andrew, *War and the Culture of Politeness: The Case of The Tatler and The Spectator*

MacDonald, Hugh, *The Law and Defamatory Biographies in the Seventeenth Century*

Mackie, Erin, *Periodical Eidolatry*

Martyn, John and Paul Slack, *Government and Information in Seventeenth-Century England*

McCullough, Peter, *Print Publication and Religious Politics in Caroline England*

McElligott, Jason, *The Politics of Sexual Libel: Royalist Propaganda in the 1640s*

McRae, Andrew, *Satire and Sycophancy: Richard Corbett and Early Stuart Royalism*

McShane, Angela, *The Roasting of the Rump: Scatology and the Body Politic in Restoration England*

McTague, John, *The New Atalantis Arrests: A Reassessment*

Noble, Yvonne, *Light Writing From a Dark Winter: The Scriblerian Annus Mirabilis*

Novak, Maximillian E., *A Vindication of the Press and the Defoe Canon*

Patterson, Paul B., *Harley, Defoe, Trapp and the 'Faults on Both Sides' Controversy*

Peacey, Jason, *'My Friend the Gazetier': Diplomacy and News in Seventeenth-Century Europe*

Peacey, Jason, *Print, Publicity, and Popularity, the Projecting of Sir Balthazar Gerbier 1642-1662*

Peacey, Jason, *The Struggle for Mercurius Britannicus: Factional Politics and the Parliamentarian Press, 1643–1646*

Peacey, Jason, *Print Culture and Political Lobbying during the English Civil Wars*

Peacey, Jason, *Politics, and the Forging of Royalist Newspapers during the English Civil War*

Pincus, Steve, *'Coffee politicians does create' Coffeehouses and Restoration Political Culture*

Poston, Lawrence, *Defoe and the Peace Campaign, 1710-1713: A Reconsideration*

Randall, David, *Epistolary Rhetoric, the Newspaper, and the Public Sphere*

Randall, David, *Joseph Mead, Novellante: News, Sociability, and Credibility in Early Stuart England*

Randall, David, *Providence, Fortune, and the Experience of Combat: English Printed Battlefield Reports, circa 1570-1637*

Ransome, Mary, *The Press in the General Election of 1710*

Raymond, Joad, *Describing Popularity in Early Modern England*

Raymond, Joad, *The newspaper, public opinion, and the public sphere In the seventeenth century*

Robins, Brian, *John Marsh and Music Making in Eighteenth-Century England*

Rogers, Pat, *Defoe's Distribution Agents and Robert Harley*

Rogers, Pat, *Nameless Names, Pope Curll and Uses of Anonymity*

Roscoe, E. S., *Robert Harley Earl of Oxford Prime Minister 1710-1714*

Rose, Mark, *The Public Sphere and the Emergence of Copyright: Areopagitica, the Stationers' Company, and the Statute of Anne*

Roulston, Chris, *Space and the Representation of Marriage in Eighteenth-Century Advice Literature*

Scarborough King, Rachael, *The Manuscript Newsletter and the Rise of the Newspaper 1665–1715*

Bateson, Thomas, *Relations of Defoe and Harley*

Schwoerer, Lois G., *Press and Parliament in the Revolution of 1689*

Shaaber, Matthias A., *The History of the First English Newspaper*

Sharpe, Kevin, *Crown, Parliament and Loyalty, Government and Communication in Early Stuart England*

Sirluck, Ernest, *Areopagitica and a Forgotten Licensing Controversy*

Slack, Paul, *Government and Information in Seventeenth-Century England*

Slaughter, Will, *Upright Piracy Understanding the Lack of Journalism in Eighteenth Century Britain*

Smith, J. H., *Thomas Baker and 'The Female Tatler'*

Snyder, Henry L., *Daniel Defoe, Arthur Maynwaring, Robert Walpole, and Abel Boyer: Some Considerations of Authorship Author(s):*

Snyder, Henry L., *Daniel Defoe, the Duchess of Marlborough, and the 'Advice to the Electors of Great Britain'*

Sowerby, Scott, *Opposition to Anti-Popery in Restoration England*

Speck, W. A., *Political Propaganda in Augustan England*

Squibbs, Richard, *Civic Humorism and the Eighteenth Century Periodical Essay*

Stern, Simon, *From Author's Right to Property Right*

Thomas, Peter D. G., *The Beginning of Parliamentary Reporting in Newspapers, 1768-1774*

Thompson, Elbert N. S., *War Journalism Three Hundred Years Ago*

Tubb, Amos, *Mixed Messages: Royalist Newsbook Reports of Charles I's Execution and of the Leveller Uprising*

Wagner, Darren, *Leaky Bodies, Bawdy Books, Gonorrhoea and Reading in Eighteenth-Century England*

Walker, James, *The Secret Service under Charles II and James II*

Walker, R. B., *The Newspaper Press in The Reign of William III*

Williams, J. B., *The Newsbooks and Letters of News of the Restoration*

Williamson, Raymond, *The Grub-Street Journal, With Particular Reference to His Attacks on Richard Bentley, Richard Bradley and William Cheselden*

ACKNOWLEDGEMENTS

No work is produced in isolation and I have quite a few people who have helped and encouraged me. I can't put them into a specific order because they all helped me in different ways. But high on the list must come Jennifer Ferguson, who read the final draft all the way through twice and made helpful suggestions. Pam Croft and Jon Barber also read the drafts of the first few chapters and liked them. So I am grateful for their positive feedback. Chris Bennett, County Archivist at Hertfordshire Archives and Local Studies, was generous with his time and knowledge on copyright. Catherine Lennon has been a supportive friend for many years and has always been encouraging and interested. On a professional level I must thank the team at Amberley for their encouragement and assistance. Finally I must thank my family. Elaine and Richard, my sister and brother-in-law, have been really supportive. Michael, my husband, persuaded me to approach Amberley in first place and my daughter, Charlotte, is simply lovely.

INDEX

Also available from Amberley Publishing

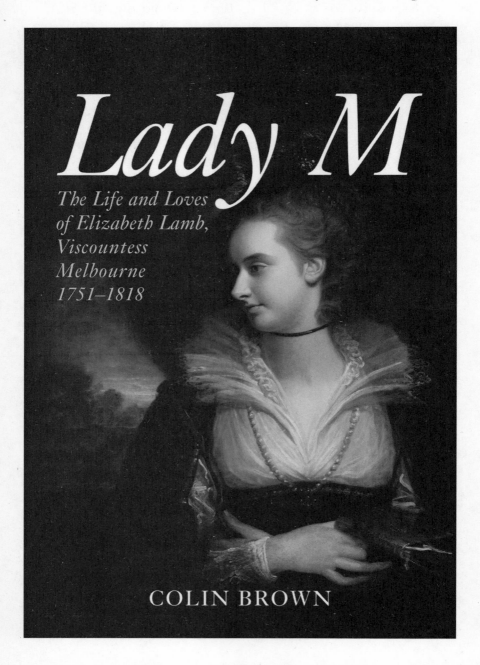

Lady M

The Life and Loves
of Elizabeth Lamb,
Viscountess
Melbourne
1751–1818

COLIN BROWN

Available from all good bookshops or to order direct
Please call **01453–847–800**
www.amberley-books.com